**Change and Continuity
In Twentieth-Century America**

Change and Continuity
in Twentieth-Century America

Edited by

John Braeman

Robert H. Bremner

Everett Walters

Ohio State University Press

INTRODUCTION

THIS is the first in a series of annual volumes devoted to the history of the United States since 1890 that will be published by the Ohio State University Press. The series, whose over-all title is MODERN AMERICA, is intended to facilitate publication of scholarly articles in all areas of recent American history. The editors hope that MODERN AMERICA will provide a publication outlet for monographic studies as well as synthetic and interpretative essays.

The events of the past seventy-five years have produced significant changes in nearly every aspect of American life. In a period as brief as the span of human lifetime, however, it is to be expected that old and familiar elements will mingle with and temper the forces of change and novelty. The editors have, therefore, chosen *Change and Continuity in Twentieth-Century America* as the theme of the first volume of MODERN AMERICA. Each of the essays in the book is concerned in some manner with the relation of tradition and innovation.

In the 1960's, the United States stands as one of the two global superpowers. Many historians date the emergence of America as a world power from the Spanish-American War and the acquisition of the Philippines. But did the events of 1898 result in fundamental changes in the principles and practice of American foreign policy? Richard W. Leopold, in "The Emergence of America as a World Power: Some Second Thoughts," concludes that the years between 1898 and 1920 witnessed no such decisive change. "In 1920, as in 1898," Leopold writes, "the average citizen thought the United States could be a world power and still adhere to the practices of an earlier day."

One of the outstanding trends of the twentieth century has been the increasingly important role played by the federal government in safeguarding the public health, morals, and welfare. In the nineteenth century such activities were the responsibility of the states under their reserved police power. The assumption of these new responsibilities by the federal government involved formidable political and constitutional obstacles. John Braeman's "The Square Deal in Action: A Case Study in the Growth of the 'National Police Power' " makes a study in depth of the passage of one of the milestones in this development—the meat inspection law of 1906.

The greatest advance in federal activity in behalf of the public welfare came during the New Deal in response to the exigencies of the Great Depression. William E. Leuchtenburg, in "The New Deal and the Analogue of War," shows how Americans used the imagery of war to describe the country's plight in the 1930's and how New Dealers drew upon the legacy of the World War I mobilization for their proposals. "The legacy of the war," Leuchtenburg asserts, "was to prove a mixed blessing. Useful as a justification for New Deal actions, it also served to limit and divert the reformers in ways that had not been anticipated." The shortcomings of the war analogy were in large part responsible for the New Deal's failure to face up to "the real problems of the relation of order to liberty which the power of the twentieth century creates."

This conclusion raises the question whether the New Deal was as much of a turning point in American history as many historians have believed. Richard S. Kirkendall examines the problem in "The Great Depression: Another Watershed in American History?" Kirkendall argues that the role of change in the 1930's has been overemphasized and the importance of continuity neglected. "The leading developments of the depression decade which are associated with the New Deal," he contends, "should not be viewed as radical new beginnings in American history but chiefly as significant parts of a large-scale transformation of American capitalism that had been under way for at least half a century before the 1930's."

A significant aspect of the transformation of American capitalism has been the change in the relations between government and business. The extent of laissez faire in the nineteenth century has been much exaggerated; yet the businessman at the beginning of this century remained largely free from governmental restraint. The situation today is much changed, but the business decision-maker is still the key figure in the economy. Arthur M. Johnson shows, in his "Continuity and Change in Government-Business Relations," that the keynote of the changing relationship between business and government has been "a basic pragmatism."

Perhaps the most striking feature of the transformation of American capitalism in the twentieth century has been the rise of a powerful labor movement. Big labor has become, in John Galbraith's phrase, a major "countervailing power" to big business. David Brody, in "The Emergence of Mass-Production Unionism," examines the revolutionary breakthrough of unionization in the mass-production industries in the 1930's. While not underrating the importance of the formation of the CIO, or of a sympathetic government acting through the Wagner Act and the National Labor Relations Board, Brody finds that the coming of World War II was decisive in the triumph of unionism in the mass-production industries.

Even before mass unionization, the average American worker enjoyed a standard of living that was the envy of his European fellows. Historically, the United States has been regarded as the land of plenty for all. But observers have in recent years increasingly lamented the persistence of poverty in the affluent society. Robert H. Bremner, in "Poverty in Perspective," finds that the discovery of poverty in the United States is not new to this generation—and he shows how changing interpretations of poverty and its causes reflect fundamental changes in American ideas and social attitudes.

The editors extend their thanks to the contributors, to the many historians who have expressed interest in MODERN AMERICA, and to Weldon A. Kefauver of the Ohio State University Press. Without Mr. Kefauver's co-operation and assistance, this volume would not have been possible.

The next two volumes in the series are in preparation. One will be devoted to "The 1920's Revisited"; the other to "American Foreign Policy in the Twentieth Century."

JOHN BRAEMAN
ROBERT H. BREMNER
EVERETT WALTERS

CONTENTS

**Change and Continuity
in Twentieth-Century America**

The Emergence of America as a World Power: Some Second Thoughts

RICHARD W. LEOPOLD

EARLY in 1901 a foreign diplomat declared that, during his brief residence in Washington, he had observed two different nations—the United States before the War with Spain and the United States after that conflict.[1] This remark has been quoted frequently to indicate the profound impact of the contest with Spain upon American foreign policy. According to this interpretation, the "splendid little war," as that inveterate phrasemaker John Hay called it, did more than terminate the bloodshed in Cuba and liberate the island from Spanish misrule. It also constituted a decisive factor in transforming the continental republic into an overseas empire, an empire with possessions in not only the Caribbean and the central Pacific but also the western Pacific and the South China Sea.

There can be little doubt that the years 1898 and 1899 formed some sort of watershed in the growth of the role

1. Archibald Cary Coolidge, *The United States as a World Power* (New York, 1908), p. 121. For a recent analysis of this problem, different in purpose from the present one, see Ernest R. May, "Emergence to World Power" in John Higham (ed.), *The Reconstruction of American History* (New York, 1962), pp. 180–96.

of the United States in world affairs. The passionate debate between the imperialists and the anti-imperialists impressed upon men at the time that the republic had to choose between tradition and innovation. The foes of colonies warned that to embark upon the path of empire would undermine the cherished policy of isolationism and thrust the country into the maelstrom of international rivalries. Such a departure from old ways would bring endless complications abroad, impede the reform movement at home, enhance the influence of the military in national affairs, and fly in the face of the democratic heritage. Contemporary historians likewise concluded that an important change had occurred. In 1903 John Bassett Moore, already an experienced diplomat and recognized student of international law, contributed to the seventh volume of the *Cambridge Modern History* a chapter entitled "The United States as a World-Power (1885–1902)." In the winter of 1906–7, Archibald Cary Coolidge, professor of European history at Harvard University, delivered at the Sorbonne a series of lectures which he subsequently published as *The United States as a World Power*. And in December, 1907, there appeared as the final narrative volume in the "American Nation" series, which was a co-operative enterprise designed to synthesize the findings of the first generation of the self-styled scientific historians, a book written by John H. Latané of The Johns Hopkins University, bearing the title of *America as a World Power, 1897–1907*. For the next half-century most writers, scholarly or popular, dated the emergence of the United States as a world power from the late 1890's and attributed to that new status varying degrees of change in American foreign policy.

Then, in 1960, the eminent diplomatic historian, Thomas A. Bailey, warned against the dangers of repeating clichés and questioned whether the United States had suddenly burst forth as a world power to the thunder of Commodore

George Dewey's guns in Manila Bay on May 1, 1898. In his presidential address before the Pacific Coast Branch of the American Historical Association, Bailey argued that the United States had been a world power since July, 1776. He defined a world power as "a nation with sufficient power in being, or capable of being mobilized, to affect world politics positively and over a period of time." He pointed out that in territory, population, natural resources, military strength, and moral force the United States met that definition. He also noted that in the century after independence the young republic had exerted its influence in all parts of the globe—in Europe, Asia, and Africa, as well as in the Americas. It had held aloft the torch of democracy and self-determination; it had broken down the commercial exclusiveness of Japan; it had become a granary for Europe. Statesmen of the major powers regarded the United States as part of the global equipoise; citizens of backward nations benefited from the endeavors of American educators and missionaries. The giant of the Western Hemisphere did not live unto itself.[2]

Bailey's address was timely but not entirely convincing. It is healthy, of course, to have old concepts challenged. His distinction between a world power and a great power is helpful, although one might question his secondary argument that the United States joined the ranks of great powers at the close of the Civil War. And certainly historians would do well to take a long look backward, to make sure of the actual role of the young republic in world affairs before 1898, if they are to describe accurately its position after that date. But in his own backward glance Bailey seems to have created an occasional straw man ready to be demolished. No reputable scholar maintains that the

2. Thomas A. Bailey, "America's Emergence as a World Power: The Myth and the Verity," *Pacific Historical Review*, XXIX (1961), 1–16.

destruction of Spain's decrepit squadron in Manila Bay and of her more modern vessels off Santiago two months later, in itself, catapulted the United States to world-power status. Such metamorphoses do not occur overnight. Similarly, it remains to be demonstrated that before 1898 the European chanceries very often considered seriously the response of the government in Washington to the power struggle outside the Western Hemisphere. The Franco-Prussian War, the clash over the Black Sea Straits, and the contest for empire in Africa are cases in point. As late as 1895, Russia, Germany, and France brought extreme pressure upon Japan during the peace negotiations with China without worrying about the reaction in America.

Two developments in the 1890's made the United States a different world power from the kind Bailey describes for the century after 1776. The first was the annexation of distant colonies which gave the nation a stake in the equilibrium of East Asia. Largely for economic reasons— the fear of closed markets and the desire for railroad and mining concessions—a concern for the future of China grew rapidly in the decade between President Grover Cleveland's indifference to the Sino-Japanese fighting over Korea in 1894–95 and President Theodore Roosevelt's peacemaking in the Russo-Japanese War of 1904–5. This concern might have come about even if there had been no crusade to free Cuba, but it was certainly hastened by the decision to retain the Philippines. The second development, stemming from the first, was a belief among the people that the country's position had changed—for better or for worse. One cannot read widely in the writings of contemporaries—businessmen, educators, clergymen, politicians, and military strategists—without detecting a new note of confidence, a new awareness of leadership, a new realization of the role the republic might play on the global stage. These broadened horizons were evident in newspapers, magazines, pamphlets, consular reports, trade journals, and congressional debates. That the American people accepted the diplomatic consequences of being a world power is, however, another matter.

The purpose of this essay is not to fix the exact date on which the United States became a world power or could rightly claim to have become a great power. Rather it seeks to look ahead, beyond the exciting events of 1898–99, to determine what effect this new position had upon subsequent foreign policy. What light do the decades between 1898 and 1917 throw upon change and continuity in twentieth-century America? Do those years mark the end of one era and the start of another? Did the acquisition of colonies bring the advantages the imperialists had promised or the evils their opponents had predicted? Were novel steps taken in world affairs? Which time-honored principles were modified or abandoned? What happened to isolationism, neutrality, the Monroe Doctrine, non-intervention, and other familiar guidelines?[3]

There can be no denying that overseas annexations led to and coincided with changes in American foreign policy. The addition of the Hawaiian Islands, Puerto Rico, Guam, the Philippines, Wake, and Tutuila between July, 1898, and December, 1899, posed unprecedented problems of administration and defense. The triumph of imperialism required the establishment of a colonial agency, the modernization of the army, the redeployment of the navy, and the institution of inter-service planning. It also caused a reversal in long-standing attitudes toward other great powers—England, Germany, and Russia at once, Japan a little later.[4]

3. For a definition of these principles and their earlier development, see Richard W. Leopold, *The Growth of American Foreign Policy: A History* (New York, 1962), pp. 17–65.

4. No citations will be given for the familiar facts that appear in this and succeeding paragraphs. For a critical evaluation of the sources from which they have been drawn, see the bibliographical

East Asia was one region where diplomacy revealed America's new position. After raising the Stars and Stripes in the South China Sea and in the Mariana Islands, the United States had to watch more closely the balance of power in the Orient. The threatened partition of China, the uncertain future of Korea, and the troublesome immigration dispute with Japan confronted men in Washington with difficult decisions. It is hardly surprising that they displayed greater activity than their predecessors. Secretary of State John Hay tried to redefine American aims in China through his circular notes of September 6, 1899, and July 3, 1900. In the summer of 1900, President William McKinley ordered ground forces from the Philippines and California to join a multinational expedition assembled to relieve the legations in Peking besieged by the insurgent Boxers. Still more prophetic was the willingness of President Roosevelt five years later to extend his good offices, and ultimately his mediation, to terminate the war then raging between Russia and Japan over Korea and Manchuria. Back in 1894, President Cleveland had asserted that the conflict then in progress between China and Japan over the same lands touched no vital interest of the United States. Thus, whereas the Sino-Japanese peace in 1895 was written at Shimonoseki under pressure from Russia, France, and Germany, the settlement of 1905 was signed at Portsmouth, New Hampshire, under the auspices of the United States.

The dozen years from the Portsmouth Treaty to the entrance into the First World War saw the American government continue to enlarge its role in the diplomacy of East Asia. Through an exchange of notes with Ambassador Kogoro Takahira on November 30, 1908, Secretary of State Elihu Root sought by all peaceful means to promote the sta-

---

essay in Leopold, *The Growth of American Foreign Policy*, pp. 819–48. Titles that are particularly relevant to this article are discussed in a bibliographical note.

bility of the Pacific area and to support the independence and integrity of China, including equality of opportunity for commerce and industry within her borders. Each party to this exchange promised to respect the territorial possessions of the other in the Pacific; it was a bilateral non-aggression pledge that foreshadowed one provision of the Four-Power Treaty of December 13, 1921. A year later Root's successor, Philander C. Knox, tried by diplomatic measures to wrest from Russia and Japan control of two key railways in Manchuria and to place them in Chinese hands. More than Hay and Root, who preceded him, or than William Jennings Bryan and Robert Lansing, who followed him, Knox endeavored to bolster his policies in East Asia by enlisting the aid of the financial community.

In the Caribbean, too, the years after 1898 brought change, but it was less precipitate and more predictable. The outmoded Clayton-Bulwer Treaty of 1850 gave way on November 18, 1901, to the second Hay-Pauncefote agreement which freed the United States to build, operate, and defend an interoceanic canal. The Monroe Doctrine, already enlarged by Secretary of State Richard Olney's dictum of July 20, 1895, was stretched further by the Roosevelt Corollary of December 6, 1904. During the Anglo-Venezuelan boundary controversy Olney had boasted that "today the United States is practically sovereign on this continent" and declared that his government would insist upon and supervise the peaceful settlement of territorial disputes between a European and a New World nation. Following the unexpectedly hostile reaction at home to the Anglo-German blockade of the Venezuelan coast in 1902, Roosevelt argued that the United States must exercise an international police power to prevent American states, guilty of flagrant wrongdoing and chronic impotence, from providing a justification for the use of armed force by a country from outside of the Western Hemisphere. Protectorates were set up in Cuba and Panama by the treaties of May 22, and November 18, 1903, in the Dominican Republic by a *modus vivendi* of April 1, 1905 (later regularized by a treaty of February 8, 1907), and in Nicaragua by a less formal arrangement in May, 1910. The assumption of these responsibilities by the United States prompted Great Britain, increasingly apprehensive over the naval race with Germany, to begin in December, 1904, transferring all large warships from the West Indies to the North Sea, thus leaving the American fleet predominant. Perhaps these developments would have occurred even if the McKinley administration had not ousted Spain from Cuba and dismembered the Spanish Empire in the Caribbean and the Pacific; certainly they were hastened by what transpired in 1898 and 1899.

The United States looked like a world power, also, in its response to mounting international tensions throughout the globe. For the first time American delegates participated in European conferences to discuss problems of war and peace. They were present at The Hague in 1899 and 1907 to deal with the machinery of arbitration, mediation, and inquiry; with the means of regulating hositlities on land and sea; and with the measures for reducing the burden of armaments. They also attended at London, in 1909–10, a gathering which labored to formulate a code of neutral rights and belligerent practices. The United States became a member of the misnamed Permanent Court of Arbitration at The Hague in 1899, and eight years later Secretary Root offered a far-sighted plan for a more effective international tribunal. Every administration from Grover Cleveland to Woodrow Wilson searched for a workable formula by which the compulsory arbitration of certain classes of disputes might be incorporated in bilateral treaties. But the most dramatic act on the world stage came in 1905 when President Roosevelt employed his good offices to help to bring the

Russo-Japanese War to a close and to liquidate, through a multipartite conference at Algeciras, a dangerous Franco-German quarrel over Morocco. Not until May, 1914, when Wilson permitted Colonel Edward M. House to explore in Europe possible means of averting an armed clash between the rival alliance systems did the United States again act so directly to preserve world peace. Once the World War had broken out, Wilson tried constantly to serve as peace-maker—at first, in a disinterested attempt to end the bloodshed; later, in a desperate effort to avoid American involvement.

To many people, in 1917, the intervention of the United States in the war seemed a logical consequence of the republic's emergence as a world power. The breakdown of traditional neutrality, the forging of economic entanglements, and the manifestation of passionate attachment to rival belligerents threatened the old indifference to the outcome of a major European conflict. Wilson was unable to apply the customary rules of neutrality without hurting Germany or to introduce a more realistic code without penalizing England. The sale of munitions and the extension of loans and credits gave American manufacturers and financiers a tangible stake in the battle, while the cotton-grower and wheat-producer feared the loss of a lucrative market on the Continent. The assiduous efforts of rival propagandists to mold American opinion and the apparent commitment of articulate groups to one side or the other frightened the President and undercut his plea of August 19, 1914, for his countrymen to be "impartial in thought as well as in action." Thus, where Roosevelt could act as peacemaker in 1905 without any fear of having the nation embroiled if he failed, Wilson knew in 1916 that failure would bring involvement. On May 27 of that year, he warned: "We are participants in the life of the world. . . .

What affects mankind is inevitably our affair as well as the affair of the nations of Europe and of Asia." [5]

How did informed citizens of 1917 interpret American intervention? Wilson's explanation was that the status of a belligerent had been thrust upon the republic. The recent course of imperial Germany, he told Congress on April 2, was "nothing less than war against the government and people of the United States." Wilson spoke of vindicating maritime rights, violations of which cost American lives, not of insuring an Allied victory or preserving a favorable equipoise in Europe and Asia. Honor, not security, was stressed. But in his much-quoted address the President discussed the aims of intervention as well as the causes, and he sketched the goals for which he asked America to give of her blood and her might. By sublimating a war to uphold national rights into a crusade for all mankind, he bolstered the notion that the United States, in the face of a global cataclysm, was responding as befitted a world power.

Others shared Wilson's belief that by April, 1917, traditional neutrality was no longer feasible and historic isolationism was both obsolete and unwise. From the outset, Herbert Croly's *New Republic* had viewed the war in the broadest terms; on November 7, 1914, an editorial had proclaimed "The End of American Isolation." One of its foremost writers, Walter Lippmann, supported intervention because it would maintain Anglo-American control of the Atlantic shipping lanes, a motive he would stress more strongly and with much more validity after June, 1940. Lippmann also wanted the United States to enter the war because he felt such a move would aid in creating a league of nations. Many scholars and publicists, such as George Louis Beer, Roland G. Usher, Walter E. Weyl, and H. H.

5. Ray Stannard Baker and William E. Dodd (eds.), *The New Democracy* (*The Public Papers of Woodrow Wilson* [6 vols; New York, 1925–27]), II, 185.

Powers, advocated some form of collective action that would bring to a close this nation's abstention from global responsibility.[6]

The foregoing is some evidence for the idea that the triumph of imperialism in 1898–99 led to a reorientation of American foreign policy. What can be said for the thesis that the acquisition of an overseas empire did not change decisively traditional principles and practices?

First, there was the rapid decline in a zeal for colonies. Far from embarking on a big program of annexation, the United States gained, between December, 1899, and April, 1917, only the Canal Zone and the Danish West Indies. The former was obtained in November, 1903, solely to provide a route for the interoceanic canal; the latter, in August, 1916, primarily to keep them out of German hands. How do we account for the sudden subsidence of expansionist sentiment? The battle waged by the anti-imperialists in 1899 and 1900 was partly responsible. The insurrection in the Philippines, with the shocking atrocities on both sides, was also a factor. But the best explanation lies in the nature of the imperialist impulse. On neither economic nor strategic grounds did the United States in 1898 need outposts in the western Pacific. American industrialists and bankers did not require dependencies in which to sell surplus manufactures or to invest surplus capital. The urge for colonies under McKinley was, as Walter E. Weyl asserted in April, 1917, "an unripe imperialism."[7] Its roots were largely emotional; and when those emotions found an outlet in a successful war, the movement withered. In the Caribbean, to be sure, the strategic roots of imperialism nourished the growth of protectorates, but these last represented a limited and temporary type of control. And they posed less diffi-

6. Robert Endicott Osgood, *Ideals and Self-Interest in America's Foreign Relations: The Great Transformation of the Twentieth Century* (Chicago, 1953), pp. 115–34.

7. Walter E. Weyl, *American War Policies* (New York, 1917), p. 53.

cult problems of defense than did the Philippines located 6,000 miles from San Francisco.

Revealing, too, was the failure to create a central colonial office. Supervision of the lands acquired in 1898 and afterward was divided. The Navy Department took over the smaller islands of Guam and Tutuila and, later, of St. Thomas, St. John, and St. Croix. The War Department governed the Canal Zone directly but handled the Philippines and, after 1909, Puerto Rico through a Bureau of Insular Affairs. Hawaii enjoyed territorial status and came nominally under the Interior Department. Uninhabited Wake, like Midway, required no formal rule. The Bureau of Insular Affairs had the makings of a colonial office, but its authority was too restricted. To some persons, it seemed handicapped by being in the War Department under an army officer rather than in the State Department under a civilian. Significantly, both Congress and the public quickly lost interest in colonial problems; despite prodding by the executive, Congress passed few important laws dealing with the new possessions from 1902 to 1916.

Equally disappointing was the inability of the army and navy to meet fully the challenges of world power. The reforms urged by Secretary of War Root between 1901 and 1903 could have come—indeed should have come—whether or not the United States acquired colonies. An increase in the authorized strength of the ground forces, the abolition of permanent assignments to staff posts in Washington, the revival of the special-service schools, the creation of an Army War College, the overhaul of the antiquated militia system, and the establishment of a general staff corps were changes long overdue. Yet Root merely scratched the surface of the deep-seated evils of the militia system, and his general staff corps had to undergo further development before it operated efficiently. Nor did Root do everything that was necessary. He deferred the tactical reorganization of the field troops, and his attempt to secure co-ordination with the navy was confined to an ineffectual Joint Army-Navy Board, founded in July, 1903. Although the army made more progress in the fifteen years before Sarajevo than in the thirty after Appomattox, it did not keep pace with its European counterparts and was never prepared to discharge completely the increased functions that came with empire.

The same can be said of the navy. Superficially that service was less in need of change. It had performed brilliantly against Spain and had escaped the scandals which plagued the War Department. Still, with new doctrines and tactics being adopted across the Atlantic and with new responsibilities for colonies being faced across the Pacific, the navy could not depend upon its existing loose command structure. In a typical compromise between tradition and innovation, Secretary John D. Long created by departmental order on March 13, 1900, a General Board, composed of nine officers and presided over by the Admiral of the Navy, a rank revived for Dewey. The General Board's main duties were to draft war plans, study construction, recommend additional facilities and deployment, and counsel the secretary. Its role, however, was purely advisory. It issued no orders and, lacking legislative sanction, could be abolished by any future secretary. It was better than anything that had gone before, but it was not enough. In 1909 Secretary George von Lengerke Meyer instituted the aide system which placed four officers, responsible to him, in charge of fleet operations, personnel, material, and inspection. Not until Congress enacted statutes in 1915 and 1916 for an Office of the Chief of Naval Operations did the sea arm possess anything resembling the general-staff principle.

More serious still was the navy's incapability of protecting some of the colonies acquired in 1898. Contrary to the claims of the expansionists, certain islands—notably the Philippines—weakened rather than strengthened the military position of the United States. The reasons were two in number. First, the fleet was never big enough or balanced enough to control the sea lanes stretching from the Caribbean to the western Pacific. Second, the vessels that were available lacked safe anchorages and repair facilities in distant waters. For these deficiencies the Congress was largely, though by no means entirely, to blame.

Measured by the yardstick of the past, the record of the legislature seemed satisfactory. Appropriations rose steadily from $48,099,969 for the fiscal year 1900 to $149,763,563 for fiscal 1916. The number of battleships in commission increased from five on January 1, 1900, to thirty-seven on October 1, 1916.[8] By 1907 the United States Navy ranked second only to Great Britain in total tonnage. But to improve upon the nineteenth century was not enough for a world power, and figures can mislead. The commissioning late in 1906 of H.M.S. "Dreadnought," the first all big-gun battleship, rendered obsolete every existing battleship and compelled nations to start building afresh. This event coincided with a growing opposition to Roosevelt's construction policy, an opposition that caused the United States to lose ground as the Anglo-German race quickened. Since most admirals wished to allot the bulk of available funds to dreadnoughts, the American fleet soon found itself sorely lacking in cruisers, battle and scout, and badly trailing in destroyers, submarines, and auxiliaries. Not until August, 1916, did Congress pass, under pressure from the advocates of preparedness, a three-year program designed to achieve a well-rounded fleet that would be second to none.

The want of adequate overseas bases can be explained on several grounds. One was the decline of popular interest in the colonies. A second was congressional apathy or, perhaps, a reluctance of the lawmakers to devote funds to installations which did not benefit their constituents directly. There was more enthusiasm on Capitol Hill for

8. B. R. Tillman, Jr. (comp.), *Navy Yearbook* [*1916*] (Washington, D.C., 1916), pp. 581, 638. This title appears also as *Senate Document No. 555*, 64th Cong., 2d Sess.

installations inside the continental United States than out-side. Finally, the army and navy could not agree on the location of the main base in the Philippines. The navy desired Olongapo on Subic Bay; the army, Cavite on Manila Bay. This inter-service quarrel reached a climax just before Roosevelt left the White House. On November 11, 1909, William Howard Taft endorsed a recommendation from the Joint Board that no major base be established in the Pacific west of Hawaii and that efforts be concentrated on Pearl Harbor. This decision accepted a fact which had become evident in the preceding years, that the Imperial Japanese Navy dominated the area beyond the International Date Line.

If after 1899 colonial and military practice revealed the limits within which the new world power must operate, a similar hesitation can be detected in its policy in East Asia. The goal of the open door, as defined by Hay on July 3, 1900, remained constant, but the obstacles to its realization grew more formidable. First Russia, then Japan, and then the two antagonists in concert infringed upon the territorial integrity of China and violated the principle of equal commercial opportunity for all. Roosevelt's peacemaking in 1905 marked the end of an era with Japan. In the ensuing decade an intermittent controversy over immigration, a muted rivalry over sea power, and an open clash over economic rights in Manchuria indicated how fully the vital interests of both nations were in conflict. And in the years before the First World War, as in those after it, the American people and their elected representatives were unwilling to put force behind their avowed policy in the Orient. No one stated the dilemma better than a leading expansionist of 1898. Writing to Taft on December 22, 1910, former President Roosevelt said:

> Our vital interest is to keep the Japanese out of our country, and at the same time to preserve the good will of Japan. The vital interest of the Japanese, on the other hand, is in Manchuria and

Korea. It is therefore peculiarly our interest not to take any steps as regards Manchuria which will give the Japanese cause to feel, with or without reason, that we are hostile to them, or a menace—in however slight a degree—to their interests. Alliance with China, in view of China's absolute military helplessness, means of course not an additional strength to us, but an additional obligation. . . . As regards Manchuria, if the Japanese choose to follow a course of conduct to which we are adverse, we cannot stop it unless we are prepared to go to war, and a successful war about Manchuria would require a fleet as good as that of England, plus an army as good as that of Germany. The "open-door" policy in China was an excellent thing, and will I hope be a good thing in the future, so far as it can be maintained by general diplomatic agreement; but as has been proved by the whole history of Manchuria, alike under Russia and under Japan, the "open-door" policy, as a matter of fact, completely disappears as soon as a powerful nation determines to disregard it, and is willing to run the risk of war rather than forego its intention.[9]

Roosevelt's cautious realism did not go unheeded. Secretary Knox had already accepted without protest Japan's absorption of Korea on August 29, 1910, and after one failure he did not again seek to upset the Russo-Japanese domination of the Manchurian railway system. In May, 1915, after Bryan's vacillation during the crisis precipitated by the twenty-one demands Japan presented to China in January, Wilson did strive, and with some success, to keep to a minimum the concessions wrung from the government at Peking. But the future of the open door was still unclear when, after the United States entered the war, Lansing and Kikijuro Ishii temporarily smoothed over mutual differences in an ambiguous executive agreement of November 2, 1917.

In the Western Hemisphere the triumph of imperialism did not transform American policy. The developments after

9. Elting E. Morison *et al.* (eds.), *The Letters of Theodore Roosevelt* (8 vols.; Cambridge, 1951–54), VII, 189–90.

1899 were more a consummation than a change. There it
was possible for the United States to play a more active
role without departing from traditional isolationism or
neutrality. What had been breached was the principle of
not interfering in the internal affairs of other nations.
The first instance came in Spain's Cuban colony in April,
1898; subsequent actions under the Roosevelt Corollary
or special treaties with Cuba and Panama also violated a
historic non-interventionism. Beginning in 1906, however,
the men in Washington sought to allay suspicion and promote hemispheric cordiality. In that year Secretary Root
made an unprecedented goodwill tour of South America
and attended the Third International Conference of American States at Rio de Janeiro. In 1907 he did much to see
that eighteen New World republics participated in the
Second Hague Conference. Indeed, he had been largely
responsible for delaying that meeting for one year so that
it would not conflict with the gathering at Rio. In 1907,
too, the United States and Mexico sponsored a Central
American Peace Conference at Washington, and in 1912
Secretary Knox visited ten Caribbean countries.

The advent of the Democrats brought even more strenuous efforts to forge a good-neighbor policy. "One of the
chief objects of my Administration," Wilson asserted on
March 11, 1913, "will be to cultivate the friendship and
deserve the confidence of our sister republics." [10] At Mobile
on October 27, he promised: "The United States will never
again seek one additional foot of territory by conquest." [11]
During 1914 Wilson and Edward M. House drew up
a four-point Pan-American pact which contained many
ideas he later wrote into the League of Nations Covenant.
It guaranteed the territorial integrity of the signatories,

10. Arthur S. Link, *Wilson: The New Freedom* (Princeton, N.J.,
1956), p. 320.
11. Baker and Dodd (eds.), *The New Democracy*, I, 67.

required an amicable settlement of all pending boundary disputes, made obligatory the use of arbitration or inquiry in certain types of controversies, and experimented with an arms embargo to keep the peace. But the outbreak of the World War prevented serious consideration of the project, while several moves by Wilson and William Jennings Bryan marred this quest for inter-American harmony. The most serious of these was the creation of a fifth protectorate in Haiti, further interference in the Dominican Republic, and an entanglement in the revolution and counterrevolution in Mexico.

There were limits, also, to how far the United States would go in helping avert wars. From 1899 to 1914, the republic broke new ground by attending the two Hague Conferences, by facilitating the peacemaking at Portsmouth, by concerning itself with a quarrel over Morocco, and by negotiating numerous treaties requiring the arbitration of certain kinds of disputes. Yet never did the government tie its hands for the future, commit itself irrevocably to a course of action, or surrender an iota of sovereignty. In consenting to the Act of Algeciras of April 7, 1906, and to the Hague Convention of October 18, 1907, the Senate added reservations designed to maintain inviolate the Monroe Doctrine and the policy of isolationism. The first of these disclaimed any intention "to depart from the traditional American foreign policy which forbids participation by the United States in the settlement of political questions which are entirely European in their scope." The second insisted that "nothing contained in this convention shall be so construed as to require the United States of America to depart from its traditional policy of not intruding upon, interfering with, or entangling itself in the political questions of policy or internal administration of any foreign state; nor shall anything contained in the said convention be construed to imply a relinquishment by the United States of its traditional attitude toward purely American questions." [12] The only bilateral arbitration agreements to pass the Senate exempted disputes affecting "the vital interests, the independence, or the honor" of the signatories and disputes concerning the interests of third parties. Differences of a legal nature and those relating to the interpretation of a treaty alone had to be arbitrated.

Two outstanding Republicans clearly defined the commitment of the United States to world peace in this period. "In all these matters where I am asked to interfere between two foreign nations," Roosevelt wrote to Ambassador Whitelaw Reid in London on August 3, 1905, "all I can do is this. If there is a chance to prevent trouble by preventing simple misunderstanding, or by myself taking the first step . . . when it has become a matter of punctilio with the two parties . . . then I am entirely willing and glad to see if I can be of any value in preventing the misunderstanding from becoming acute to the danger point. If, however, there is a genuine conflict of interest which has made each party resolute to carry its point even at the cost of war, there is no use of my interfering. . . . " [13] On January 24, 1906, Henry Cabot Lodge defended in the Senate Roosevelt's dispatch of representatives to Algeciras. "The policy and interest of the United States alike demand the peace of the world," he said, "and it is not to be supposed for a moment that we are never to exert our great moral influence or to use our good offices for the maintenance of the world's peace. . . . In entangling alliances, of course, no man wants to engage this country; we have no concern with the wars of Europe; no one for a moment would think

12. William M. Malloy (comp.), *Treaties, Conventions, International Acts, Protocols and Agreements between the United States of America and Other Powers, 1776–1909* (2 vols.; Washington, D.C., 1910), pp. 2183, 2247. This title appears also as *Senate Document No. 357*, 61st Cong., 2d Sess.

13. Morison, *The Letters of Theodore Roosevelt*, IV, 1298.

of engaging us in a position where we might be involved in them . . . but . . . the phrase 'entangling alliances' does not mean that we should not unite with other nations on commercial questions . . . or in the promotion of those great and beneficent objects which are embodied in international conventions." The presence of American delegates, he concluded, "will make for the advancement of our commerce in Morocco and will also make for what is infinitely more important, the peace of the world." [14]

Did the experience of the years from 1914 to 1917 persuade the American people to enlarge that commitment? Did they agree with Wilson that neutrality was "no longer feasible or desirable where the peace of the world is concerned"? Did they endorse his "concert of free people," his league of nations, as a war aim? The evidence is overwhelming that they did not. In April, 1917, Wilson and his associates, as well as intellectuals like Lippmann and Weyl, were in a minority. Few citizens feared that Germany would wrest control of the Atlantic; not even the President or his secretary of the navy knew at that time of the alarming inroads the submarine was making on British shipping. The war on land appeared to be a stalemate, with little prospect of a German victory. An invasion of American soil seemed very unlikely. With considerable reluctance and an air of resignation, most Americans concurred in Wilson's assertion that "the right is more precious than peace" and that they must "accept gage of battle with this natural foe to liberty."

The debate in Congress revealed how few legislators followed the President beyond his immediate goals—the defense of American rights and the destruction of Prussian autocracy. A handful of critics, like Senators Robert M. La Follette and George W. Norris or Representatives Claude Kitchin and Fred A. Britten, rejected Wilson's basic premise, arguing that the United States should have and could have stayed out. They would have denied that America's

14. *Congressional Record*, 59th Cong., 1st Sess., p. 1470.

emergence as a world power obligated her to fight in order
to preserve the existing order in Europe or in Asia. The
more ardent Republican interventionists, like Lodge or
Senator James W. Wadsworth, carefully refrained from
supporting the league-of-nations idea. They appealed rather
for bipartisanship in a war against the forces of barbarism.
They were the ones most likely to recognize the need for a
changed foreign policy; they reflected the views of Roosevelt, Hay, Root, and others who had shaped the course of
the imperial republic after 1898. Most of this group favored
a postwar alliance with England and France but said little
on that point in April, 1917. Still other Republicans, and a
few Democrats, stood closer to La Follette and Norris on
the best policy for the future. While ready to vindicate
national honor by armed force, they saw no need to depart
from traditional practices after the guns were stilled. Thus
Senator Warren G. Harding insisted that he was "not voting
for war in the name of democracy" but rather in behalf of
"the maintenance of just American rights." William E.
Borah was more explicit in separating the quarrel with
Germany from the creation of a future league. There can
be, he told the Senate, "but one sufficient reason for com-
mitting this country to war, and that is the honor and
security of our own people and our own Nation. . . . I join
no crusade; I seek or accept no alliances; I obligate this
Government to no other power. I make war alone for my
countrymen and their rights, for my country and its
honor." [15]

Certainly the subsequent battle over the Versailles Treaty
disclosed a widespread unwillingness to join Wilson in pro-
claiming the abandonment of isolationism and neutrality.
The rejection of the League Covenant cannot be attributed,
as it often has been, solely to personal enmities, partisan
rivalries, and parochial outlooks. In seeking to break with
the past, the President moved too far, too fast. The American people were not prepared to assume the moral leader-

15. *Congressional Record*, 65th Cong., 1st Sess., p. 253.

ship he asked of them or to embrace the type of collective security he envisaged. In 1920, as in 1898, the average citizen thought the United States could be a world power and still adhere to practices of an earlier day. In the interlude between the two World Wars, the policy-makers had to settle for a compromise between traditional nineteenth-century principles and Wilson's more ambitious objectives. These leaders reflected the experience of 1898 to 1917 by taking unprecedented steps to achieve regional non-aggression pacts, arms-control agreements, membership in an international court, and pledges to renounce war as an instrument of national policy. They also eliminated some of the excrescences of the imperialist adventure. But they were still loath to forge permanent alliances or to promise in advance to use armed force in a future crisis, even though the new world power of 1898 had become the Old World's creditor of 1921. It would take the lessons learned from the futility of that compromise and from the agony of 1940 to 1945 to effect a true revolution in American foreign policy. As we look back from the troubled present, we can see more clearly than did the older historians that the emergence of the United States as a world power after the clash with Spain and the interwar compromise after the struggle against Germany—while representing change— were at most transitional stages in a process that culminated in the global commitments and constant involvement which characterize American foreign policy today.

BIBLIOGRAPHICAL NOTE

Although many able scholars have dealt with American foreign policy in the period from 1898 to 1917, none has produced a comprehensive analysis of the United States as a world power. The best overview is in the first hundred pages of Foster Rhea Dulles, *America's Rise to World Power, 1898–1954* (New York, 1955), a volume in "The New American Nations Series" edited by Henry Steele Commager and Richard B. Morris. It rests, however, entirely on printed materials.

Works on the basic guidelines of American foreign policy in this period are spotty. There is no systematic treatment of neutrality or isolationism. Selig Adler, *The Isolationist Impulse: Its Twentieth-Century Reaction* (London, 1957) is helpful for popular sentiment, as opposed to governmental policy, but devotes less than forty pages to the years before 1917. For neutrality, one must look to books whose primary concern is the years 1914 to 1917. Two works by Dexter Perkins do justice to the Monroe Doctrine—his heavily documented *The Monroe Doctrine, 1867–1907* (Baltimore, 1937) and the less detailed *Hands Off: A History of the Monroe Doctrine* (Boston, 1941). The latter was reissued in 1955, with little change, under the subtitle. John A. Logan, Jr., *No Transfer: An American Security Principle* (New Haven, 1961) is a useful supplement. Studies of the open door, non-intervention, and recognition would be welcome.

Until recently an understanding of the emergence of the United States as a world power has been obscured by the myths and distortions surrounding the War with Spain. Although the foes of colonies lost the fight over the peace treaty and the election of 1900, they won the battle of words that followed. Ever since 1917, but especially in the 1930's, there has been a distinct anti-imperialist tinge to most books relating to McKinley, armed intervention in Cuba, and the decision to retain the Philippines. Several facts account for that coloration. Many writers disliked the economic and social ideas of the twenty-fifth president. Some found his religiosity unpalatable. Others accepted the contemporary lampoons which pictured him as a puppet of Mark

Hanna and the trusts. Still others swallowed the nonsense contained in H. H. Kohlsaat's memoirs regarding his alleged ignorance of geography and military matters.[16] Most influential of all, was *The Martial Spirit* by Walter Millis, a journalist without previous experience in historical writing. Published in 1931, when the author's pacifism was in full flower and most Americans had rejected the white man's burden, it stressed the satiric aspects of the war. Using only obvious printed sources and some of them uncritically, Millis produced an amusing but highly oversimplified chronicle whose pages have since been a gold mine for professors seeking humor for their lectures. These teachers often overlook the fact that Millis called his book "an essay in history" and not a history or work of scholarship.[17]

If *The Martial Spirit* strengthened the anti-imperialist caricature of McKinley and the assumptions of economic

16. H. H. Kohlsaat, *From McKinley to Harding: Personal Recollections of Our Presidents* (New York, 1923) has badly misled a large number of historians who, in quoting or summarizing the following sentences, have denigrated McKinley. "I visited the President a few days after the victory [at Manila Bay]. McKinley said: 'When we received the cable from Admiral Dewey telling of their taking of the Philippines I looked up their location on the globe. I could not have told where those darned islands were within 2,000 miles!' Some months later he said: 'If old Dewey had just sailed away when he smashed the Spanish fleet, what a lot of trouble he would have saved us" (page 68). Actually, McKinley knew exactly where the islands were. He had let stand since February 25, 1898, a preliminary order to Dewey—who held the temporary rank of commodore, not admiral—from Assistant Secretary Roosevelt to prepare for an attack on Manila in case of war with Spain. On April 24 McKinley presided over a White House conference which directed Dewey to sail at once from Hong Kong. For the next week Washington papers carried full stories of the impending battle, replete with maps and pictures. Furthermore, McKinley never envisaged Dewey's sailing away after the battle. Without consulting Congress or awaiting Dewey's formal report, McKinley decided on May 2 to send army units to enable Dewey to hold Cavite and eventually move on Manila. On these two episodes, see Leopold, *The Growth of American Foreign Policy*, pp. 150–52, 180–82.

17. Walter Millis, *The Martial Spirit* (Cambridge, 1931), p. 413.

determinists, a scholarly effort by Julius W. Pratt five years later rescued American imperialism from being fitted into the classic mold of John A. Hobson. In *Expansionists of 1898,* originally prepared as lectures, Pratt paid relatively little attention to the origins of the Cuban crusade but concentrated on the growth of a new manifest-destiny sentiment in the 1880's and on the debate over the annexation of Hawaii in the 1890's. In two self-contained chapters, however, he analyzed the attitude of the business and religious community, mostly through specialized periodicals, and found that most manufacturers and financiers opposed a bold foreign policy until the eve of war. Only when they saw that the conflict would be brief and not check recovery from the long depression did they embrace imperialism. Pratt's findings have, properly, greatly influenced later writers.[18]

For almost twenty years no one undertook a major study of McKinley or the War with Spain. Several minor or tangential publications filled gaps or corrected earlier interpretations. William E. Livezey, John A. Garraty, and Howard K. Beale developed the ideas of those ardent expansionists —Mahan, Lodge, and Roosevelt—but in the process reinforced the false notion that this trio directly affected McKinley's decisions.[19] Other important imperialists, like Senator Cushman K. Davis, were neglected, while key men of the President's inner circle, notably William R. Day,

18. Julius W. Pratt, *Expansionists of 1898: The Acquisition of Hawaii and the Spanish Islands* (Baltimore, 1936), especially pp. 230–316. The most systematic attempt to explain American imperialism in terms of the drive for outlets for surplus manufactures, capital, and population is in Charles A. Beard, *The Idea of National Interest: An Analytical Study of American Foreign Policy* (New York, 1934), a work done in collaboration with G. H. E. Smith.

19. William E. Livezey, *Mahan on Sea Power* (Norman, Okla., 1947); John A. Garraty, *Henry Cabot Lodge: A Biography* (New York, 1952); Howard K. Beale, *Theodore Roosevelt and the Rise of America to World Power* (Baltimore, 1956).

were ignored. Beale, moreover, exaggerated Roosevelt's role in ordering Dewey, in case of war, to attack the Philippines and wrongly attributed to him a prewar desire to annex the archipelago.[20] Books by Sylvester K. Stevens and William A. Russ, Jr., have supplemented, but not markedly altered, Pratt's story of events in Hawaii.[21] George W. Auxier has demonstrated that yellow journalism was not confined to New York.[22] Orestes Ferrara's sketch of the diplomacy of the great powers before 1898 was translated into English.[23] In a widely quoted essay Richard Hofstadter linked the impulse for adventure abroad with the frustration and discord at home—what he calls "the psychic crisis of the 1890's." He also correctly distinguished the forces making for intervention in Cuba from those responsible for retention of the Philippines.[24]

Then in 1959 appeared the first of four major contributions to comprehending the emergence of the United States as a world power. *In the Days of McKinley* by Margaret

20. On February 25, 1898, according to Beale, "The Assistant Secretary had seized the opportunity given by Long's absence to insure our grabbing the Philippines without a decision to do so by either Congress or the President, or least of all the people" (p. 63). Such a conclusion is unwarranted by the facts and is unfair to McKinley. The latter could have revoked the order at any time in the next two months but chose not to do so. Instead, on April 24 he directed that it be put into effect. There is no evidence that Roosevelt on February 25 or McKinley on April 24 looked upon this military operation as a means "to insure our grabbing the Philippines."

21. Sylvester K. Stevens, *American Expansion in Hawaii, 1842–1898* (Harrisburg, Pa., 1945); William A. Russ, Jr., *The Hawaiian Revolution, 1893–1894* (Selinsgrove, Pa., 1959) and *The Hawaiian Republic (1894–98) and Its Struggle to Win Annexation* (Selinsgrove, Pa., 1961).

22. George W. Auxier, "Middle Western Newspapers and the Spanish-American War, 1895–1898," *Mississippi Valley Historical Review*, XXVI (1940), 523–34.

23. Orestes Ferrara, *The Last Spanish War*, trans. William E. Shea, (New York, 1937).

24. Richard Hofstadter, "Manifest Destiny and the Philippines," in Daniel Aaron (ed.), *America In Crisis* (New York, 1952), pp. 172–200.

Leech is not a complete biography or the work of a specialist in the period. The author devotes 500 of the 600 pages to the presidential years, and most of those center upon the war. Except for the diary of George B. Cortelyou, which had been kept from scholars for her benefit, she draws upon little new material, and her grasp of the political and military problems of the day is not always sure. Yet by an impressionistic technique and a sympathetic approach, Miss Leech has produced a good portrait of McKinley, a thoroughly credible one that testifies to his virtues and only slightly underplays his shortcomings. She has demonstrated that the President was no weakling and made all of the key decisions once the war had begun. Hers is a long overdue corrective that must be taken into account by all who henceforth discuss the era.[25]

The second contribution came in 1961. Ernest R. May's *Imperial Democracy: The Emergence of America as a Great Power* is the product of a highly competent scholar who places his subject in a broad setting. Focusing on the period from the uprising in Hawaii in January, 1893, to the Senate's vote on the peace treaty in February, 1899, it covers more ground and probes more deeply than Pratt's lectures. May describes fully the Venezuelan boundary controversy in order to illustrate Europe's sudden realization that the transatlantic giant must be reckoned with. His best chapters trace Spain's futile moves to muster European support against intervention in Cuba; in these he has exploited the manuscript and printed files of the Continental foreign offices. He is also very good in analyzing American public opinion, though his treatment of McKinley's decision to retain the Philippines is less convincing than that of the President's yielding on intervention in Cuba. By August, 1898, McKinley was master of the situation. Far from hav-

25. Margaret Leech, *In the Days of McKinley* (New York, 1959).

ing to avoid being crushed by the steamroller of popular sentiment—the figure is May's—he did much by word and deed to arouse that sentiment.[26] Since the personal papers of McKinley's circle are either non-existent or unrewarding, May might have enlarged his knowledge of the cabinet's deliberations by a more extensive investigation of newspapers and military records in the National Archives. But all in all, his is an impressive volume with which future scholars must begin.

The last two contributions followed in 1963. H. Wayne Morgan's *William McKinley and His America* does not alter the portrait drawn by Leech, but it is a much sounder historical study. The author has dug more deeply into newspapers and manuscripts, both private and archival; and if he tends to explain rather than to appraise many of the President's acts, he is not uncritical. Morgan offers the fullest and best account of the prewar negotiations with Spain; his story of the peacemaking is good but a little imprecise.[27] He follows Pratt on the attitude of the business community; he differs from May in stressing less the impact of public opinion. Although he argues that McKinley virtually decided to retain the Philippines on May 2, 1898, when, on the basis of incomplete reports, he dispatched ground troops to aid Dewey, his evidence is not convincing. Morgan does not even try to explain why the cabinet, having given no thought before May 1 to what would be done in event of a victory in Manila Bay, moved so promptly. A

26. Ernest R. May, *Imperial Democracy: The Emergence of America as a Great Power* (New York, 1961). The allusion to the steamroller is on page 257.

27. Syracuse, N. Y., 1963. For example, Morgan fails to make clear the exact sequence of events leading to the telegram of October 28, 1898, from John Hay to William R. Day instructing the peace commissioners to demand all of the Philippines. For a statement on how an error in the *Foreign Relations* volume for 1898 has misled historians, see Richard W. Leopold, "The *Foreign Relations* Series: A Centennial Estimate," *Mississippi Valley Historical Review*, XLIX (March, 1963), 598 n. 12.

failure to answer a few unresolved, and perhaps insoluble, questions of war and peace is the chief weakness of this highly creditable but too hastily published book.

The New Empire: An Interpretation of American Expansion, 1860–1898 by Walter LaFeber emphasizes the economic factors making for the acquisition of overseas possessions. It could initiate a modification of the prevailing consensus among historians that has minimized material considerations in the coming of the war with Spain. The first half of the volume describes the persistence of territorial ambitions from 1865 to 1889 and analyzes the intellectual, strategic, and economic elements in the new manifest destiny. The second half maintains that a quest for new markets dominated the diplomacy of the 1890's as the United States reacted to developments in Brazil, Venezuela, Central America, Cuba, Hawaii, and China. The author has done an impressive job of research and reveals an inquiring mind in the questions he raises. He insists that colonies were sought, not for their own sake, but as a means of opening up markets to relieve the glut of industrial and agricultural goods at home. Thus, anticolonialists like Cleveland, Gresham, and Olney were as eager as expansionists like Lodge, Beveridge, and Reid to help the businessman. LaFeber does not pretend to deal fully with the decision to wage war or to retain colonies; he is content "to stress the operative economic forces and to point out the interaction of events in Asia, Cuba, and the American business community." [28] He is most convincing on this interaction; for, although he has produced a stimulating essay that must be read by all specialists in foreign policy, he has hurt his case by carelessness with facts, haste in

28. *The New Empire: An Interpretation of American Expansion, 1860–1898* (Ithaca, N.Y., 1963), ix. A paper read by William Appleman Williams before the Mississippi Valley Historical Association at Cleveland on April 30, 1964, also emphasized the quest for new markets as an explanation of the triumph of imperialism in 1898.

composition, and an eagerness to force evidence into a preconceived mold.

The question of how the United States acted as a world power has attracted less attention than why or when the republic gained that status. To be sure there are, for the years 1899 to 1914, many excellent works on American policy in the Caribbean and East Asia. Others describe the changed relations with the great powers; a few of these draw upon recently opened files of the Public Record Office in London.[29] Julius W. Pratt has traced lucidly the administration of the new empire; and although he did not tap the unprinted files of the Bureau of Insular Affairs and other governing bodies, his conclusions are not likely to be altered.[30] Among the policy-makers, Roosevelt, Hay, Root, and Wilson have been well covered; more needs to be done on Taft, Knox, Bryan, and Lansing.[31] Beale's study of

29. Charles S. Campbell, Jr., *Anglo-American Understanding, 1898–1903* (Baltimore, 1957), and A. E. Campbell, *Great Britain and the United States, 1895–1903* (London, 1960).

30. Julius W. Pratt, *America's Colonial Experiment: How the United States Gained, Governed, and In Part Gave Away a Colonial Empire* (New York, 1950). Whitney T. Perkins, *Denial of Empire: The United States and Its Dependencies* (Leyden, 1962), is a carefully executed work which not only brings up to date the analysis in Pratt but also discusses more fully the administration of individual territories under American rule.

31. Beale, *Theodore Roosevelt and the Rise of America to World Power;* William H. Harbaugh, *Power and Responsibility: The Life and Times of Theodore Roosevelt* (New York, 1961); Tyler Dennett, *John Hay: From Poetry to Politics* (New York, 1933); Philip C. Jessup, *Elihu Root* (2 vols.; New York, 1938); Richard W. Leopold, *Elihu Root and the Conservative Tradition* (Boston, 1954); Arthur S. Link, *Wilson* (3 vols. to date; Princeton, N.J., 1947–   ). Henry F. Pringle, *The Life and Times of William Howard Taft* (2 vols.; New York, 1938) is good on domestic affairs but fails to do justice to foreign policy. There are useful sketches of Knox, Bryan, and Lansing in Norman A. Graebner (ed.), *An Uncertain Tradition: American Secretaries of State in the Twentieth Century* (New York, 1961); the one on Bryan by Richard D. Challener is especially good. The picture of Lansing after 1914 can be filled out by Daniel M. Smith, *Robert Lansing and American Neutrality, 1914–1917* (Berkeley, Calif., 1958) and by Burton F. Beers, *Vain Endeavor: Robert Lansing's Attempt to End the American-Japanese Rivalry* (Durham, N.C., 1962).

Roosevelt, while uneven in places, is particularly good on the peace of Portsmouth and the quarrel over Morocco. Still to come are reliable accounts of United States policy with respect to compulsory arbitration, the Second Hague Conference, and attempts to strengthen the machinery for peace from 1907 to 1914.[32] Pilot essays have shown what can be done with the ideas of military leaders and the drafting of war plans when previously classified manuscripts are made available.[33]

The last decade has seen the historiography of the First World War come of age. Gone are the passionate attacks upon and defenses of Wilson—and the straining to draw lessons from the past—which marred so many writings of the 1920's and 1930's. Books by Arthur S. Link, Ernest R. May, Marion C. Siney, and Karl E. Birnbaum, to mention only a few, are notable for their detachment and their approach.[34] May's careful probing into German sources and his intelligent sampling of scattered British records give

32. Calvin DeArmond Davis, *The United States and the First Hague Peace Conference* (Ithaca, N.Y., 1962) is a helpful monograph.

33. Fred Greene, "The Military View of American National Policy, 1904–1940," *American Historical Review*, LXVI (1961), 354–77; Louis Morton, "War Plan ORANGE: Evolution of a Strategy," *World Politics*, XI (1959), 221–50; Albert C. Stillson, "Military Policy without Political Guidance: Theodore Roosevelt's Navy," *Military Affairs*, XXV (1961), 18–31; Richard D. Challener, "The Military and the Formulation of American Foreign Policy, 1900–1914," a paper read before the American Historical Association on December 28, 1958. See also, William R. Braisted, *The American Navy in the Pacific, 1897–1907* (Austin, Tex., 1958).

34. Link, *Wilson: The New Freedom; Wilson: The Struggle for Neutrality, 1914–1915* (Princeton, N.J., 1960); *Wilson the Diplomatist: A Look at His Major Foreign Policies* (Baltimore, 1957); *Woodrow Wilson and the Progressive Era, 1910–1917* (New York, 1954). Ernest R. May, *The World War and American Isolation, 1914–1917* (Cambridge, 1959) does not really discuss isolationism. Marion C. Siney, *The Allied Blockade of Germany, 1914–1916* (Ann Arbor, Mich., 1957). Karl E. Birnbaum, *Peace Moves and U-Boat Warfare: A Study of Imperial Germany's Policy toward the United States, April 18, 1916–January 9, 1917* (Stockholm, 1958). For an appraisal of the writings of the 1920's and 1930's, see Richard W. Leopold, "The Problem of American Intervention, 1917: An Historical Retrospect," *World Politics*, II (1950), 405–25.

authority to his analysis of American policy. In his third volume, Link delved even more deeply into the British side, while his fourth will draw upon additional private collections in England and upon the hitherto closed French archives. At last we shall be on firm ground in watching Wilson's diplomacy, and House's, as it unfolded in the major capitals of the world. The final word has not yet been written on the problems inherent in the theme of this paper—whether the American people went to war in 1917 to uphold their maritime rights, forestall a German victory, or make the world safe for democracy and whether they intended, by intervening, to abandon isolationism and neutrality. But on all these points Robert E. Osgood's volume, cited above, has important things to say.[35]

35. Osgood, *Ideals and Self-Interest in America's Foreign Relations.* Edward H. Buehrig, *Woodrow Wilson and the Balance of Power* (Bloomington, Ind., 1955) is suggestive but not wholly conclusive.

The Square Deal in Action: A Case Study in the Growth of the "National Police Power"

JOHN BRAEMAN

BY 1906, the Progressive movement was beginning to move into high gear at the national level. Safely elected in his own right, Theodore Roosevelt was growing increasingly alarmed at the multiplying signs of unrest. The marked jump in the Socialist vote in the 1904 elections appeared "ominous." "The dull, purblind folly of the very rich men; their greed and arrogance, . . . and the corruption in business and politics," he complained to Secretary of War William Howard Taft in March, 1906, "have tended to produce a very unhealthy condition of excitement and irritation in the popular mind. . . ." [1] In response, T.R. called for positive action by the federal government against corporate wrong-doing and social evils.[2] In his annual message of December, 1905, Roosevelt had laid down the basic principles of the program which would become known as the

1. Theodore Roosevelt to Charles Ferris Gettemy, February 1, 1905, in Elting E. Morison *et al.* (eds.), *The Letters of Theodore Roosevelt* (8 vols.; Cambridge, 1951–54), IV, 1113; Roosevelt to William Howard Taft, March 15, 1906, *ibid.*, V, 183.

2. For a perceptive account of T.R.'s program, see George E. Mowry, *The Era of Theodore Roosevelt, 1900–1912* (New York, 1958), pp. 197–225.

"New Nationalism." "The fortunes amassed through corporate organization," the chief executive warned Congress, "are now so large, and vest such power in those that wield them, as to make it a matter of necessity to give to the sovereign—that is, to the government, which represents the people as a whole—some effective power of supervision over their corporate use." The states could not do the job; only the federal government could deal with problems that had become nationwide in scope. Recent court decisions, however, had led to "a very unfortunate condition of things, under which these great corporations doing an interstate business occupy the position of subjects without a sovereign, neither any State government nor the National Government having effective control of them." The time had come, T.R. concluded, "to assert the sovereignty of the National Government by affirmative action." [3]

There were, however, formidable hurdles, constitutional no less than political, to carrying out this program. The Constitution granted no general police power to the national government; Congress was given no authority "to make," in the classic words of Chief Justice Lemuel Shaw of the Massachusetts Supreme Court, ". . . all manner of wholesome and reasonable laws . . . not repugnant to the constitution, as they shall judge to be for the good and welfare of the commonwealth, and of the subjects of the same." [4] If Congress were to undertake an ambitious program of national regulation and supervision of the economy, then it must act under one of its enumerated powers. Of the enumerated powers, none appeared more inviting as a vehicle for what Robert E. Cushman has called the "national police power" than the commerce clause.[5] But how far could

3. Hermann Hagedorn (ed.), *The Works of Theodore Roosevelt* (20 vols.; National Edition; New York, 1926), XV, 270–73.

4. Leonard W. Levy, *The Law of the Commonwealth and Chief Justice Shaw* (Cambridge, 1957), pp. 247–54.

5. Robert E. Cushman, "The National Police Power under the Commerce Clause of the Constitution," Part I, *Minnesota Law Review*, III, No. 5 (April, 1919), 289–303.

Congress undertake, under the cloak of the commerce clause, to regulate business activities within the states? As of 1906, the constitutional picture remained unclear.[6]

Chief Justice John Marshal, in *Gibbons* v. *Ogden* (1824), had defined federal authority under the commerce clause in sweeping terms. Before 1887, however, the commerce clause was interpreted primarily as a barrier against state interference with the free flow of interstate commerce rather than as a positive grant of power to Congress.[7] The first major positive exercise of the commerce power by the federal government came in the Interstate Commerce Commission Act of 1887. Subsequent court decisions emasculated the legislation by denying the Interstate Commerce Commission rate-fixing powers; these decisions, however, rested upon the question of Congress's intent and not its constitutional authority. Justice David J. Brewer, speaking for the majority in *Interstate Commerce Commission* v. *Cincinnati, New Orleans and Texas Pacific Railway Co.* (1897), affirmed that "Congress might itself prescribe the rates; or it might commit to some subordinate tribunal this duty. . . ." But, he held, Congress had not done so in the 1887 legislation. ". . . If Congress had intended to grant such a power to the Interstate Commerce Commission," Brewer reasoned, "it cannot be doubted that it would have used language open to no misconstruction, but clear and direct." [8]

6. In preparing the following survey, I am deeply indebted to: Edward S. Corwin, *The Commerce Power versus States Rights* (Princeton, N.J., 1936), *passim;* Henry Rottschaefer, *The Constitution and Socio-Economic Change* (Ann Arbor, Mich., 1948), pp. 13–24, 28–32; Alfred H. Kelly and Winfred A. Harbison, *The American Constitution: Its Origins and Development* (New York, 1955), pp. 543–608; and Alpheus T. Mason and William M. Beaney, *The Supreme Court in a Free Society* (Englewood Cliffs, N.J., 1959), pp. 114–17, 151–92.

7. James W. Hurst, *Law and the Conditions of Freedom in the Nineteenth-Century United States* (Madison, Wis., 1956), pp. 44–51.

8. I. L. Sharfman, *The Interstate Commerce Commission: A Study in Administrative Law and Procedure* (4 Parts in 5 vols.; New York, 1931–37), I, 11–35, 45; William Z. Ripley, *Railroads: Rates and Regulations* (New York, 1912), pp. 441–86; *Interstate Commerce Commission* v. *Cincinnati, New Orleans and Texas Pacific Railway Co.*, 167 U.S. 479 (1897).

Thus, T.R. in picking railroad-rate regulation as the opening target in his campaign for national supervision of the economy was making a shrewd move. Not merely could he count upon strong popular backing spearheaded by the shippers' organizations, but he stood on sound constitutional ground. That Congress itself could fix rates was not at issue in the struggle that followed. Its giving that authority to the Interstate Commerce Commission represented more of a stumbling block. Many "men of disinterested conviction as well as those who were sheer obstructionists" had qualms about the constitutionality of Congress delegating its legislative power—that is, its power to make rates—to an administrative body. But the Supreme Court in the Cincinnati, New Orleans and Texas Pacific Railway case had indicated that Congress could do so. Nor did the "railroad" senators concentrate their fire upon this question. The fight in the Senate raged over the question of how far the rate-making authority to be granted the Interstate Commerce Commission should be hedged by court review.[9] Important as the Hepburn Act was in setting a "precedent, accepted by the courts and enlarged by later Congresses, . . . [for] government by administrative commission,"[10] its adoption did not constitute a major step forward in the extension of the national police power. Its significance, a leading authority acknowledged, "was not primarily in the wider scope of Federal control."[11]

The railroads were generally recognized as within the scope of federal authority. But could this authority reach to encompass business activities carried on within the states? This question came to the fore in the debate over

9. John M. Blum, *The Republican Roosevelt* (Cambridge, 1958), pp. 73–105; Mowry, *The Era of Theodore Roosevelt*, pp. 201–6; Sharfman, *The Interstate Commerce Commission*, I, 40–52; Ripley, *Railroads: Rates and Regulations*, pp. 494–521; F. H. Dixon, "The Interstate Commerce Act as Amended," *Quarterly Journal of Economics*, XXI, No. 1 (November, 1906), 22–51.

10. Blum, *The Republican Roosevelt*, p. 105.

11. Ripley, *Railroads: Rates and Regulations*, p. 500.

antitrust legislation. Did Congress have the authority to prohibit combinations in manufacturing simply because the goods made were intended for interstate commerce? The upshot of congressional doubts was the purposefully vague phraseology of the Sherman Act which left to the courts to decide if combinations in manufacturing were—or were not—included within the ban. The Supreme Court's decision, in *United States* v. *E. C. Knight Co.* (1895), appeared to strike a fatal blow to future use of the commerce clause as a vehicle for expansion of the national police power. In rejecting the government's suit for dissolution of the sugar trust, Chief Justice Melville Fuller, speaking for an eight to one majority, drew a sharp distinction between manufacturing and commerce. "Slight reflection will show," Fuller declared, "that if the national power extends to all contracts and combinations in manufacture, agriculture, mining, and other productive industries, whose ultimate result may affect external commerce, comparatively little of business operations and affairs would be left for state control."

If not overturned, or at least modified, the Knight decision would have made impossible future use of the commerce clause as a vehicle for the national police power. There is no question but that this was the overriding issue in the minds of the majority. ". . . The power of a State to protect the lives, health, and property of its citizens, and to preserve good order and the public morals, . . . is," Fuller explained, "a power originally and always belonging to the States, not surrendered by them to the general government. . . . " This police power was "essentially exclusive"; therefore, "the relief of the citizens of each State from the burden of monopoly . . . was left with the States to deal with. . . . " That interstate commerce "might be indirectly affected was not enough" to warrant congressional interference in the sphere belonging to the states. "It is vital," the Chief Justice insisted, "that the independ-

ence of the commercial power and of the police power, and
the delimitation between them, however sometimes perplexing, should always be recognized and observed. . . .
[This] is essential to the preservation of . . . our dual form
of government; and acknowledged evils, however grave and
urgent they may appear to be, had better be borne, than the
risk be run, in the effort to suppress them, of more serious
consequences by resort to expedients of even doubtful constitutionality." [12]

More than any other decision, the Knight case was responsible for that never-never land Roosevelt complained
about in which neither the federal government nor the states
could act. In subsequent decisions, however, the Court
backtracked. In *Addyston Pipe and Steel Co.* v. *United
States* (1899), the Supreme Court held that an agreement
among pipe manufacturers to fix prices and divide markets
was illegal under the Sherman Act. This decision, according to a leading authority on the subject, represented, "in
practice, if not in theory," a departure from the restricted
view of interstate commerce taken in the Knight case. The
decision in the Northern Securities case (1904) represented
a further step in revitalizing the Sherman Act. That law
included within its ban, the majority opinion by Justice
John M. Harlan ruled, "combinations . . . among *private*
manufacturers or dealers whereby *interstate or international commerce* is restrained. . . . " The following year in
Swift & Co. v. *United States* (1905), a unanimous Court
approved the "current of commerce" doctrine that would in
the New Deal provide the rationale for an unprecedented
expansion of federal authority under the commerce clause.[13]

12. Hans Thorelli, *The Federal Antitrust Policy: Origination of
an American Tradition* (Baltimore, 1955), pp. 164–232, 445–48;
United States v. *E. C. Knight Co.*, 156 U.S. 1 (1895); Arnold M. Paul,
*Conservative Crisis and the Rule of Law: Attitudes of Bench and
Bar, 1887–1895* (Ithaca, N.Y., 1960), pp. 179–84.

13. Thorelli, *The Federal Antitrust Policy*, pp. 452–77; Mason and
Beaney, *The Supreme Court in a Free Society*, pp. 151–56.

The full significance of the Swift decision was not immediately apparent. And important as were these decisions in
revitalizing the Sherman Act, their significance for the
future development of the national police power remained
limited. The constitutional rationale for federal antitrust
legislation was the power Congress enjoyed under the commerce clause "for the promotion and protection of interstate
commerce itself"—a power that included the authority "to
keep interstate commerce free from the obstacles and inter-
ferences resulting from monopoly and other combinations
and conspiracies designed to destroy free competition and
restrain trade." [14] Crucial for the future development of
the national police power was Congress's authority to bar
goods from interstate commerce as a weapon with which to
force compliance with its regulations. This question came
before the Court in *Champion* v. *Ames* (1903). In a five
to four decision the Court upheld an 1895 federal law ban-
ning the shipment of lottery tickets in interstate commerce.

The majority decision, written by Justice Harlan, harked
back to *Gibbons* v. *Ogden*. " . . . The power of Congress to
regulate commerce among the States," Harlan declared, "is
plenary" and thus not limited by the reserved powers of the
states. Since the power to regulate included the power to
prohibit, Congress could, Harlan held, bar lottery tickets
from interstate commerce "for the purpose of guarding the
people of the United States against the 'widespread pesti-
lence of lotteries'. . . ." Here was a clear-cut avowal of
a national police power under the cloak of the commerce
clause. The minority bemoaned this invasion of states'
rights. "The power of the State to impose restraints and
burdens on persons and property in conservation and promotion of the public health, good order, and prosperity is,"
Chief Justice Fuller argued, "a power originally and always
belonging to the States, not surrendered by them to the

14. Cushman, "The National Police Power under the Commerce
Clause," I, 303, 310–12.

General Government. . . . " Authority to suppress lotteries "belongs to the States and not to Congress." "To hold that Congress has general police power," Fuller complained, "would be to hold that it may accomplish objects not entrusted to the General Government, and to defeat the operation of the Tenth Amendment. . . . "

The door appeared open for a sweeping extension of the national police power. But how far open? Harlan denied that his decision gave Congress carte blanche "arbitrarily [to] exclude from commerce among the States any article, commodity or thing, of whatever kind or nature, or however useful or valuable, which it may choose, no matter with what motive. . . . " Although Congress's power over interstate commerce was not limited by the reserved power of the states, that power, Harlan warned, "may not be exercised so as to infringe rights" protected by the due process clause of the Fifth Amendment. The courts must decide in any given instance whether Congress has exceeded the proper limits of its authority. "The whole subject is too important," Harlan concluded, "and the questions suggested by its consideration are too difficult of solution, to justify any attempt to lay down a rule for determining in advance the validity of every statute that may be enacted under the commerce clause." [15]

A possible test of the extent of the national police power under the commerce clause was pending before Congress at the beginning of 1906. This was the bill for a federal pure food and drug law. The pressures for congressional action were growing in strength. The work of Dr. Harvey Wiley, chief of the Bureau of Chemistry of the Department of Agriculture, had awakened the public to the dangers of adulterated foods and quack drugs. Samuel Hopkins

15. *Champion* v. *Ames*, 188 U.S. 321 (1903). An excellent discussion of the significance of the decision is given by Robert E. Cushman, "The National Police Power under the Commerce Clause of the Constitution," Part II, *Minnesota Law Review*, III, No. 6 (May, 1919), 381–88.

Adams' exposé of patent-medicine nostrums in *Collier's,* "The Great American Fraud," was creating a nation-wide sensation.[16] In his annual message of December, 1905, Roosevelt had urged "that a law be enacted to regulate inter-state commerce in misbranded and adulterated foods, drinks, and drugs." The federal authority must intervene, T.R. de-clared, "to secure the health and welfare of the consuming public." [17]

Despite the growing clamor for action, the powerful inter-ests threatened by the law continued to stymie action with loud attacks upon the measure's constitutionality. "If the Federal Government should regulate Inter-state traffic in drugs on the basis of their therapeutic value," complained the Committee on Legislation of the Proprietary Association of America, "why not regulate traffic in theology, by exclud-ing from transportation, all theological books which Dr. Wiley and his assistants, upon examination, should find to be 'misleading in any particular'?" [18] Although the Senate passed the bill on February 21, the possibility of House action appeared dim.[19] Then came an unexpected bombshell. This was the furor that followed the publication, on Febru-ary 15, of Upton Sinclair's *The Jungle*—and Theodore Roosevelt brilliantly exploited the popular excitement the book created to help overcome congressional obstructionism and constitutional scruples, and push through a bold exten-sion of the national police power.

Sinclair was a struggling young novelist and enthusiastic

16. Mark Sullivan, *Our Times, 1900–1925* (6 vols.; New York, 1925–35), II, 471–83, 496–536; Louis Filler, *Crusaders for American Liberalism* (Yellow Springs, O., 1950), pp. 142–63; James H. Young, *The Toadstool Millionaires: A Social History of Patent Medicines in America before Federal Regulation* (Princeton, N.J., 1961), pp. 205–39; Oscar E. Anderson, Jr., *The Health of a Nation, Harvey W. Wiley and the Fight for Pure Food* (Chicago, 1958), esp. pp. 120–81.

17. Hagedorn, *The Works of Theodore Roosevelt*, XV, 326.

18. Young, *The Toadstool Millionaires*, p. 237.

19. Anderson, *The Health of a Nation*, pp. 180–88.

convert to socialism. He had intended *The Jungle* as a "Socialist novel" that would "open the eyes of the American people to the conditions under which the toilers get their bread"—a novel that would, in his words, *"blow the top off of the industrial tea-kettle."* He spent seven weeks in the stockyards district of Chicago gathering background material. He had picked "Packingtown," he explained, because "I knew this was a place where modern commercial forces held complete sway. . . . "[20] As background color for his story, Sinclair included a frightening and unforgettable picture of the filth of the slaughterhouses, the sharp practices of the packers, and the farce of the existing government inspection. There were the hogs dead of cholera turned into lard; the sales of meat from carcasses condemned by government inspectors as tubercular; the potted chicken made of tripe, beef suet, and waste ends of veal; the rancid butter "oxidized" by a forced-air process, rechurned with skim milk, and sold as fresh; and most spectacular, the tales of men in the cooking rooms falling into the vats and being overlooked for days "till all but the bones of them had gone out to the world as Durham's Pure Leaf Lard!"[21]

The Jungle had first been serialized in the Socialist weekly *Appeal to Reason,* beginning February, 1905. But finding a book publisher who would handle so explosive a story was more difficult. Five publishers fearfully rejected the book; finally Walter Hines Page of Doubleday, Page & Company

20. Upton Sinclair, *The Autobiography of Upton Sinclair* (New York, 1962), pp. 99–112; Sinclair, *The Brass Check, A Study of American Journalism* (Pasadena, Calif., [1919]), p. 27; Sinclair, "The Condemned-Meat Industry: A Reply to Mr. J. Ogden Armour," *Everybody's Magazine,* XIV, No. 5 (May, 1906), 608–16; Sinclair, "What Life Means to Me," *Cosmopolitan Magazine,* XLI, No. 6 (October, 1906), 593; *Appeal to Reason,* September 17, 1904, December 31, 1904, January 21, 1905, January 28, 1905, March 4, 1905.

21. Upton Sinclair, *The Jungle* (Signet Classic Edition; New York, 1960), pp. 41–42, 66–67, 98–102.

offered to publish it if he could verify its truthfulness. After running their own check, the Doubleday officials were "convinced that *The Jungle* told the truth." [22] The advance publicity billed the novel as "a searching expose of . . . the flagrant violations of all hygienic laws in the slaughter of diseased cattle, the farce of government inspection, and the whole machinery of feeding a world with tainted meat." [23] The first reviews were skeptical. Even the most sympathetic found the book "overdrawn" and "exaggerated as to facts"; the more hostile denounced it as a tissue of "exaggeration and falsification." [24] But with each passing day, public interest grew. Twenty-five thousand copies were sold within a month-and-a-half of publication. While its Socialist message went largely unheeded, its disclosures about what Sinclair called the "condemned-meat industry" struck a responsive public. ". . . I aimed at the public's heart," Sinclair lamented, "and by accident I hit it in the stomach." [25]

The times were ripe for *The Jungle*. As early as the 1870's European countries were complaining that American meats were not wholesome and healthful, and had begun to

22. Sinclair, *The Brass Check*, pp. 32–34; *The Autobiography of Upton Sinclair*, pp. 114–16; *Appeal to Reason*, February 25, November 18, December 16, 1905; Isaac F. Marcosson, *Before I Forget, A Pilgrimage to the Past* (New York, 1959), pp. 95–98; Walter Hines Page to James Wilson, March 8, 1906, Office of the Secretary of Agriculture, Record Group 16, Solicitor's Office Correspondence, File 74, National Archives.

23. *Chicago Inter Ocean*, January 27, 1906; *Chicago Record-Herald*, February 26, 1906.

24. *Independent*, LX, No. 2991 (March 29, 1906), 740–41; *Bookman*, XXIII (April, 1906), 195–97; *Public Opinion*, XL, No. 15 (April 14, 1906), 476, 479–80; *Chicago Inter Ocean*, March 3, 1906; *Outlook*, LXXXII (March 31, 1906), 758; *Dial*, XL, No. 476 (April 16, 1906), 262; *Reader*, VII, No. 5 (April, 1906), 564; J. Ogden Armour, "The Packers and the People," *Saturday Evening Post*, CLXXVII, No. 37 (March 10, 1906), 6.

25. *Chicago Inter Ocean*, March 31, 1906; Sinclair, "What Life Means to Me," p. 594.

restrict or prohibit imports from this country. To meet this threat to the American export trade, Congress had passed the act of March 3, 1891, requiring ante mortem inspection of all cattle, sheep, and hogs whose meat was intended for export or sale across state lines and authorizing post mortem inspection at the discretion of the Secretary of Agriculture.[26] Even with this legislation, suspicions continued that all was not well in the stockyards. The "embalmed meat" scandal during the Spanish-American War had created a furor. Starting in January, 1905, the distinguished British medical journal, *The Lancet,* had run a series of articles assailing the Chicago packing houses as dirty and unsanitary and calling for stricter federal inspection. Later that year, muckraker Samuel Merwin, in a *Success Magazine* article on the monopolistic practices of the Beef Trust, raised the question, "Are Packers, as Is very often Charged, deliberately Selling Diseased Meat?" and answered in the affirmative.[27]

The prestige of the Beef Trust was at a low ebb. Its arrogance in price-fixing had aroused bitter resentment, and indictments were pending against five meat-packing companies and seventeen of their officers—including J. Ogden Armour, Louis F. Swift, Edward A. Cudahy, and Ira N. Morris—for violation of the Sherman Antitrust Law.[28] The

26. A. D. Melvin, "The Federal Meat Inspection Service," in U.S. Bureau of Animal Industry, *Twenty-third Annual Report, 1906* (Washington, D.C., 1908), pp. 69–78; Fred W. Powell, *The Bureau of Animal Industry: Its History, Activities and Organization* (Baltimore, 1927), pp. 1–14, 128–30; John M. Gaus and Leon O. Wolcott, *Public Administration and the United States Department of Agriculture* (Chicago, 1940), pp. 165–71.

27. Margaret Leech, *In the Days of McKinley* (New York, 1959), pp. 316–22; *Lancet,* January 9, 1905, pp. 49–52, January 14, 1905, pp. 120–23, January 21, 1905, pp. 183–85, January 28, 1905, pp. 258–60; and Samuel Merwin, "The Private-Car Abuses," *Success Magazine,* VIII, No. 131 (April, 1905), 249–54.

28. U.S. Federal Trade Commission, *Report on the Meat-packing Industry, 1919* (6 vols.; Washington, D.C., 1918–20), I, 46–48; II, 11–25; Arthur M. Johnson, "Theodore Roosevelt and the Bureau of Corporations," *Mississippi Valley Historical Review,* XLV, No. 4

public was prepared to believe the worst about the packers —and that public had become increasingly pure-food conscious.

The furor reverberated in Washington. In mid-February of 1906 the Department of Agriculture appointed a committee of departmental experts, consisting of John Mohler, chief pathologist of the Bureau of Animal Industry, R. P. Steddom, chief of the bureau's inspection division, and George P. McCabe, solicitor for the department, to investigate the federal inspection service in Chicago. Secretary of Agriculture "Tama Jim" Wilson amended the department's meat-inspection rules and regulations to require that the packing houses "be kept in a clean and sanitary condition." Orders went out to the local inspectors to tighten up the procedures for destroying condemned carcasses. "If the conditions described by Mr. Sinclair actually exist," Secretary Wilson assured *The Jungle*'s publisher, the abuses will immediately "be corrected." [29]

As the furor continued, the White House took a hand. Sinclair himself had sent Roosevelt a copy of the book. Commissioner of Corporations James R. Garfield brought over another copy. Although thinking that its conclusions were "too pessimistic," Garfield advised that its charges against the packers warranted investigation. So did Indiana's Senator Albert J. Beveridge. While scornful of Sinclair's "pathetic belief" in socialism, Roosevelt invited him to the White

---

(March, 1959), 578–82. See also *United States* v. *Armour & Co. et al.*, 142 Fed. 808 (1906).

29. Testimony of A. D. Melvin before the House Committee on Agriculture, 59th Cong., 1st Sess., *Hearings . . . on the So-called "Beveridge Amendment" to the Agricultural Appropriation Bill (H.R. 18537) . . .* (Washington, D.C., 1906), pp. 241–43; Bureau of Animal Industry, *Twenty-third Annual Report, 1906*, p. 346; A. D. Melvin to S. E. Bennett, March 30, 1906, and April 7, 1906, Records of the Bureau of Animal Industry, Record Group 17, General Correspondence, 1895–1906, File 320, National Archives; James Wilson to Doubleday, Page & Company, March 5, 1906, Office of the Secretary of Agriculture, R.G. 16, Solicitor's Office Correspondence, File 74, National Archives.

House for a talk and assured him that "the specific evils you point out shall, if their existence be proved, and if I have the power, be eradicated." [30] The public-be-damned attitude shown by the Beef-Trust people in the past, T.R. confessed to Secretary Wilson, "convinces me that there is very little they will stop at." [31]

About the middle of March, Frank N. Doubleday sent the President advance proofs of three articles that were scheduled for publication in the May issue of *The World's Work* under the over-all title of "Selling Diseased Meat": one by Dr. W. K. Jaques, former head of the city's meat inspection at the Chicago stockyards, who had been dismissed because of his too vigorous action in destroying condemned meat; another by Thomas H. McKee, the Doubleday lawyer who had gone to Chicago to check upon *The Jungle*; and a third by Dr. Caroline Hedger, a physician in the packing-house district. All assailed the existing federal inspection as a farce that did not protect the consuming public from unwholesome and diseased meats. *The Jungle* could be dismissed as mere fiction, or socialistic claptrap; but such accusations in a reputable magazine could not be ignored. The explosiveness of the charges led Roosevelt to have second thoughts about the wisdom of an investigation by experts from the Department of Agriculture since the department was, in the public mind, a defendant in the case.[32]

Secretary Wilson, aware of the difficulty, had himself suggested an independent investigation by Commissioner of

30. Theodore Roosevelt to Upton Sinclair, March 9, March 15, 1906, Roosevelt Papers (Library of Congress); *The Autobiography of Upton Sinclair*, pp. 118–19; Albert J. Beveridge to Albert Shaw, July 1, 1906, Beveridge Papers (Library of Congress).

31. Theodore Roosevelt to James Wilson, March 12, 1906, Morison, *The Letters of Theodore Roosevelt*, V, 176–77.

32. W. K. Jaques, "A Picture of Meat Inspection," *World's Work*, XII, No. 1 (May, 1906), 7491–505; Caroline Hedger, "The Unhealthfulness of Packingtown," *ibid.*, 7507–510; Thomas H. McKee, "The Failure of Government Inspection," *ibid.*, 7510–514; Theodore Roosevelt to F. N. Doubleday, March 22, 1906, Roosevelt Papers.

Labor Charles P. Neill; Roosevelt took up the suggestion and recommended that Neill take along New York social worker James B. Reynolds. A former professor of political economy at Catholic University of America, Neill had been appointed Commissioner of Labor in 1905, and he served as Roosevelt's chief trouble shooter in labor and social-welfare questions. Reynolds, a lawyer turned social worker, was head worker at the University Settlement and had long been active in "good-government" causes in New York City. "I want to get at the bottom of this matter," T.R. instructed the two men, "and be absolutely certain of our facts when the investigation is through." [33]

Meanwhile, the three departmental experts had completed their investigation, and on April 3 they submitted their report. Roosevelt was not pleased with the result. The report was a long, detailed, and highly technical document which, the chief executive complained, "did not give me the clear, definite answers I wish to the charges made." At his behest, they made a second report on April 13, this one consisting of rebuttals to specific charges levied in *The Lancet, The World's Work,* and *The Jungle*.[34] The investigators found the charges of unsanitary conditions grossly exaggerated. Sinclair, they charged, "in his anxiety to be as sensational and 'yellow' as possible" had "selected the worst possible condition which could be found in any establishment as typical of the general conditions existing. . . . " The accusations of negligence and even malfeasance on the part of the federal inspectors were "willful and deliberate misrepresentations of fact."

33. Theodore Roosevelt to Charles P. Neill, March 22, 1906, *ibid.;* to James Wilson, March 22, 1906, Morison, *The Letters of Theodore Roosevelt,* V, 190.

34. Theodore Roosevelt to Upton Sinclair, April 11, 1906, *ibid.,* V, 208–9; to James Wilson, April 11, 1906, Wilson to Roosevelt, April 11, 1906, Roosevelt to Charles P. Neill, April 16, 1906, Roosevelt Papers.

The departmental experts did, however, acknowledge grave defects in the existing inspection system. The federal inspectors had no authority under the law to destroy animals rejected at the ante mortem inspection; they were disposed of under local regulations, which permitted the sale of such animals at auction and their slaughter at packing houses not subject to federal inspection. Acting under the authority given him by the 1891 law, the Secretary of Agriculture required a post mortem inspection at plants covered by federal inspection. But the inspectors had no legal authority to destroy meat found unsound and unhealthful; such meat was in practice destroyed under the threat of the withdrawal of the inspection. Most importantly, the packers' compliance was voluntary—a matter of business—and not compulsory. Although the existing law effectively barred the export of meats without the government stamp of approval, there was no similar provision to protect the American consumer. The law prohibited the transportation in interstate commerce of carcasses "or the food products thereof" that had been inspected and condemned; but there was nothing in the law, the report confessed, "to forbid any carrier from accepting for interstate transportation carcasses and food products which have not had Federal inspection."

Nor were these the only shortcomings. Once the carcasses were passed, the federal inspectors had no authority over the conditions under which the finished products were prepared. The government label on canned meats, for instance, meant no more than that the carcass had been inspected at the time of slaughter. It was no warranty that the meat was fresh or even healthful. The recent amendment to the rules notwithstanding, the Department of Agriculture had no legal authority to enforce sanitary regulations in the packing houses. The only weapon it had was to withdraw its inspectors from the plant; but, as the head of the Bureau

of Animal Industry admitted in testimony before the House
Committee on Agriculture, this threat was more illusory
than real. "There is," Secretary Wilson insisted, "no lack
of vigilance on our part, as far as we have authority in
inspecting meats. But our authority is limited. . . ." And
even if the department had the authority, it lacked the
funds to police all the packing houses. " . . . I have found
it impossible," the Secretary complained, "to get money
enough to appoint as many inspectors as I think necessary
to do the work completely. . . ." Because of the inadequacy
of its appropriation, the department had to turn down
requests from packing houses for inspection. "We occupy a
disagreeable position in this Department," Wilson lamented
to the chairman of the Senate Committee on Agriculture.
"We are held responsible for the work and do not have men
or money enough to do it." [35]

   T.R. sent the report of the departmental experts to Neill
and Reynolds for their information, and the two special
commissioners reported their own findings to the President
early in May. The major emphasis of their report was
on the negative side of the picture. They found the build-
ings badly lighted and ventilated; the floors and work-
tables, tubs, meat racks, and conveyors filthy, rotten, and
blood-soaked; workmen's aprons blood-soaked and filthy;
men climbing with dirty shoes or sitting in filthy clothes on
tables where meat was handled; workmen spitting or even
urinating on the floors; meat for canning or for sausage
thrown in heaps on the floors; scraps of all kinds, including pieces of rope and pigskin, turned into "potted ham";

   35. Bureau of Animal Industry, *Twenty-third Annual Report,*
1906, pp. 406–56; House Committee on Agriculture, *Hearings . . .*
on the so-called "Beveridge Amendment," p. 243; James Wilson to
Redfield Proctor, May 22, 1906, Wilson Papers (in possession of Mrs.
Albert Lehninger, Owings Mills, Md.). I wish to thank Professor
Willard Hoing, of Baldwin-Wallace College, who is preparing a biography of Wilson, for references from the Wilson Papers.

and cans of meat moldy with age heated to "liven up" the
contents, relabeled, and placed on sale. Whereas the Department of Agriculture report did not touch upon working
conditions in the packing houses, the Neill-Reynolds report
showed in detail how thousands of workers were "forced
to spend their working hours under conditions . . . which
are a constant menace not only to their own health, but to
the health of those who use the food products prepared
by them."

Despite their sharper indictment of the packers, Neill
and Reynolds made much the same recommendations as did
the experts from the Department of Agriculture. The crux
of the difficulty was that the existing inspection system
was confined by law to passing on the healthfulness of the
animals at the time of slaughter and the federal inspectors
had no authority over the conditions under which the finished products were prepared. The remedy was to give
the inspectors authority to supervise all stages in the production of meat and meat products; authorize the Department of Agriculture to lay down and enforce rules and
regulations covering sanitation; and, most importantly, bar
the shipment in interstate commerce of all meats not
government-inspected and approved.[36] By early May, the
legal staff of the Department of Agriculture had drafted
a bill to close the loopholes in the existing law. To forestall
the danger of an insufficient appropriation by Congress, the
bill provided, Secretary Wilson told the chairman of the
Senate Committee on Agriculture, "that the packers should
pay for the inspection." [37]

36. The initial report was given in person; the writing of the
formal statement was not completed until June 2. The text is printed
in *House Document 873*, 59th Cong., 1st Sess. (June 4, 1906), pp. 3–11.
The recommendations of the Department of Agriculture experts are
given in Bureau of Animal Industry, *Twenty-third Annual Report,
1906*, pp. 441–42.

37. Theodore Roosevelt to Charles P. Neill, May 4, 1906, Roosevelt
Papers; James Wilson to Redfield Proctor, May 22, 1906, Wilson
Papers.

As the investigation proceeded, Roosevelt had received a steady barrage of letters and telephone calls from Upton Sinclair. A front-page story in the *Chicago Tribune* of April 10 reported that the investigators sent out by the Department of Agriculture had given the lie to *The Jungle* and that the chief executive intended to pillory the book and Sinclair in his forthcoming "The Man with the Muck-Rake" speech. The always excitable novelist immediately raised the cry of "whitewash." This outburst confirmed Roosevelt's suspicions about Sinclair's temperamental instability. But he was too much of a moralist to permit flagrant wrong-doing to pass unchastened, and political no less than moral considerations required a full airing of the scandal. He assured Sinclair that he had no intention of attacking *The Jungle* in his speech or of doing anything else "until I have data on which to base action." The departmental report was merely preliminary; he needed more information before acting. ". . . You *must* keep your head," he chided the novelist. ". . . I intend before I get through to be able to have authoritative reasons for saying 'proved,' or 'unproved,' . . . of each specific charge advanced against the packers."[38]

No less excited were the packers. The uproar had alarmed them, and they feared that official government confirmation of unsanitary conditions in their plants would be financially ruinous. A representative of the packers had approached Neill while he was in Chicago and pleaded with him to withhold his report, promising that any "reasonable, rational, and just" recommendations would be carried out

38. *Chicago Tribune,* April 10, 1906; Upton Sinclair to Theodore Roosevelt, April 10, 1906, and memorandum of telephone calls from Sinclair, April 11, 1906, Roosevelt Papers; Roosevelt to Sinclair, April 11, 1906, Morison, *The Letters of Theodore Roosevelt,* V, 208–9. Sinclair was temporarily reassured (Sinclair to Roosevelt, April 12, 1906, Roosevelt Papers) and later conceded that Neill and Reynolds "had made a most thorough and elaborate investigation . . . " (Sinclair to Roosevelt, June 1, 1906, Roosevelt Papers).

within thirty days. Then he could return, make a new investigation, and publish that as his report. When the Commissioner replied that he was not authorized "to make any trades," Louis F. Swift went directly to the President with a promise to remedy any shortcomings found if the chief executive would not publish the report. But T.R. replied that voluntary action by the packers would not suffice. Shocked and indignant at the "hideous" conditions found in the packing houses, he insisted that "it is absolutely necessary that we shall have legislation which will prevent the recurrence of these wrongs." [39]

One of the most interested readers of *The Jungle* had been Senator Albert J. Beveridge of Indiana. The Hoosier lawmaker was in the midst of a transition in his political beliefs: aware of the multiplying signs of popular unrest, he was moving toward a more progressive stance than he had taken in his earlier years in the Senate. Always eager to bask in the spotlight, he saw immediately the possibility of garnering personal glory by introducing the legislation needed for meat inspection. When he told the President that he was preparing such a bill, T.R. said, "Bully," and invited him to consult with Neill and Reynolds. By the beginning of May, he was hard at work drafting, he confided to a Chicago publisher-friend, "one of the most important bills which has been presented to Congress for a long while. . . ." Then one evening he met Secretary of Agriculture Wilson at dinner at Gifford Pinchot's and learned that the department was preparing its own bill. Not wanting someone else to introduce a bill upon which he had been working, he asked the President

39. Testimony before the House Committee on Agriculture, *Hearings . . . on the So-called "Beveridge Amendment,"* pp. 95–99; Louis F. Swift to William Loeb, Jr., May 24, 1906, Roosevelt Papers; Theodore Roosevelt to James W. Wadsworth, May 26, 1906, Morison, *The Letters of Theodore Roosevelt,* V, 282–83.

if he could sponsor the administration measure in the upper chamber.[40]

When the Secretary sent over the departmental bill, Beveridge found it less carefully drawn than his own and "rejected it in toto excepting only the section on fees. . . ." In consultation with Wilson, A. D. Melvin, chief of the Bureau of Animal Industry, Garfield, Neill, and Reynolds, he continued rewriting and revising the bill. By mid-May, he had the final draft in hand. Although Secretary Wilson gave his approval, T.R. still hesitated to commit himself when Beveridge asked that he send Congress a special message transmitting the Neill-Reynolds findings.[41] While having no qualms about harming the packers, Roosevelt feared lest any further loss of confidence in American meat products, in this country and abroad, injure the livestock-raisers. Having just won the bitter fight over the Hepburn railroad-rate bill, that canny politician wanted no undue haste in bearding the packers. "The matter is one of such far-reaching importance," he explained to Neill, "that it is out of the question to act hastily. We must be absolutely sure of our ground and must be able to form a rough forecast of the effects." [42]

But the ever impatient Beveridge would brook no further delay. On Monday, May 21, three days after Senate passage of the Hepburn bill, he introduced his bill in the upper chamber. The bill provided for a mandatory post mortem inspection of all cattle, sheep, swine, and goats whose meat

40. John Braeman, "Albert J. Beveridge: From Imperialism to Progressivism" (Ph.D. dissertation, The Johns Hopkins University, 1960), pp. 282–84; Albert J. Beveridge to John C. Shaffer, May 11, 1906, to Albert Shaw, July 1, 1906, Beveridge Papers.

41. James Wilson to Albert J. Beveridge, May 14, 1906, Beveridge to Albert Shaw, July 1, 1906, *ibid.;* Theodore Roosevelt to Beveridge, May 23, 1906, Morison, *The Letters of Theodore Roosevelt,* V, 281–82.

42. Theodore Roosevelt to Charles P. Neill, May 23, 1906, Roosevelt Papers.

was to be sold in interstate or foreign commerce; for the destruction of any carcasses found "unfit for human food"; for the inspection and dating of all meat products and canned meats; for the use of "none but healthful materials and ingredients fit for human food" in their preparation; for the destruction of "all such products" found "to be impure, unsound, composed of unhealthful ingredients, or which have been treated with or contain any dyes or deleterious chemicals of any kind or which are otherwise unfit for human food."

The Secretary of Agriculture was authorized to draw up rules and regulations governing sanitary conditions, "and it shall be the duty of the inspectors herein provided for to inspect the sanitary conditions of said establishments as well as the animals slaughtered and the meat products therein prepared. . . ." No meat product was to be sold "under any other than a true name which shall accurately describe said food product. . . ." After January 1, 1907, "no person, firm, or corporation shall transport" from one state to another any meats or meat products that have not been "inspected, examined, and marked as 'inspected and passed,' in accordance with the terms of this act. . . ." Violations would be punished by a fine of not more than $10,000, or by imprisonment for not more than two years, or by both. If the packers appealed any ruling by an inspector, the decision of the Secretary of Agriculture would be "final and conclusive."

Beveridge realized that all these safeguards could be nullified by an insufficient force of inspectors. Shortage of funds had nullified much of the value of the existing inspection law. The danger was not immediate since the uproar over the scandals would guarantee a generous appropriation for the present. But the meat industry would continue to grow, and the popular excitement would pass. Then the packers could trap Congress into voting an insufficient appropriation with the ever popular cry of economy. To avert this danger, his bill authorized the Secretary of Agriculture to charge the packers a fee for each animal inspected to defray the cost of inspection. The funds available for the inspection service would thus automatically keep pace with the growth of the industry.[43] His proposal was, Beveridge exclaimed to a friend, "the most perfect meat inspection bill in the world—that looks like an extravagant statement, but it is true." [44]

The bill would remedy the abuses in the meat-packing industry. But no one could miss the wider bearings. A Hamiltonian, Beveridge had long believed "that the Constitution must steadily grow . . . as the people grow, and furnish scope for the people's power and the Nation's necessities in exact proportion as the people's power and the Nation's necessities enlarge." Congress had the authority, he insisted, to do whatever was "necessary for the preservation of the morality and uprightness of our people." Such power was "inherent" in the federal government "as an incident to sovereignty." [45] And as he moved towards progressivism, the Hoosier lawmaker became increasingly concerned with the necessity of expanding the power of the national government to deal with business wrongdoing. His meat-inspection bill represented a major step forward in meeting that need. It was, Beveridge boasted to magazine editor Albert Shaw, "THE MOST PRONOUNCED EXTENSION OF FEDERAL POWER IN EVERY DIRECTION EVER ENACTED, INCLUDING EVEN THE RATE BILL ITSELF." [46]

43. *Congressional Record*, 59th Cong., 1st Sess. (May 21, 1906), p. 7127; (May 25, 1906), pp. 7420–21.

44. Albert J. Beveridge to Henry W. Bennett, May 28, 1906, Beveridge Papers.

45. Albert J. Beveridge, *The Meaning of the Times and Other Speeches* (Indianapolis, 1908), pp. 1–19.

46. Albert J. Beveridge to Albert Shaw, May 26, 1906, Beveridge Papers.

The news of the introduction of the bill aroused a flurry of excitement among the packers. Themselves too much in disrepute to take the lead, they galvanized the stock-raisers into action. A close working partnership had been forged between the packers and the major livestock-raisers represented by the American National Livestock Association, and a flood of telegrams and letters came to the White House from the cattlemen pleading that T.R. withhold publication of the Neill-Reynolds report lest the resulting uproar destroy the foreign market for American meats. Two spokesmen for the livestock interests, William E. Skinner and W. L. Carlisle, met with Roosevelt on Thursday, May 24, and told him that the packers had promised to implement in their establishments all sanitary improvements found necessary. While disclaiming any wish to injure the "innocent" livestock-raisers of the country, the chief executive reiterated that legislation was required to prevent any recurrence of the wrongs found. If the packers were sincere, he insisted, they should join forces with the administration in passing effective legislation such as the Indiana senator's bill.[47]

The next day, May 25, Beveridge forced the issue by presenting his bill as an amendment to the pending Agricultural Appropriation Bill. The Senate had to go on record, and the Hoosier lawmaker warned his colleagues that if a fight were made against the amendment, he would make a speech that would shock the country. Joining the fray, Roosevelt repeated his warning that he would make public the Neill-Reynolds report unless satisfactory legislation was passed. To underline what the report involved, he had Commissioner Neill outline his findings to the repre-

47. *Chicago Daily Drovers Journal and Farm News*, January 31, February 2, May 24–25, 1906; *Chicago Record-Herald*, May 24–25, 1906; *Chicago Inter Ocean*, May 24–25, 1906; *Chicago Tribune*, May 25, 1906.

sentatives of the livestock men and leading senators from
the western cattle-raising states. After meeting with Neill,
Skinner had a conference with Beveridge. When the
Hoosier refused to postpone his demand for a vote on his
amendment, Skinner telephoned the packers for instructions. In a momentary panic, they agreed to offer no opposition. Thereupon the Senate passed the amendment without
a dissenting vote.[48] Heartened by this showing, the President hoped for a swift House approval. If the lower chamber
approved the Senate amendment, he told the chairman of
the House Committee on Agriculture, the feared Neill-
Reynolds report need not be published. If a snag developed,
he warned, publication would follow.[49]

The President's appeal fell on deaf ears. Almost immediately the packers regretted their weakness. One industry
spokesman after another hastened to deny that conditions
were amiss in their packing houses and assailed the Senate
amendment as hastily drawn, too rigid, and unconstitutional. The labeling provision in the Senate amendment,
the packers complained, would force the scrapping of long-
established brand names. Even worse was the provision
for dating canned meats. Properly canned meats could
stand for years without spoiling, a spokesman for the
packers declared. Dating the cans would simply prejudice the consumer against buying stored goods. Another
sore point was the provision forbidding the use of "any
dyes or deleterious chemicals of any kind"; the packers
wanted permission to use preservatives in amounts not
injurious to health. The loudest complaints were against

48. Albert J. Beveridge to Albert Shaw, May 26, 1906, Beveridge
Papers; *Chicago Record-Herald,* May 26, 1906; *Chicago Daily Drovers
Journal and Farm News,* May 26, 1906; *Chicago Tribune,* May 26,
1906; *Chicago Inter Ocean,* May 26, 1906; *Congressional Record,* 59th
Cong., 1st Sess. (May 25, 1906), pp. 7420–21.

49. Theodore Roosevelt to James W. Wadsworth, May 26, 1906,
Morison, *The Letters of Theodore Roosevelt,* V, pp. 282–83.

the fee provision. The packers, the president of the National Packing Company remonstrated, were losing a million dollars a year on animals which they had purchased but which were condemned on post mortem inspection and destroyed. That they should shoulder the extra burden of paying the salaries of the government inspectors "does not seem just fair. . . ."

Underlying the issues of preservatives, dates, labels, and even dollars and cents was the question of power—whether the packers themselves or outsiders would regulate conditions in their plants. Government inspection could not be avoided, but the packers wished to salvage as much as possible of what they regarded as private enterprise from governmental interference. Under the Senate amendment, an inspector could shut down an entire plant as unsanitary, and the decision of the Secretary of Agriculture would be final. Such action, the packers claimed, would amount to confiscation of their property without due process of law, and they demanded the right to appeal to the courts from any ruling of the Department of Agriculture. The issue, the general manager of Nelson Morris & Company told the House Committee on Agriculture, was "our right to control our own business." What the packers opposed, Thomas E. Wilson declared, "is a bill that will put our business in the hands of theorists, chemists, sociologists, etc., and the management and control taken away from the men who have devoted their lives to the upbuilding and perfecting of this great American industry. . . ." [50]

50. *Chicago Tribune*, May 26, 28–29, June 7–9, 1906; *Chicago Record-Herald*, May 26, 31, June 7–8, 1906; *Chicago Inter Ocean*, May 26–28, June 5–8, 10, 1906; *Chicago Daily Drovers Journal and Farm News*, May 26, 28, June 7–8, 1906; *Indianapolis Star*, May 31, 1906. The fullest statement of the packers' objections to the Senate amendment was given in the testimony of Thomas E. Wilson, general manager of Nelson Morris & Company, before the House Committee on Agriculture, *Hearings . . . on the So-called "Beveridge Amendment,"* pp. 5–94. Louis Filler makes some perceptive comments on the last point in his "Progress and Progressivism," *American Journal of Economics and Sociology*, XX, No. 3 (April, 1961), 296–97.

The packers had powerful friends in the House of Representatives. A ranking member of the House Committee on Agriculture, William Lorimer, the notorious "blond boss" of Chicago and a long-time ally of the packers, vowed that "this bill never will be reported by my committee—not if Little Willie can help it." [51] Committee chairman James W. Wadsworth, a wealthy stock-raiser from New York's Genessee Valley, dismissed the charges against the packers as mere sensationalism. Himself a large-scale cattle-raiser, he found "the whole thing . . . *most costly* to my foreign trade." The President, the New York congressman complained, had "let his imagination ran [sic] away with him" after reading "that horrid, untruthful book" and "sent two sociologists to inspect something they knew nothing about. Those men simply threw mud over everything and everybody." [52]

Wadsworth and Lorimer could rally strong backing in the House at large. Speaker "Uncle Joe" Cannon could not ignore the weight of the packers' influence in Illinois Republican circles.[53] The livestock interests were clamoring that the packers would recoup any fees paid by reducing the prices paid for livestock,[54] and most congressmen from western districts were responsive to the wishes of the livestock men. Many other lawmakers shied at enacting so far-reaching an increase in the authority of the federal government over private industry. "The passage of the meat inspection amendment as it came from the Senate

51. *Chicago Record-Herald*, May 24, 1906. A biographical sketch of Lorimer is in the *Dictionary of American Biography, Supplement One* (New York, 1944), pp. 511–12.

52. Biographical information on Wadsworth is in Alden Hatch, *The Wadsworths of the Genesee* (New York, 1959), pp. 99–111. For his reaction to the Senate amendment: *Chicago Tribune*, May 29, 1906; James W. Wadsworth to Matilda Gay, August 5, 1906, Wadsworth Family Papers (Library of Congress).

53. *Chicago Inter Ocean*, May 27, 1906.

54. *Chicago Daily Drovers Journal and Farm News*, June 8, 1906; *Chicago Inter Ocean*, May 27, June 10, 1906; *Chicago Tribune*, June 3–5, 1906.

would mean the ultimate federalization of every single industry in America," complained Indiana congressman E. D. Crumpacker. "Carried to its logical conclusion the same principle would prohibit any corn, or hay, or cotton from interstate commerce unless it is grown according to rules laid down by the secretary of agriculture." [55]

In his private talks with House leaders, T.R. continued to wield the threat of publication of the Neill-Reynolds report to force swift approval of the Senate amendment.[56] But the sensational write-ups filling the newspapers undercut the effectiveness of this weapon. Although he had promised the President to say nothing until a thorough investigation of his charges had been made, Sinclair was not the man to remain silent long. He wrote first for *Collier's* and then for *Everybody's* articles repeating and elaborating his attack. After their return from Chicago, Neill and Reynolds briefed him on their findings; but when Roosevelt continued to withhold the report, he grew more and more restive, publicly calling upon the chief executive to release it. When no action followed, the novelist leaked to the *New York Times* the substance of the still secret report. In a separate interview with the *Times*, Sinclair supplied additional lurid details supported by affadavits he had gathered. From the *Times*, the stories were picked up by newspapers throughout the country.[57]

55. *Indianapolis Star*, May 29, 1906.

56. *Chicago Record-Herald*, May 27, 29, 1906; *Chicago Inter Ocean*, May 27, 29, 1906; *Chicago Tribune*, May 29, 1906; Theodore Roosevelt to Murdo Mackenzie, May 27, 1906, to James W. Wadsworth, May 29, 1906, Roosevelt Papers.

57. Upton Sinclair to Theodore Roosevelt, April 10, 1906, *ibid.;* Upton Sinclair, "Stockyard Secrets," *Collier's, The National Weekly,* XXXVI, No. 26 (March 24, 1906), 24; Sinclair, "The Condemned-Meat Industry: A Reply to Mr. J. Ogden Armour," *Everybody's Magazine,* XIV, No. 5 (May, 1906), 608–16; *New York Times,* May 28–29, 1906; Sinclair, *The Brass Check,* pp. 41–43. Roosevelt angrily denounced Sinclair for making "utterly reckless statements which you have failed to back up by proof" (Roosevelt to Sinclair, May 29,

The damage had been done, the packers felt. The time for a peaceful accommodation had passed. Wadsworth and Lorimer proceeded to rewrite the Senate amendment to suit the packers. Their draft allowed the use of preservatives in quantities that would not be unhealthful; permitted continuance of established brand names; replaced the fee provision with a yearly appropriation; and added a court-review provision to the effect that any firm injuriously affected by a departmental ruling could appeal "the legality or constitutionality of such ruling" in the federal courts. The inspection was limited to the post mortem examination of the carcasses; the provision for the inspection and dating of meat products and canned meats was struck out. Most importantly, noted the solicitor for the Agriculture Department, the provision barring "the interstate transportation of *uninspected* meat" was "entirely omitted from the draft." [58] Thus the new law would be no more effective than the old. After a conference with his advisers, Roosevelt lashed out at the proposed substitute. ". . . It seems to me," he admonished Representative Wadsworth, "that each change is for the worse and that in the aggregate they are ruinous, taking away every particle of good from the suggested Beveridge amendment." [59]

His hand forced, Roosevelt had to carry out his threat. On Monday, June 4, he transmitted to Congress the Neill-

---

1906, Morison, *The Letters of Theodore Roosevelt*, V, 287–89). The gist of this letter was reported by T. R.'s friend, John Callan O'Laughlin, in the *Chicago Tribune*, May 31, June 1, 1906.

58. "Memorandum [from George P. McCabe] for the Secretary of Agriculture. Comparing the draft of the Bill left with Doctor Melvin by Representatives Wadsworth and Lorimer, with the amendment to the Appropriation Act of the Bureau of Animal Industry, as passed by the Senate," May 31, 1906; a second memorandum entitled "Changes in the Beveridge Amendment Proposed by The House Draft," May 31, 1906, Office of the Secretary of Agriculture, Record Group 16, Solicitor's Office Correspondence, File 74, National Archives.

59. Theodore Roosevelt to James W. Wadsworth, May 31, 1906, Morison, *The Letters of Theodore Roosevelt*, V, 291–92.

Reynolds report accompanied by a special message urging adoption of the Senate amendment. The conditions in the packing houses, he told the lawmakers, "are revolting." The loopholes in the existing law have left the door open "to traffic in diseased or spoiled meats." New legislation was necessary "which will enable the inspectors of the General Government to inspect and supervise from the hoof to the can the preparation of the meat food product." For a moment, the President had wavered on the fee question. But Secretary of Agriculture Wilson reminded him of how difficult it had been to obtain sufficient appropriations for the existing inspection service. Persuaded, T.R. in his message came out strongly in favor of meeting the expenses of the inspection by a fee paid by the packers for each animal slaughtered. Without this provision, he warned, "the whole purpose of the law can at any time be defeated through an insufficient appropriation. . . ." [60]

The lines of battle were drawn. On Friday, June 1, after learning that T.R. had rejected the proposed substitute, Lorimer had made a hasty trip to Chicago to consult with the packers and returned breathing defiance. The Neill-Reynolds report, he told a reporter, was "a gross exaggeration of the conditions." The leading packers joined in issuing a statement denying the charges made in the report as "slanders." Interviewed in Paris J. Ogden Armour declared that the President had "a strong personal animus against the packers of Chicago and is doing and will do everything in his power to discredit them and their business." Full-page advertisements in the newspapers invited the public to visit the packing houses and judge for themselves if the charges were true. Two University of Illinois scientists

60. *House Document 873*, 59th Cong., 1st Sess. (June 4, 1906), pp. 1–11. For T.R.'s temporary wavering on the fee provision, Theodore Roosevelt to James W. Wadsworth, May 29, 1906, Roosevelt Papers; to Albert J. Beveridge, May 29, 1906, Morison, *The Letters of Theodore Roosevelt*, V, 289; to Wadsworth, May 31, 1906, *ibid.*, 291–92.

reported that their own investigation of the packing houses made "it impossible for us to believe the horrible stories recently appearing in print, or that anything approaching the described conditions really exists."

The business community rallied behind the packers. Officers of the Illinois Manufacturers' Association and the Chicago Commercial Association joined in assailing the President for his "thoughtlessness" in releasing the Neill-Reynolds findings "before there was an opportunity to establish the correctness." The directors of the Chicago Board of Trade went officially on record as deploring "the one-sided report recently issued which has given rise . . . to a sensational agitation fraught with serious and far-reaching injurious results." A special investigating committee from the National Association of Manufacturers, consisting of St. Louis stove-manufacturer J. W. Van Cleave, Indianapolis carriage-maker David M. Parry, and Chicago industrialist Elliott Durand, concluded that the charges of unsanitary conditions in the packing houses were "the result of a conspiracy" against the packers which involved high officials in Washington.[61]

The newspapers were filled with alarmist stories about contemplated foreign action to bar American meats as well as about a sharp drop in meat sales within the country. Bewailing the impending ruin of the stock-raiser and farmer, spokesmen for the livestock industry demanded speedy action to restore confidence in American meats— and speedy action meant legislation on the packers' terms. Inspired telegrams and letters poured into Congress and the White House.[62] But the President stood firm. While regretting the harm done to the livestock-raisers, he blamed

61. *Chicago Tribune*, June 3–5, 7, 15, 1906; *Chicago Daily Drovers Journal and Farm News*, June 4, 6, 13, 1906; *Chicago Record-Herald*, June 5, July 15, 1906; *Chicago Inter Ocean*, June 5, 10, 1906.

62. *Chicago Daily Drovers Journal and Farm News*, June 2, 4, 8, 1906; *Chicago Inter Ocean*, June 6, 8, 10–11, 13, 1906; *Chicago Tribune*, June 4–5, 1906.

the injurious publicity upon "the wicked folly of the beef-packers in fighting the legislation. . . ." The messages of protest coming to the White House, he complained to a middle-western senator, "are evidently all prepared by the same person." [63]

Events were moving rapidly to a climax. In an effort to reach an accommodation, T.R. had the Department of Agriculture send Wadsworth a draft bill that "would provide an inspection which would safeguard the health of the people and would, at the same time, be a workable measure." [64] Wadsworth and Lorimer then conferred with Louis Swift and Thomas E. Wilson, general manager of Nelson Morris & Company, at their rooms in the Willard Hotel. The two congressmen were prepared to make a bow toward the White House. The provision barring the shipment in interstate commerce of uninspected meats was restored. So was the provision for the inspection of meat products and canned meats—although not the provision requiring the dating of such products. On the other points at issue, however, Wadsworth and Lorimer would not yield. On the showdown vote, the House Committee on Agriculture divided eleven to seven—with nine Republicans and two Democrats for, three Democrats and four Republicans against—in favor of the Wadsworth-Lorimer substitute. On June 14, the committee formally reported the substitute to the House.[65]

63. Theodore Roosevelt to Elmer J. Burkett, June 8, 1906; to Col. John N. Simpson, June 13, 1906, Roosevelt Papers.

64. George P. McCabe to James W. Wadsworth, June 2, 1906; "Memorandum [from George P. McCabe] for the Secretary," June 4, 1906, Office of the Secretary of Agriculture, Record Group 16, Solicitor's Office Correspondence, File 74, National Archives.

65. *Chicago Tribune*, June 11, 13–14, 1906; *Chicago Inter Ocean*, June 12, 1906. The text of the substitute with Wadsworth's explanation of the changes made is given in *House Report 4935*, 59th Cong., 1st Sess. (June 14, 1906), pp. 1–7. There were two minority reports filed the following day: *House Report 4935, Part 2*, 59th Cong., 1st Sess. (June 15, 1906), pp. 1–3, and *House Report 3468, Part 2*, 59th Cong., 1st Sess. (June 15, 1906), pp. 1–3.

The President was furious. The committee substitute, he complained, did not provide for the nighttime surveillance of the packing houses, a measure required to prevent the illicit practices said to take place after the plants were shut. Nor could he approve the provision in the substitute which would waive for one year the civil-service requirement in the appointment of new inspectors. The majority report explained that the Department of Agriculture would need the year's delay in which to prepare and hold the examinations for appointing the inspectors under civil service. The chief executive, on the other hand, saw a more sinister purpose: during that year, the posts would remain patronage appointments subject to the recommendations of the congressmen from the meat-packing district—men widely regarded as under the thumb of the packers—and the inspectors so named would continue in office during good behavior.

Another point in dispute involved the dating of canned meats. Was this—or was it not—an essential safeguard for the consumer? Even more of a stumbling block was the question of fees. The draft bill prepared by the Department of Agriculture had tried to resolve this issue by giving the Secretary stand-by authority to levy fees "if the appropriations made by Congress shall be inadequate to carry out the provisions of the Act. . . ." But the House committee rejected this solution and instead provided for a permanent appropriation of $1,000,000 a year. Since that sum would barely meet the estimated cost of the expanded inspection for the first year, the inspection service would remain at the mercy of yearly appropriations from Congress. These provisions, T.R. fumed, "are so bad that in my opinion if they had been deliberately designed to prevent the remedying of the evils complained of they could not have been worse."

But what most agitated the President was the provision in the substitute conferring upon the packers the right of appeal to the federal courts from "any of the rulings or decisions provided for in this act." Having accepted the inevitability of federal inspection, the packers and their congressional allies sought to transfer final say from the Department of Agriculture to the federal courts. As in the fight over the Hepburn bill, this question became the focal point of contention. Under the broad court review provision in the substitute, a federal judge could review the findings of an inspector or the Secretary of Agriculture, *de novo*, upon the facts. ". . . You would have," Roosevelt admonished Wadsworth, "the functions of the Secretary of Agriculture narrowly limited so as to be purely ministerial; and when he declared a given slaughterhouse unsanitary, or a given product unwholesome, acting upon the judgment of the Government experts, you would put on the judge, who had no knowledge whatever of the conditions, the burden of stating whether or not the Secretary was right."

Not that T.R. denied the right of judicial review. "Congress cannot take away the constitutional right of the packers, or of anyone else, to the protection of the courts," he conceded. But this judicial review should be confined to the strictly procedural question of whether or not the Secretary's method of reaching his decision in any given case had been fair to the packers, and should not include a judicial reappraisal of the facts of the case. The broad court review provided for in the substitute would, on the contrary, place before the courts substantive questions of fact upon which they were not qualified to pass. He was the more sensitive on this point because of the recent decision by Federal District Judge J. Otis Humphrey in the packers' antitrust suit which freed the individual packers from prosecution. Referring bitterly to the "immunity bath" given the packers, T.R. charged that the committee substitute "would make any judge whom the packers chose to designate, and not the experts of the Department of Agriculture, the man to decide on any question of any kind which the packers thought it worth while to dispute." This broad court review provision, T.R. insisted, "will nullify the major part of the good which can be expected from the enactment of this law." [66]

"You are wrong, 'very, very wrong,' in your estimate of the Committee's Bill," Wadsworth replied. Assailing the President for "impugning the sincerity and the competency of a Committee of the House of Representatives," the New York congressman defended the substitute as "as perfect a piece of legislation, to carry into effect your own views on this question, as was ever prepared by a Committee of Congress." He could not see how a provision guaranteeing the packers their constitutional rights of appeal to the courts when their property rights were threatened "can be justly or properly objected to." Lorimer remained as defiant as ever. Regardless of what the President said, the Chicagoan vowed, he would stand by the substitute. At a meeting on Friday morning, June 15, a majority of the house committee resolved to "stand pat." [67]

This impasse placed Speaker of the House "Uncle Joe" Cannon in an embarassing plight. He was under pressure from his home state to back the substitute, and his personal inclinations favored private enterprise against governmental interference. But as the leader of the Republican party in the House, he shrank from a bitter, last-ditch fight with a chief executive of his own party on so politically explosive an issue. So that Friday he went up to the White House for a talk with Roosevelt. He found T.R.,

66. Theodore Roosevelt to James W. Wadsworth, June 14, 1906, Wadsworth to Roosevelt, June 15, 1906, Roosevelt to Wadsworth, June 15, 1906, Roosevelt to Albert J. Beveridge, June 15, 16, 1906, Beveridge to Roosevelt, [June 16, 1906]; Roosevelt to George P. McCabe, June 16, 1906, Roosevelt to William B. Howland, June 20, 1906, Roosevelt Papers. A detailed comparison of the House committee substitute with the Senate amendment was made by John Callan O'Laughlin in the *Chicago Tribune*, June 14, 1906.

67. James W. Wadsworth to Theodore Roosevelt, June 15, 1906, Roosevelt Papers; *Chicago Tribune*, June 15–16, 1906.

himself, worried about splitting the party, amenable to peace feelers. To work out the details, the Speaker sent over that afternoon Representative Henry C. Adams of Wisconsin. A respected member of the House Committee on Agriculture, Adams was not tarred with the packers' brush, and as former food commissioner in his home state, was a long-time advocate of stringent pure-food legislation. The Wisconsin lawmaker and T.R. quickly reached an understanding.[68]

Department of Agriculture solicitor George P. McCabe and James Reynolds, who were present at the meeting, proceeded to draw up a new bill with the agreed-upon changes. The one-year waiver on the civil-service requirement was dropped; provision was made for dating canned meats; the Secretary of Agriculture was given stand-by authority to levy fees if the appropriations from Congress proved insufficient; and the broad court-review provision was struck out. If those changes were adopted, T.R. indicated, the House bill "will become as good as the Beveridge amendment. . . ."[69] The next day, Adams called an informal meeting of the available members of the House committee to discuss the matter. With Lorimer and Wadsworth away for the weekend, the members present went along with their Wisconsin colleague. The President appeared to have won nearly every point in his fight.[70]

68. *Chicago Tribune*, June 16, 1906; Theodore Roosevelt to James W. Wadsworth, June 15, 1906, Morison, *The Letters of Theodore Roosevelt*, V, 298–99; to Joseph G. Cannon, June 16, 1906, *ibid.*, 301; to Nicholas Murray Butler, June 16, 1906, Roosevelt Papers. A biographical sketch of Adams by Harvey W. Wiley is in the *Dictionary of American Biography*, I, 69.

69. George P. McCabe to Theodore Roosevelt, June 15, 1906, June 16, 1906; George P. McCabe to Henry C. Adams, June 16, 1906, Office of the Secretary of Agriculture, R. G. 16, Solicitor's Office Correspondence, File 74, National Archives; Theodore Roosevelt to James W. Wadsworth, June 15, 1906, and Theodore Roosevelt to Albert J. Beveridge, June 16, 1906, Morison, *The Letters of Theodore Roosevelt*, V, 298–99, 300–301.

70. *Chicago Tribune*, June 17, 1906; *Chicago Inter Ocean*, June 17, 1906.

Wadsworth and Lorimer returned furious, vowing no retreat. But the Speaker was not willing to see the impasse renewed. When the full committee met Monday, he paid them a visit to urge peace with the White House. There would be no fees. Cannon joined with the committee majority in rejecting the provision giving the Secretary of Agriculture stand-by authority to levy fees as an infringement upon Congress's control of the purse. On the other hand, the permanent appropriation was raised to $3,000,000 a year—a sum that would provide sufficient leeway for the future growth of the meat industry. Although still balking at dating canned meats, the committee agreed to eliminate the civil-service waiver and to make more explicit the provision giving the inspectors access to the packing houses at all times, "by day or night, whether the establishment be operated or not." Most importantly, the committee agreed to strike out the court-review provision if the words in the Senate amendment making the judgment of the Secretary of Agriculture "final and conclusive" were cut out. With that done, Wadsworth explained, the court-review provision became "unnecessary." [71]

Roosevelt gave his approval when Cannon brought over the committee's draft that afternoon. The provision in the Senate amendment making the Secretary of Agriculture's decision "final and conclusive" might, he conceded, be taken to violate the Constitution by appearing to deny appeals of any kind to the courts. As in the Hepburn bill fight, the question of court review was left in (to use John M. Blum's phrase) "purposeful obscurity." T.R. had won his major point. The remaining questions presented no further difficulties. The permanent appropriation of $3,000,000 a year

71. *Chicago Tribune*, June 18–19, 1906; *Chicago Inter Ocean*, June 18–19, 1906; *Chicago Daily Drovers Journal and Farm News*, June 19, 1906; *Chicago Record-Herald*, June 19, 1906. The text of the revised House committee substitute appears in the *Congressional Record*, 59th Cong., 1st Sess. (June 19, 1906), pp. 8720–21; Wadsworth's explanation, *ibid.* (June 19, 1906), pp. 8721–22.

would, he conceded, allow sufficient leeway for the future growth of the industry without yearly fights over the budget. He was not happy about the defeat of the provision for dating canned meats; but he was not prepared to risk loss of face by insisting upon what he regarded a minor detail.[72] The Committee reported its substitute the next day, Tuesday, June 19, with White House approval, and the House approved with scant debate.[73]

But when the agricultural appropriation bill was returned to the Senate, new difficulties appeared. Assailing the packers for their sins, Beveridge protested that the consumer had a right to know whether his canned meat was five years old or five days old. To conceal the age of the meat *"is a fraud* on the consumer." No less crucial was the retention of the fee provision. The government seal of inspection, he told the Senate, would be worth millions of dollars in advertising to the packers. " . . . *Why should the people pay for the packers' inspection, instead of the packers paying for their own inspection?"* The meat industry would continue to grow in the future. But could Congress be depended upon to vote the additional funds after the uproar passed? Was not the packers' aim to cripple the inspection service?

Senator Francis Warren of Wyoming, a leading sheep-raiser and spokesman for the livestock interests in the upper chamber, protested that if the packers were forced to pay for inspection, they would defray the cost by reducing the price paid to the stock-raiser and raising the price charged the consumer. Beveridge replied that if the packers could so easily shift the burden, why did they so bitterly fight the provision? As it is, he argued, packers paid the

72. Theodore Roosevelt to Albert J. Beveridge, June 16, 1906, Morison, *The Letters of Theodore Roosevelt,* V, 300–301; to Redfield Proctor, June 18, 1906, Roosevelt Papers; *Chicago Tribune,* June 19, 1906; *Chicago Inter Ocean,* June 19, 1906; *Chicago Record-Herald,* June 19, 1906.

73. *Congressional Record,* 59th Cong., 1st Sess. (June 19, 1906), pp. 8720–29.

lowest and charged the highest the market allowed. The chairman of the Senate Committee on Agriculture, Redfield Proctor of Vermont, who though nearly crippled with rheumatism had returned to Washington to oversee passage of effective meat-inspection legislation, backed the Indiana senator. The Senate then voted overwhelmingly to disagree to the House substitute and stand by its version.[74]

Although unwilling to reopen the fee question, T.R. did plead with the House leaders to restore the provision for dating canned meats.[75] But his plea was of no avail. The House conferees continued to insist that canned meats could stay for years without spoiling. To put the date on American canned meats would only hurt their sale abroad in competition with the products of other countries which did not require dating. The House conferees were even more adamant against any provision for fees. Finally, on Friday, June 29, with the session drawing rapidly to a close, Proctor, the spokesman for the Senate conferees, advised his colleagues to bow "to make sure of the greater good. . . ." Swift action by the Senate followed.[76] The next day, Roosevelt signed the agricultural appropriation bill with the meat-inspection amendment into law.[77] That law, the chief executive cabled the American ambassador in London to inform British purchasers, "can and will guarantee the fitness in all respects of . . . meat containing [the] Government stamp." [78]

74. *Ibid.* (June 20, 1906), pp. 8763–70, (June 23, 1906), pp. 9016–27. On Proctor's physical condition, Redfield Proctor to Theodore Roosevelt, June 13, 1906, Roosevelt Papers.

75. Theodore Roosevelt to Joseph G. Cannon, June 26, 1906, Morison, *The Letters of Theodore Roosevelt,* V, 317.

76. *Chicago Inter Ocean,* June 27–30, 1906; *Chicago Tribune,* June 27–30, 1906; *Congressional Record,* 59th Cong., 1st Sess. (June 27, 1906), pp. 9376–78; (June 28, 1906), pp. 9569–75; (June 29, 1906), pp. 9655–56, 9664–65.

77. Roosevelt sent the pen with which he signed the bill to Beveridge in appreciation of his role in securing the legislation, Theodore Roosevelt to Albert J. Beveridge, June 30, 1906, Morison, *The Letters of Theodore Roosevelt,* V, 326–27.

78. Andrew J. Giles to Theodore Roosevelt, July 2, 3, 1906, Roosevelt to Whitelaw Reid, July 7, 1906, Roosevelt Papers.

The passage of the meat-inspection amendment provides a case study in the Square Deal. First there was the popular demand for reform triggered by a sensational exposé, the resistance of powerful business interests and their supporters in Congress, the wielding of the "big stick" by T.R., and finally his retreat on minor issues to achieve what he regarded as his major aim. In the end, the amendment's sponsor boasted, "we have secured nearly everything we went after. . . ." [79] But the legislation was not passed without a bitter fight—and it was only T.R.'s masterful handling of the political situation that carried the day. There has been in recent years much criticism to the effect that T.R. was no more than a lukewarm reformer who settled too readily for half a loaf.[79a] Yet such criticism fails to take into account the political climate in which he had to operate. The battle over the meat-inspection amendment

79. *Chicago Tribune,* June 30, 1906.

79a. A variant on this theme has been expressed in a recent book by Gabriel Kolko, *The Triumph of Conservatism: A Reinterpretation of American History, 1900–1916* (New York, 1963), pp. 98–108. Mr. Kolko denies that the big packers opposed the Beveridge amendment "save in two particulars"—the fee provision and the dating of canned meats. On the contrary, Mr. Kolko argues, the big packers favored stricter federal regulation to end the competitive advantage enjoyed by their smaller competitors not reached by the existing inspection system.

In light of the evidence presented in this paper, I believe Mr. Kolko's interpretation is untenable. Mr. Kolko misses what was the crucial issue involved in the fight over the meat inspection law. In support of his thesis, he quotes from the testimony of Thomas E. Wilson, general manager of Nelson Morris & Co., before the House Committee on Agriculture to the effect that the packers favored stricter inspection. But Mr. Kolko fails to note that this statement was followed by Wilson's plea to the committee to save the packers from "a bill that will put our business in the hands of theorists, chemists, sociologists, etc., and the management and control taken away from the men who have devoted their lives to the upbuilding and perfecting of this great American industry . . . " (House Committee on Agriculture, *Hearings . . . on the So-called "Beveridge Amendment,"* p. 5). At issue in the struggle over the court-review provision was the question of control—and on this issue Roosevelt took his stand and won his point.

exhibits the strength of the standpat forces. Despite the popular excitement, a key participant acknowledged, Congress would never have acted "if Roosevelt had not picked up his big stick and smashed the packers over the head with it and their agents in the House and Senate." [80]

The uproar over the meat scandal spurred Congress into passing the long-blocked pure food and drug law.[81] This law, coming on the heels of the Hepburn railroad-rate bill and the meat-inspection amendment, was the third epoch-making piece of legislation passed in the first session of the Fifty-ninth Congress. The Hepburn Act "settled once for all the fundamental dominance of public over private interests in the functioning of the railroad industry." [82] Despite its shortcomings, the pure food and drug act of 1906 laid the groundwork for the present-day legislation that protects the American consumer from adulterated food and quack drugs.[83] Except for minor amendments, the 1906 statute remains the basic law under which the meat-inspection service operates today.[84] Most importantly, as a perceptive newspaperman observed, the three laws marked "a radical departure from previous governmental methods. In each case there is a marked tendency toward the centralization of power in the United States and a corresponding decrease in the old time sovereignty of the states, or of the individual." [85]

Of the three, the meat-inspection law represented perhaps the boldest extension of the so-called national police

80. Albert J. Beveridge to Francis Baker, August 1, 1906, Beveridge Papers.

81. Anderson, *The Health of a Nation*, pp. 188–96; Young, *The Toadstool Millionaires*, pp. 239–43.

82. Sharfman, *The Interstate Commerce Commission*, I, 39.

83. Young, *The Toadstool Millionaires*, pp. 247–62.

84. U.S. Department of Agriculture, *Regulations Governing the Meat Inspection of the United States Department of Agriculture* (Washington, D.C., 1957), pp. 186–95.

85. *Chicago Tribune*, June 24, 1906.

power. Under the cloak of the commerce clause, federal inspectors were empowered to supervise directly activities carried on within the states. But would the courts approve? The first test came over the pure food and drug act. A unanimous Supreme Court in *Hipolite Egg Company* v. *United States* (1911) upheld the exclusion of adulterated and misbranded food and drugs from interstate commerce as "within that breadth of discretion . . . Congress possesses in the execution of the powers conferred upon it by the Constitution." In *McDermott* v. *Wisconsin* (1913), the Court reaffirmed that Congress had "full power to keep the channels of [interstate] commerce free from the transportation of illicit or harmful articles, to make such as are injurious to the public health outlaws of such commerce and to bar them from the facilities and privileges thereof." [86]

The same constitutional principle underlay the meat-inspection law. The broad authority given the Secretary of Agriculture under that law to prescribe rules and regulations governing the inspection service was challenged as an unconstitutional delegation of legislative authority to an administrative officer. But Federal District Judge Edwin S. Thomas in *United States* v. *Cudahy Packing Co. et al.* (1917) held that Congress could "delegate authority to the proper administrative or executive officer to make administrative rules, violations of which may be punished as public offences where the act of legislation which delegates the authority ordains that this be done. . . ." [87] The following year, in *Pittsburgh Melting Company* v. *Totten* (1918), Justice William R. Day, speaking for a unanimous Supreme Court, took pains in a case involving a limited technical question to affirm that "the enactment of the statute was within the power of Congress in order to prevent interstate

86. *Hipolite Egg Company* v. *United States*, 220 U.S. 45 (1911); *McDermott* v. *Wisconsin*, 228 U.S. 115 (1913).

87. *United States* v. *Cudahy Packing Co. et al.*, 243 Fed. 441 (1917).

and foreign shipment of impure or adulterated meat-food products." [88]

Nor did the question of the scope of judicial review cause difficulties. The much-feared flood of litigation in the federal courts over departmental rulings never materialized. When the question of whether a given product was a "meat-food product" covered by the act came before the Supreme Court in *Pittsburgh Melting Company* v. *Totten* (1918), the justices unanimously sustained the Department of Agriculture, without, however, dealing with the larger question of the scope of judicial review. The following year, in *Houston* v. *St. Louis Independent Packing Company* (1919), the Court explicitly confirmed its adherence to "narrow" review. Whether or not the name of a given meat product was false and deceptive, Justice John H. Clarke ruled for a unanimous Court, "is a question of fact, the determination of which is committed to the Secretary of Agriculture . . . , and the law is that the conclusion of the head of an executive department on such a question will not be reviewed by the courts, where it is fairly arrived at with substantial evidence to support it." The record shows that the Secretary "in promulgating the regulation complained of acted on substantial evidence and with sufficient reason. . . ." ". . . Under such circumstances as we have here," Clarke concluded, "this court will not review . . . the decision of the Secretary of Agriculture." [89] This position was reaffirmed in the case of *Brougham* v. *Blanton Manufacturing Company* (1919). ". . . The decision of the department," Justice Joseph McKenna held for the unanimous court, "unless arbitrary, is conclusive." [90]

The meat inspection law represented a landmark in the growth of the national police power—and its sponsor in the

88. *Pittsburgh Melting Company* v. *Totten*, 248 U.S. 1 (1918).

89. *Houston* v. *St. Louis Independent Packing Company*, 249 U.S. 479 (1919).

90. *Brougham* v. *Blanton Manufacturing Company*, 249 U.S. 495 (1919).

Senate was eager to push forward with new applications of the principle to remedy newly exposed evils. In December, 1906, Beveridge introduced in the upper chamber a bill to exclude from interstate commerce "the product of any factory or mine that employs children under the age of fourteen years." "The meat inspection bill gives an absolutely satisfactory precedent," wrote an enthusiastic Gifford Pinchot in congratulating the Indiana senator, "and the remedy would be complete and instantaneous." When states' rights men assailed the measure as an unconstitutional invasion of the reserved powers of the states, Beveridge replied that the decision of the Supreme Court in *Champion* v. *Ames* "absolutely settled" the constitutionality of his bill. "If this law is unconstitutional," he told T.R., "then at least a dozen laws already on our statute books, prohibiting various articles from interstate commerce, are also unconstitutional." [91]

Roosevelt, unwilling to risk his prestige in a cause doomed to defeat and dubious about the measure's constitutionality, withheld his support. Without the chief executive's backing, Beveridge could make no headway. [92] But the seed he had planted came to fruition under the Wilson administration with the adoption of the Keating-Owen bill in 1916. The act forbade the shipment in interstate commerce of any products manufactured in whole or in part by children under fourteen or from any mine employing children under sixteen. The act was "the high peak of Wilsonian progressivism"—and alarmed conservatives saw in the law the precedent for an even wider extension of the national police power. If the child-labor law were constitutional, the Wash-

91. Albert J. Beveridge to Gifford Pinchot, November 12, 1906, Pinchot to Beveridge, November 22, 1906, Pinchot Papers (Library of Congress); Beveridge to Harriet Lake, November 22, 1907, Beveridge to Theodore Roosevelt, November 11, 1907, Beveridge Papers.

92. John Braeman, "Albert J. Beveridge and the First National Child Labor Bill," *Indiana Magazine of History*, LX, No. 1 (March, 1964), 1–36.

ington spokesman for the National Association of Manufacturers complained, the door would be open for Congress to bar shipment "of any commodity produced in whole or part by the labor of men or women who work more than eight hours, receive less than a minimum wage, or have not certain educational qualifications." [93]

At this juncture, however, the Supreme Court interposed a check. In *Hammer* v. *Dagenhart* (1918), the Court, in a five to four decision, declared the law unconstitutional. To distinguish the case from previous decisions upholding legislation barring goods from interstate commerce, the majority opinion, written by Justice Day made "the character of the particular subjects dealt with" the controlling factor in determining the law's validity. In the other cases, the articles prohibited were themselves harmful or deleterious; goods made by child labor, on the contrary, "are of themselves harmless." Thereupon Day revived the distinction made in the Knight case between commerce and manufacturing. The "mere fact," he held, that the goods "were intended for interstate commerce transportation does not make their production subject to federal control under the commerce power." Hence the child-labor law violated the Tenth Amendment. "To sustain this statute," Day concluded, ". . . would sanction an invasion by the federal power of the control of a matter purely local in its character, and over which no authority has been delegated to Congress in conferring the power to regulate commerce among the States." [94]

The decision in *Hammer* v. *Dagenhart* loomed as an insuperable obstacle to further development of the national police power. The political climate of the 1920's made the constitutional question largely an academic one. But with the New Deal the issue was once again joined. The out-

93. Arthur Link, *Woodrow Wilson and the Progressive Era, 1910–1917* (New York, 1954), pp. 226–27.
94. *Hammer v. Dagenhart,* 247 U.S. 251 (1918).

come of the bitter struggle was the switch in time that saved nine. By 1941, the triumph of the national police power was complete. In *United States* v. *Darby* (1941), the Court upheld the Fair Labor Standards Act of 1938. Speaking for a unanimous Court, Justice Harlan Fiske Stone explicitly repudiated *Hammer* v. *Dagenhart*. Under its "plenary" power over interstate commerce, Congress can, Stone declared, "by appropriate legislation regulate intrastate activities where they have a substantial effect on interstate commerce." Giving the national police power its most sweeping definition, Stone held that Congress had practically unlimited power to bar from interstate commerce "articles whose use in the states for which they are destined it may conceive to be injurious to the public health, morals or welfare. . . ." [95]

Underlying this triumph of the national police power was a fundamental change in the nation's political outlook. In the nineteenth century, most Americans looked to their state governments as the proper instrumentalities for promoting the health, morals, and welfare of society. With the nationalizing of business and the resulting complexity of social relationships, men began to look to the federal government to solve problems that had grown beyond the capacity of the individual states to handle. Nowadays when an evil is discovered, the immediate reaction is that Congress should pass a law. This change in popular attitudes is reflected in today's advertising. Firms proudly boast that their products are prepared under United States government supervision. The fight over the meat-inspection amendment had its share in creating this public consciousness. During the excitement aroused by Upton Sinclair's *The Jungle*, the federal government stepped forward as the defender of the public well-being. The lesson was not forgotten—and later events would reinforce its message.

95. *United States* v. *Darby*, 312 U.S. 100 (1941).

The New Deal and the Analogue of War*

WILLIAM E. LEUCHTENBURG

THE metaphors a nation employs reveal much about how it perceives reality. The unconscious choice of symbols bares the bedrock of its beliefs. Moreover, the words people use are not neutral artifacts; they shape ideas and behavior. Just as the psychoanalyst listens for slips of the tongue or strange incongruities of ideas to help him understand the patient, or the literary critic studies the symbols in a poem or novel, so the historian finds it rewarding to explore the imagery a particular period has used, consciously or unconsciously, to interpret its experience.

In the months and years that followed the stock market crash of 1929, America searched for some way to make comprehensible what was happening. Sometimes people thought of the Great Depression as a breakdown of a system, sometimes as the product of the machinations of evil

*The writer is indebted to David Brody, Clarke Chambers, Bernard Cohen, Paul Conkin, Robert Cross, Bertram Gross, Charles Hirschfeld, Richard Hofstadter, Robert Holt, Henry Kaiser, Val Lorwin, Warren Miller, Carl Resek, James Shideler, and Rexford Tugwell for helpful comments on an earlier draft of this essay. The essay was originally presented as a paper at the meetings of the American Historical Association in New York in December, 1960, and was substantially revised when the writer was a Fellow at the Center for Advanced Study in the Behavioral Sciences, Stanford, California, 1961–62.

or stupid men, sometimes as the visitation of a plague like the Black Death. But from the very first, many conceived the depression to be a calamity like war or, more specifically, like the menace of a foreign enemy who had to be defeated in combat. Occasionally, the analogue of war was a general one, more often it referred specifically to World War I. When President Hoover summoned the leading industrialists to meet in Washington, one financial journal commented: " 'Order up the Moors!' was Marshal Foch's reply at the first battle of the Marne. . . . 'Order up the business reserves,' directed President Hoover as pessimistic reports flowed in from all quarters, following the stock market crash." [1]

For the rest of his years in office, Hoover resorted constantly to the imagery of war to describe the depression.[2] In one of his addresses, he claimed that the country had just won its "battle of Chateau-Thierry" and must "reform [its] forces for the battle of Soissons." "Again and again he used military terms in describing the struggle in which he was

1. *Magazine of Wall Street*, XLV (1929), 264, cited in J. Kenneth Galbraith, *The Great Crash* (Boston, 1929), p. 143.

2. Hoover, observed George Seldes, "repeatedly used the figures of speech of war in his description of the depression. It was a skillful association of ideas, for the war was a difficult time which ended happily; it was exciting; and it was the last time the whole nation was united."—Seldes, *Years of the Locust* (Boston, 1933), p. 258. The conviction of political leaders and publicists that reference to the war would evoke a favorable response suggests some modification of the view that the "pacifist thirties" thought of World War I only with abhorrence. While they viewed war as a wasteful, inhuman social institution, many progressives also recalled World War I as an ennobling experience of sacrifice for the national welfare and as a time of economic advance. In 1931 Richard Ely wrote: "A marked difference between the general situation in the World War and our situation during Hard Times must be noticed. A war may at first be attended by a good deal of economic confusion and distress, but very soon the wages and profits mount upward and people are apparently more prosperous than ever. Returns of capital in many lines of activity are large and wages are apt to mount up to levels heretofore unknown." — Ely, *Hard Times — The Way In and the Way Out* (New York, 1931) p. 110.

engaged," recalled one of his aides. "He was the command-
ing officer at general headquarters, so visualized himself." [3]
Hoover's advisers perceived the crisis in the same terms. In
June, 1931, after the President unfolded his reparations
plan, Secretary of State Henry Stimson confided to his
diary: "We have all been saying to each other the situation
is quite like war." [4]

In addition to employing the metaphor of war to explain
the meaning of the depression, the 1930's drew on the experience of the economic mobilization of World War I for
instrumentalities to combat hard times. These are two dis-
crete themes. Some who resorted to the analogue of war
had no interest in the precedent of the wartime mobilization,
and a few who turned to the example of the mobilization
did not employ the imagery of war. Hence, it would be
possible to examine these strands separately. But so closely
did most Americans associate the metaphor of war with the
specific legacy of the war mobilization that it has seemed
more fruitful to discuss both these themes in a single context.

In the New Deal years, the two strands were inseparable.
As early as his "forgotten man" speech in the 1932 campaign, Franklin Roosevelt manipulated the analogue of war
to his advantage. In that same address, he referred to the

3. *Literary Digest*, CXIV (September 10, 1932), 4–5; *New Republic*,
LXXII (1932), 86; Theodore Joslin, *Hoover Off the Record* (Garden
City, N.Y., 1934), p. 63. "Fighting this depression is becoming more
and more like waging a war," Hoover observed. "We have the combats,
if against an unseen foe of inestimable strength. We have our men
and we have our casualties among them."—*Ibid.*, p. 182.

4. Henry Stimson MS Diary, June 15, 1931, Sterling Memorial
Library, Yale University, New Haven, Conn., Stimson MSS. For
similar assessments of the depression, see *Report of Proceedings of
the Fiftieth Annual Convention of the American Federation of Labor*
(Washington, D.C., 1930), p. 366; Henry Morrow Hyde MS Diary,
December 17, 1931, Alderman Library, University of Virginia, Char-
lottesville, Va., Hyde MSS; Justice Brandeis' dissent in *New State
Ice Co.* v. *Liebmann*, 285 U.S. 306 (1932); *Rocky Mountain News*,
March 1, 1933.

specific operations of the war mobilization, a heritage he
was to acknowledge on many occasions after his election to
the presidency. But the legacy of the war was to prove a
mixed blessing. Useful as a justification for New Deal
actions, it also served to limit and divert the reformers in
ways that had not been anticipated.

In tracing the genealogy of the New Deal, historians have
paid little attention to the mobilization of World War I.
Instead, they have centered their interest on two movements: populism and progressivism. Both were important
antecedents—a reasonably straight line may be drawn from
the Populist sub-treasury plan to the Commodity Credit
Corporation, from the Pujo committee to the Securities and
Exchange Commission. Yet in concentrating on populism
and progressivism, writers have given too little attention to
the influence of the wartime mobilization, which may have
been as great as the example of the Progressive era and
certainly was more important than populism.[5]

Much of the experience of the Progressive era proved
irrelevant to the task facing Roosevelt in 1933. Very little
in the Populist and Progressive periods offered a precedent

5. One cannot, of course, distinguish sharply between the relative
influence of World War I and progressivism since the war mobilization
was, in some respects, a logical outgrowth of the Progressive movement. (There were, too, other antecedents of the New Deal, notably
the experiments of the 1920's.) Some historians of the New Deal,
it should be noted, have been sensitive either to the indebtedness of
the Roosevelt administration to the war mobilization or to the use
the New Deal made of war imagery. See, especially, Frank Freidel,
America in the Twentieth Century (New York, 1960), p. 312; Arthur
Schlesinger, Jr., *The Crisis of the Old Order (The Age of Roosevelt)*
(Boston, 1957), pp. 37–39; Schlesinger, *The Coming of the New Deal
(The Age of Roosevelt)* (Boston, 1959), p. 176; Paul Conkin, *Tomorrow a New World: The New Deal Community Program* (Ithaca, N.Y.,
1959), pp. 50–54, 67. Most narratives, however, have not only ignored
this relationship but have minimized the significance of the political
and economic events of the war years. With respect to the war,
historians have been chiefly interested in what happened *before* our
intervention (the submarine crisis) and what happened *afterwards*
(the League of Nations fight), not with the substance of the war
experience itself.

for massive federal intervention in the economy. Many of the reforms of the prewar generation were modest ventures in regulation or attempts to liberate business enterprise rather than ambitious national programs of economic action. Moreover, in these years, reformers thought the state and the city more important arenas than the national capital.

World War I marked a bold new departure. It occasioned the abandonment of laissez faire precepts and raised the federal government to director, even dictator, of the economy. The War Industries Board mobilized production; the War Trade Board licensed imports and exports; the Capital Issues Committee regulated investment; the War Finance Corporation lent funds to munitions industries; the Railroad Administration unified the nation's railways; the Fuel Administration fixed the price of coal and imposed "coal holidays" on eastern industry; and the Food Administration controlled the production and consumption of food. The Lever Food and Fuel Control Act of 1917 gave the President sweeping powers: to take over factories and operate them, to fix a maximum price for wheat, and to license businesses in necessaries. By a generous interpretation of its powers, the War Industries Board supervised pricing, compelled corporations to accept government priorities, and forced companies to obey federal edicts on how to dispose of their products. "This is a crisis," a War Industries Board representative scolded steel-industry leaders, "and commercialism, gentlemen, must be absolutely sidetracked." [6] Actions of this character, as well as the proliferation of public corporations ranging from the United States Housing Corporation to the Spruce Production Corporation, proved important precedents for New Deal enterprises fifteen years later.[7]

6. David Brody, *Steelworkers in America: The Nonunion Era* ("Harvard Historical Monographs," XLV [Cambridge, 1960]), p. 206; *Iron Age*, May 9, 1918, pp. 1206–13.

7. If, by later standards, the experiment in controls was embryonic, it nonetheless represented an unprecedented degree of government

The field of labor relations may serve as a single example of the difference in importance of the Populist and Progressive experience and that of World War I. Prior to the war, no serious attempt had ever been made to empower the federal government to uphold the right of collective bargaining.[8] Federal action was limited to peripheral areas. When class lines were drawn in labor disputes, progressives frequently aligned themselves against the unions.[9] But in World War I, the War Labor Board proclaimed its support of union rights and, to the discomfiture of businessmen, enforced these rights. Many of the labor policies pursued in the war months would have been inconceivable a short while before. When the Smith & Wesson Arms Company of Springfield, Massachusetts, insisted on its prerogative to require workers to sign yellow-dog contracts, the War Department commandeered the plant, even though the Supreme Court had upheld the legality of such contracts.[10] The government even dared to seize Western Union when the president of the firm denied his employees the right to join

intervention. In the immense literature on the war mobilization, see Benedict Crowell and R. F. Wilson, *How America Went to War* (6 vols.; New Haven, 1921); Bernard M. Baruch, *American Industry in the War* (New York, 1941); Woodbury Willoughby, *The Capital Issues Committee and War Finance Corporation,* ("The Johns Hopkins University Studies in Historical and Political Science," LII [Baltimore, 1934]); Mê Hsin Chiang, "The United States War Industries Board, 1917–1918" (Master's thesis, Stanford University, 1937); William Clinton Mullendore, *History of the United States Food Administration 1917–1919* (Palo Alto, Calif., 1941); Waldo G. Leland and Newton D. Mereness, *Introduction to the American Official Sources for the Economic and Social History of the War* (New Haven, 1926).

8. The most ambitious federal program was the investigation conducted by the U. S. Commission on Industrial Relations (Graham Adams, "Age of Industrial Violence," [Ph.D. dissertation, Columbia University, 1962]).

9. See, for example, George E. Mowry, *The California Progressives* (Berkeley and Los Angeles, 1951), pp. 294–99.

10. "Springfield and Bridgeport," *New Republic*, XVI (1918), 185–86; Henry F. Pringle, *The Life and Times of William Howard Taft* (2 vols.; New York, 1939), II, 921.

the Commercial Telegraphers Union.[11] The panoply of procedures developed by the War Labor Board and the War Labor Policies Board provided the basis in later years for a series of enactments culminating in the Wagner National Labor Relations Act of 1935.

The war gave a home to the new class of university-trained intellectuals which had emerged in the generation before the war. While some of them had found a career in public service in state governments before 1917, few had worked in the national government, chiefly because there was so little in Washington for them to do. After the United States intervened, Washington swarmed with professors, until, one writer noted, "the Cosmos Club was little better than a faculty meeting of all the universities." [12] In all countries, he observed, professors "fought, and they managed affairs, thus refuting the ancient libellous assumption that they constituted an absent-minded third sex. . . . " [13]

Public administrators of this type represented a new force in American politics. They were advisers and technicians but, more than that, men of influence and even of power. At a time when class conflicts were sharpening, they did not reflect particular classes so much as the thrust for power

11. "Snubbing the War Labor Board," *Survey*, XL (1918), 292–93; "The Western Union and the Government," *New Republic*, XV (1918), 163–64; Pringle, *The Life and Times of William Howard Taft*, II, 919–20. For the wartime labor experience, see "Final Report of the Chairman of the Labor Division, War Industries Board, 1919," copy in Library of Congress, John P. Frey MSS, Box 15; Brody, *Steelworkers in America*, Chap. X; U. S. Department of Labor, Bureau of Labor Statistics, "National War Labor Board," in *Bulletin No. 287* (Washington, D.C., 1922); Gordon S. Watkins, *Labor Problems and Labor Administration in the United States During the World War* ("University of Illinois Studies in the Social Sciences," VIII [Urbana, Ill., 1919]); Felix Frankfurter, "New Labor Ideas Taught by War," in Edwin Wildman (ed.), *Reconstructing America* (Boston, 1919), pp. 239–44.

12. Gordon Hall Gerould, "The Professor and the Wide, Wide World," *Scribner's Magazine*, LXV (1919), 466.

13. *Ibid.*, p. 465.

of *novi homines* who had a significant role to play on the
national stage. Some like Gifford Pinchot had made their
appearance in Washington before the war, and still more
like Charles McCarthy had been active in such reform capitals as Madison and Albany, but it was the war which
offered them an unparalleled opportunity. Randolph Bourne
noted perceptively the "peculiar congeniality between the
war and these men. It is as if the war and they had been
waiting for each other." [14] Phenomena almost wholly of the
twentieth century, they came by the 1930's to have a crucial
part in shaping legislation and in manning the new agencies
which their legislation developed. The passage of the Wagner Act in 1935, for example, resulted less from such traditional elements as presidential initiative or the play of
"social forces" than from the conjunction of university-
trained administrators like Lloyd Garrison within the New
Deal bureaucracy with their counterparts on senatorial
staffs like Leon Keyserling in Senator Wagner's office.

This new class of administrators, and the social theorists
who had been advocating a rationally planned economy,
found the war an exciting adventure. The *New Republic*
liberals rejoiced that the war produced a novel kind of
democratic state which was creating a radical new order
based on the democratization of industry. ". . . During
the war we revolutionized our society," the *New Republic*
boasted.[15] These liberals distinguished themselves sharply
from the New Freedom reformers who aimed only to achieve
minor changes in the nineteenth-century tradition. Nation-
alists and collectivists, they looked toward a centralized state
which would use its powers to reshape the economy in the
interests of labor and other disadvantaged groups.[16]

14. Bourne, *Untimely Papers*, ed. James Oppenheim (New York,
1919), p. 129.
15. "The Uses of an Armistice," *New Republic*, XVII (1918), 60.
16. Charles Hirschfeld, "American Reform and World War I,"
paper delivered at the convention of the Mississippi Valley Historical
Association, Denver, Colo., April 25, 1959, pp. 3, 12–13.

Many progressives believed that Wilson's war measures signified both a fulfillment of Progressive hopes and a happy augury for the future. Enormously impressed by "the social possibilities of war," John Dewey observed that in every warring country, production for profit had been subordinated to production for use. "The old conception of the absoluteness of private property has received the world over a blow from which it will never wholly recover." [17] Thorstein Veblen, who worked for the Food Administration in 1918, thought the war created new possibilities for far-reaching social change.[18] Economists viewed the War Industries Board as "a notable demonstration of the power of war to force concert of effort and collective planning," and anticipated that lessons from the war could be applied in times of peace.[19] When Wesley C. Mitchell closed his lectures at Columbia University in May, 1918, he remarked that peace would bring new problems, but "it seems impossible that the countries concerned will attempt to solve them without utilizing the same sort of centralized directing now employed to kill their enemies abroad for the new purpose of reconstructing their own life at home."[20] "What we have learned in war we shall hardly forget in peace,"

17. John Dewey, "What Are We Fighting For?" *Independent,* XCIV (1918), 480, reprinted as "The Social Possibilities of War," in Joseph Ratner (ed.), *Characters and Events* (2 vols.; New York, 1929), II, 555. See, too, John Dewey, "A New Social Science," *New Republic,* XIV (1918), 293.

18. David Riesman, *Thorstein Veblen* (New York, 1953), p. 119; Joseph Dorfman, *Thorstein Veblen and His America* (New York, 1934), pp. 380–95.

19. Curtice N. Hitchcock, "The War Industries Board: Its Development, Organization, and Functions," *Journal of Political Economy,* XXVI (1918), 566; Irving Fisher, "Some Contributions of the War to Our Knowledge of Money and Prices," *American Economic Review,* VIII (1918), Supplement, 257–58; Joseph Dorfman, *The Economic Mind in American Civilization* (5 vols.; New York, 1946–59), III, 485–94.

20. Dorfman, *The Economic Mind in American Civilization,* III, 490.

commented Walter Weyl. "The new economic solidarity, once gained, can never again be surrendered." [21]

The end of the war left the administrators with a sense of incompletion. One writer noted unmistakable shadows of annoyance at the Cosmos Club when "the dark cloud of peace" lowered in October, 1918.[22] After the war, to the chagrin of the planners, the economic machinery was quickly dismantled, but the lesson that the war had taught—that the federal government could mobilize the nation's resources in a planned economy—was not forgotten.[23] Throughout the 1920's, the more advanced Progressives looked back fondly toward the war mobilization which seemed to have drawn a blueprint for America's future. In 1927, Rexford Tugwell lauded the war as "an industrial engineer's Utopia." He wanted to co-ordinate the economy as it had been under the War Industries Board in "America's war-time socialism." "We were on the verge of having an international industrial machine when peace broke," he wrote ruefully. ". . . Only the Armistice," he lamented, "prevented a great experiment

21. Walter Weyl, *The End of the War* (New York, 1918), pp. 303–4. Cf. Sidney Kaplan, "Social Engineers as Saviors: Effects of World War I on Some American Liberals," *Journal of the History of Ideas*, XVII (1956), 347–69. The war experience casts doubt on the familiar generalization that war is always fatal to reform. In some ways, the war dealt a severe blow to the progressive movement; in other ways, it opened up new possibilities for reform. No doubt the war resulted in more harm than good for progressivism, but it was not the totally unusable experience it has frequently been represented to be.

22. "The Demobilized Professor," *Atlantic Monthly*, CXXIII (1919), 537.

23. In the months after the armistice, economists like Wesley Mitchell sought to preserve the activities begun during the war, and men like Senator William S. Kenyon of Iowa attempted to keep alive and even expand the work of war agencies, but in vain. See Dorfman, *The Economic Mind in American Civilization*, IV, 9–11, 365; Lucy Sprague Mitchell, *Two Lives: The Story of Wesley Clair Mitchell and Myself* (New York, 1953), p. 303; Wesley C. Mitchell, *The Backward Art of Spending Money and Other Essays* (New York, 1937), pp. 42–57.

in control of production, control of price, and control of consumption." [24]

The fascination the war example held for the Progressives was a consequence of the fusion of nationalism and reform in the previous generation. Heralded by Bismarck in Germany and Joseph Chamberlain in Great Britain, this conjunction appeared in America in the martial fantasies of Edward Bellamy, in Francis Walker's critique of classical economics, in the "industrial armies" of men like Jacob Coxey, in the military forms of the Salvation Army, and in the response of certain reformers to the imperialist issues of the 1890's.[25] In the Progressive era, this association was starkly revealed in the career of Theodore Roosevelt who thought social justice and military preparedness to be two aspects of a common program.

While the confluence of nationalism and reform fascinated a number of progressive theorists, notably Brooks Adams, it was Herbert Croly who, in his seminal *The Promise of American Life,* explored the relationship most extensively. Croly set down the deep dissatisfaction of the Progressives with the quality of life in America. The homogeneity of the early republic, he wrote, had been fragmented by a century of individualism run riot. So long as the market place determined values, so long as each individual or interest was permitted to pursue its own ends with no commitment to a common ideal, the result could not help but be unsatis-

24. Rexford G. Tugwell, "America's War-Time Socialism," *Nation*, CXXIV (1927), 364–65. Cf. Donald Richberg, *Tents of the Mighty* (New York, 1930), p. 82. Even the social security movement of the 1920's was affected by the wartime precedents of government insurance and of the care and rehabilitation of veterans (Clarke Chambers to the writer, June 23, 1962). The Railroad Administration was to provide the model for the New Deal's Coordinator of Transportation.

25. In some respects, this relationship had even earlier antecedents, for example, in the special place that Lincoln and the Union cause had in the hearts of postbellum reformers. It might even be traced back as far as the congruence of reform and imperialism in the Jefferson administration.

fying, Croly reasoned. Reform had foundered because it lacked a sense of national purpose. "In this country," he observed, "the solution of the social problem demands the substitution of a conscious social ideal for the earlier instinctive homogeneity of the American nation."[26]

The war offered just such a "conscious social ideal." Through war priorities, as Bernard Baruch later explained, the economy could be "made to move in response to a national purpose rather than in response to the wills of those who had money to buy."[27] The nationalistic demands of war denied, if only for a time, the claims of the profit system. ". . . When production and distribution became really a matter of life and death, immediate and dramatic, every warring nation, after a few months of appalling waste, threw laissez-faire out of the window," noted Stuart Chase. "Wars must be won, and it was painfully obvious that laissez-faire was no help in winning them."[28] The individualistic, competitive economy of the prewar years had to submit to the discipline of conscious government direction. Not business profit but the national interest was to determine how resources were to be allocated. The old system of competition, Rexford Tugwell wrote jubilantly, "melted away in the fierce new heat of nationalistic vision."[29]

When the stock market crash of 1929 precipitated the Great Depression of the 1930's, progressives turned instinc-

26. Croly, *The Promise of American Life* (New York, 1909), p. 139. Croly rejoiced that the Spanish-American War and the subsequent imperial expansion had given "a tremendous impulse to the work of national reform" (*ibid.*, p. 169). See William E. Leuchtenburg, "Progressivism and Imperialism: The Progressive Movement and American Foreign Policy, 1898–1916," *Mississippi Valley Historical Review*, XXXIX (1952), 483–504.

27. Baruch, *American Industry in the War*, p. 29. See, too, J. M. Clark's perceptive article, "The Basis of War-Time Collectivism," *American Economic Review*, VII (1917), 772–90.

28. Stuart Chase, *A New Deal* (New York, 1933), pp. 84–85.

29. Tugwell, "America's War-Time Socialism," p. 365.

tively to the war mobilization as a design for recovery. The War Industries Board, Stuart Chase pointed out, had, like the Soviet *Gosplan,* demonstrated that "super-management" could replace "industrial anarchy." [30] George Soule contended that the war had shown that planning was neither beyond human capacity nor alien to American values. "Many of those who now advocate economic planning have been doing so, in one way or another, ever since the experiences of 1917–18, and mainly as result of the possibilities which those experiences suggested for better performance in times of peace." The same "deliberate collective effort" which had made possible a tremendous expansion of production could be turned to peacetime ends, he argued. "If that military and industrial army had been mobilized, not to kill, burn and shatter, but to substitute garden cities for slums, to restore soil fertility and reforest our waste regions, to carry out flood control, to increase the necessities of life available for those in the lower income groups, we could have achieved in a short time a large number of really desirable objectives," Soule claimed.[31]

Such men as Gerard Swope of General Electric, a veteran of the war mobilization, and Otto T. Mallery, the leading advocate of public works in the World War I era, recommended floating large federal bond issues like Liberty Bonds to finance a massive public-works program.[32] Swope wrote President Hoover: "If we were faced with war, the Presi-

30. Stuart Chase, "The Heart of American Industry," in Fred J. Ringel (ed.), *America as Americans See It* (New York, 1932), p. 30.

31. George Soule, *A Planned Society* (New York, 1933), pp. 184–87. See, too, J. Russell Smith, "The End of an Epoch," *Survey,* LXVI (1931), 333.

32. Mallery had headed a division of the War Labor Policies Board charged with developing public works during the postwar transition. For the proposals of Mallery and Father John O'Grady, see the *New York Times,* December 30, 1931. The economist Arthur Gayer recommended profiting from the Liberty Bond example by floating bonds for public works "in a war on growing suffering and distress" (Arthur D. Gayer, "Financing the Emergency Public Works Program," *American Labor Legislation Review,* XXII [1932], 75).

dent would immediately call a special session of Congress to declare war and to raise armies. This unemployment situation in many ways is more serious even than war. Therefore it is suggested that an extra session of Congress be called and the President request it to issue a billion dollars of bonds, bearing a low interest rate, and that then a campaign be organized to sell these bonds, much as the Liberty Bond campaigns were organized when we entered the war thirteen years ago." [33] The Wisconsin economist Richard T. Ely went a step farther. He proposed the creation of a peacetime army which, when a depression struck, could be expanded by recruiting from the ranks of the unemployed. Under the direction of an economic general staff, the army, Ely urged, "should go to work to relieve distress with all the vigor and resources of brain and brawn that we employed in the World War." [34]

By the middle of 1931, both businessmen and politicians were calling on President Hoover to adopt the procedures of the War Industries Board to pull the country out of the depression. When William McAdoo, who had headed the wartime Railroad Administration, proposed a Peace Industries Board in June, 1931, he found ready support. The War Industries Board, one correspondent wrote McAdoo, "accomplished wonders during the war, and there is no question but that a board established now to coordinate things in our national industries will also do wonders. This historical precedent is a great asset and ought to guide us in our national planning for the benefit of all." [35] A month later, Charles Beard urged the creation of a National Economic Council with a Board of Strategy and Planning which would follow the pattern of "the War Industries Board and other federal agencies created during the titanic effort to

33. Swope to Hoover, October 2, 1930, Columbia University, New York, Gerard Swope MSS.

34. Richard T. Ely, *Hard Times*, pp. 103–6.

35. Raphael Herman to William McAdoo, June 10, 1931, Library of Congress, McAdoo MSS, Box 359.

mobilize men and materials for the World War." [36] The following month, Representative Chester Bolton of Ohio advanced a similar proposal. "If we could have another body like the old War Industries Board," he wrote the head of Hoover's voluntary relief agency, "I believe the situation today could be greatly bettered." [37] In September, 1931, Gerard Swope came forth with the most influential of all the pre-New Deal proposals: the "Swope Plan" to stabilize employment and prices through a constellation of trade associations under a national economic council.[38] Early in 1932, a group of more than a hundred businessmen requested Hoover to declare a two-year truce on destructive competition and urged him "to consider a return to war-time experience by bringing into existence A National Economic Truce Board." [39]

The cornucopia of proposals included suggestions with widely differing ideological implications. Some called on the war example to support radical recommendations for national planning; others used the war precedent simply as a stratagem to free business of the encumbrance of the trust laws. Most of them had in common a demand for greater initiative by the federal government, and many of them—especially the public-works proposals—called for a sharp increase in government spending.

Such proposals ran far ahead of anything President Hoover and his followers would countenance. Most business-

36. Charles A. Beard, "A 'Five-Year Plan' for America," *Forum* LXXXVI (1931), 5. He also proposed gigantic agricultural and housing programs to be "financed by Freedom Bonds and sold with the zeal of war issues" (*ibid.*, p. 11).

37. Representative Chester Bolton to Walter Gifford, August 24, 1931, Library of Congress, Newton Baker MSS, Box 192.

38. J. George Frederick (ed.), *The Swope Plan* (New York, 1931); Gerard Swope, Columbia Oral History Collection, pp. 123 ff. The Collection will be cited henceforth as COHC.

39. "A Plea from 123 Representatives of Independent Industrial Units and of Labor for the Trial of a Two Years' Truce in Destructive Competition," to Herbert Hoover, February 11, 1932, copy in Harvey Williams to Robert Wagner, March 24, 1932, Wagner MSS, Georgetown University, Washington, D.C.

men seemed chary of taking the War Industries Board as a model for peacetime.[40] The President himself gave little indication of a readiness to have the federal government assume a larger role. To be sure, he signed an Employment Stabilization Bill in 1931, and gave a major share of credit for the measure to Mallery.[41] But he deplored recommendations for lavish federal spending. Ventures of this sort, the President protested, would unbalance the budget and destroy business confidence in public credit.

These doctrines received small credence from men who recalled the war expenditures. "If it is permissible for government to expend billions in wartime in the organization of production, it is no less legitimate for government in a great emergency of peacetime to do what it is also impossible for private individuals to accomplish," reasoned the distinguished economist Edwin R. A. Seligman.[42] The popular economic writer William Trufant Foster scolded:

> If any one still doubts that our economic troubles are mainly mental, let him consider what would happen if the United States

40. For the wariness of businessmen about using the War Industries Board as a model, see U. S. Congress, Senate, *Establishment of a National Economic Council*, Hearings before a Subcommittee of the Committee on Manufactures, U. S. Senate, 72d Cong., 1st Sess., on S. 6215, October 22 to December 19, 1931 (Washington, D.C., 1932), p. 174. William Appleman Williams sees men like Gerard Swope as representative of a new group of corporation executives who came out of the war with a more sophisticated approach to industrial problems, and views Herbert Hoover as their most important spokesman (Williams, *The Contours of American History* [Cleveland and New York, 1961], pp. 425–26). While this judgment seems valid for the 1920's, especially during Hoover's tenure as Secretary of Commerce, it is hardly pertinent for Hoover's presidency. The differences between Swope and President Hoover, sharply revealed by their divergent evaluations of the relevance of war to the depression, were more significant than their area of agreement.

41. Dorfman, *The Economic Mind in American Civilization*, IV, 7. Moreover, Hoover had stepped up public works right after the crash. Still, this represented far less than the progressives demanded.

42. *Ibid.*, V, 672. During the fight over the sales tax in 1932, an Oklahoma congressman hooted at the idea that budget-balancing was a patriotic duty. "Those who are so anxious to balance the budget

declared war today. Everybody knows what would happen. Congress would immediately stop this interminable talk and appropriate three billion dollars—five billion—ten billion—any necessary amount. . . .

Some day we shall realize that if money is available for a blood-and-bullets war, just as much money is available for a food-and-famine war. We shall see that if it is fitting to use collective action on a large scale to kill men abroad, it is fitting to use collective action on an equally large scale to save men at home.[43]

Although Hoover rejected the demand that he draw on the war legacy to mount a program of public works, he could not resist for long the clamor for government initiative to expand relief to the jobless. By the summer of 1931, the number of unemployed totaled eight million. William Allen White wrote: "Hundreds of thousands of men, women and children are going to suffer terribly this winter in spite of all that the natural laws of economic change can do, however soon change may start, however rapidly it may move. Yet the situation is not hopeless, for if we can recreate the dynamic altruism outside of government which moved us during the war, we can harness forces that will bring relief and make us a better and nobler people." If Hoover could arouse the "latent altruism" of the people, White believed, great sums could be raised for relief "as we raised the

---

at this time either forget or ignore the fact that we have in times past raised vast sums in emergencies to carry on wars without resorting to the general sales tax," he noted ("Soak the Poor," University of Oklahoma, Norman, Okla., Wilburn Cartwright MSS).

43. Foster, "When a Horse Balks," *North American Review*, CCXXXIV (1932), 10. John Maynard Keynes wrote: "I hope that in the future we shall . . . be ready to spend on the enterprises of peace what the financial maxims of the past would only allow us to spend on the devastations of war."—Keynes, "The World's Economic Outlook," *Atlantic Monthly*, CXLIX (1932), 525. See, too, Lewis Kimmel, *Federal Budget and Fiscal Policy, 1789–1958* (Washington, D.C., 1959), pp. 170–72.

Liberty Loan, Red Cross and Y drive funds during the war." [44]

On August 19, 1931, President Hoover named Walter S. Gifford, president of the American Telephone and Telegraph Company, to head the President's Organization on Unemployment Relief. A week later Newton Baker, a member of the Advisory Committee of the POUR, noted that Gifford seemed to be planning to organize the country along the lines of the Council of National Defense, and added: "I am going a step farther and suggest that as far as possible men with military experience in the World War be used. They have had lessons in effective and disciplined action which will be valuable." [45] That fall, the Gifford committee launched a "mobilization" to win support for local fund-raising drives. National advertisements proclaimed: "Between October 19 and November 25 America will feel the thrill of a great spiritual experience." A few weeks later, when Senator Edward Costigan of Colorado questioned the advisability of employing such techniques, Gifford responded: "We certainly did it in the war. I do not know that I like it, but, as I say, it is more or less the established practice. . . . " [46]

President Hoover made much more forceful use of the war precedent to meet the financial crisis of the autumn of 1931. In December, 1931, Hoover asked Congress to

44. White to David Hinshaw, August 10, 1931, Library of Congress, William Allen White MSS, Box 135.

45. Baker to Representative Chester Bolton, August 26, 1931, Newton Baker MSS, Box 192.

46. U. S. Congress, Senate, *Unemployment Relief*, Hearings before a Subcommittee of the Committee on Manufactures, U. S. Senate, 72d Cong., 1st Sess., on S. 174 and S. 262, December 28–30, 1931, and January 4–9, 1932 (Washington, D.C., 1932), p. 327. A year later, when Newton Baker was named to head the National Citizen's Committee for the Welfare and Relief Mobilization of 1932, the *Literary Digest* explained: "The concentrated effort is under the direct command of Newton D. Baker, who, as Secretary of War under President Wilson, mobilized the forces of the country for the war in Europe. The campaign is to be the Armageddon of the Great Depression." (*Literary Digest*, CXIV [October 8, 1932], 20).

create a Reconstruction Finance Corporation frankly modeled on the War Finance Corporation.[47] The proposal appeared to originate at about the same time in the minds of several different men: Hoover, Federal Reserve Governor Eugene Meyer, who had been managing director of the WFC, Louis Wehle, who had been the WFC's general counsel, and Senator Joseph Robinson of Arkansas.[48] All drew their inspiration from the WFC. "The RFC was a revival of the War Finance Corporation, that's all, but with expanded powers," Meyer recalled.[49] Observers were astonished by the speed with which Congress approved the RFC bill. "It puts us financially on a war basis," noted the *New Republic*.[50] When the RFC began operations, it employed many of the WFC's old staff, followed its pattern and that of the wartime Treasury in financing, and even took over, with slight modifications, the old WFC forms for loan applications.[51]

The RFC, declared one periodical, was to be the "spearhead of the economic A.E.F." [52] But Hoover and his aides in-

47. William Starr Myers (ed.), *The State Papers and Other Public Writings of Herbert Hoover* (2 vols.; Garden City, N.Y., 1934), II, 6.

48. Accounts of the origin of the RFC vary in detail. Cf. Eugene Meyer, COHC, pp. 612–13; Jackson Reynolds, COHC, pp. 152–53; Louis Wehle, *Hidden Threads of History* (New York, 1953), p. 77; U. S. Congress, Senate, *Creation of a Reconstruction Finance Corporation*, Hearings before a Subcommittee of the Committee on Banking and Currency, U. S. Senate, 72d Cong., 1st Sess., on S. 1, December 18, 19, 21, 22, 1931 (Washington, D.C., 1932).

49. Eugene Meyer, COHC, p. 613. Meyer's initiative, and the WFC model, is also stressed in Gerald Nash, "Herbert Hoover and the Origins of the Reconstruction Finance Corporation," *Mississippi Valley Historical Review*, XLVI (1959), 455–68.

50. *New Republic* LXIX (1932), 291.

51. W. Randolph Burgess, "Plans for Financial Reconstruction," Address at the Century Association of New York, April 7, 1932, Library of Congress, Ogden Mills MSS, Box 9; J. Franklin Ebersole, "One Year of the Reconstruction Finance Corporation," *Quarterly Journal of Economics*, XLVII (1933), 468; Wehle, *Hidden Threads of History*, p. 77.

52. *Literary Digest*, CXII (February 13, 1932), 9. Congress, reported the *Philadelphia Record*, had given the new agency "two billion dollars' worth of ammunition. The people are waiting to see how straight it can shoot" (*ibid.*).

sisted that the intervention of the RFC be held to a minimum. Hoover's reluctance to use the RFC as an agency in a new kind of mobilization suggested that the war analogy meant different things to different men and that it could be turned to conservative purposes as readily as to those envisaged by the progressives. While the progressives thought of the war as a paradigm for national planning, Hoover remembered it as a time when the government had encouraged a maximum of voluntary action and a minimum of disturbance of the profit system.[53] He wished the crucial decisions to be made, as they had been in wartime, by corporation leaders. He employed the metaphor of war to serve a conservative function: that of draining internal antagonisms onto a common national enemy.[54] In his address to the Republican national convention in 1932, the permanent chairman, Bertrand Snell, declared in defense of Hoover: "He solidified labor and capital against the enemy." [55]

New York's Governor Franklin D. Roosevelt sought to reap political advantage from these different perceptions of the war experience.[56] In his campaign for the Democratic presidential nomination in 1932, Roosevelt contrasted Hoover's performance with the achievements of the war mobilization. In his "forgotten man" address in Albany on April 7, 1932, Roosevelt declared that American success

53. For the determination during the war to refrain from interference with business, see Randall B. Kester, "The War Industries Board, 1917–1918; A Study in Industrial Mobilization," *American Political Science Review*, XXXIV (1940), 683; and Herbert Stein, *Government Price Policy in the United States during the World War* (Williamstown, Mass., 1939), p. 13.

54. The integrative function of war is discussed in W. Lloyd Warner, *American Life: Dream and Reality* (Chicago, 1953), p. 20.

55. *Official Report of the Proceedings of the Twentieth Republican National Convention, 1932* (New York, 1932), p. 89.

56. As the country entered the election year of 1932, the tempo of demands for a return to the war spirit quickened. See Baker Brownell to Gifford Pinchot, January 10, 1932, Library of Congress, Gifford Pinchot MSS, Box 320; John J. Pershing, "We Are at War!" *American Magazine*, CXIII (June, 1932), 15–17, 72, 74; *B. E. F. News*, July 2, 1932.

in the war had been due to leadership which was not satisfied with "the timorous and futile gesture" of sending a
small army and navy overseas, but which "conceived of a
whole Nation mobilized for war, economic, industrial, social
and military resources gathered into a vast unit." The
United States in 1932, Roosevelt asserted, faced "a more
grave emergency than in 1917," and in meeting that emergency the Hoover administration had neglected "the in-
fantry of our economic army." "These unhappy times,"
the Governor observed, "call for the building of plans that
rest upon the forgotten, the unorganized but the indispensable units of economic power, for plans like those of 1917
that build from the bottom up and not from the top down,
that put their faith once more in the forgotten man at the
bottom of the economic pyramid." [57] Less than two weeks
later, at the Jefferson Day Dinner at St. Paul on April 18,
Roosevelt repeated that the nation faced an emergency
"more grave than that of war" and once more derided
Hoover's efforts to meet the crisis. He added pointedly:

> Compare this panic-stricken policy of delay and improvisation
> with that devised to meet the emergency of war fifteen years ago.
>   We met specific situations with considered, relevant measures
> of constructive value. There were the War Industries Board, the
> Food and Fuel Administration, the War Trade Board, the
> Shipping Board and many others.[58]

The 1932 election brought the Democrats to power for
the first time since Wilson's war administration. It was
"only natural," as Swisher has observed, "that some of the

57. *The Public Papers and Addresses of Franklin D. Roosevelt*, ed.
Samuel I. Rosenman (13 vols.; New York, 1938–1950), I, 624–25. At
a Roosevelt rally in Salem, Massachusetts, James Michael Curley
made effective use of the war analogue to berate Hoover (*Salem News*,
April 6, 1932 [Holy Cross College Library, Worcester, Mass., Curley
Scrapbooks]).
58. Roosevelt, *Public Papers*, I, 631–32.

World-War leaders should return to federal office and that others should become unofficial advisers of the administration. They, like the President, thought in terms of the dramatic concentration of power in the federal government which they had helped to bring about for the defeat of a foreign enemy. It is not surprising that modes of procedure were carried over from one period to the other." [59] In the interregnum between Roosevelt's election in November, 1932, and his inauguration in March, 1933, war recollections became even more compelling. The whole political system seemed doomed to self-asphyxiation. The discords of party, the deadlock in Congress, the maxims of the classical economists, the taboos of the Constitution all seemed to inhibit action at a time when action was desperately needed. In contrast, the war was remembered as a time of movement and accomplishment.[60]

During the interregnum, the country debated a series of new proposals for utilizing the war experience to vanquish

59. Carl Brent Swisher, *American Constitutional Development* (Boston, 1943), p. 878. Senator James F. Byrnes of South Carolina later wrote: "In our efforts to find a remedy for this situation, we had no guideposts. I recalled that when I went to the House of Representatives I had firm convictions about federal-state relations and the wisdom of preserving local governments, the necessity of maintaining a balanced budget, and like subjects; but when we entered World War I in 1917, I recognized that, in a war emergency, principles as well as policies had to be temporarily subordinated to the necessity of some experimentation in order to preserve the government itself. The economic crisis now demanded a similar attitude."—Byrnes, *All in One Lifetime* (New York, 1958), pp. 69–70.

60. The President's Research Committee on Social Trends pointed to the "surprising energy and efficiency" that had emerged in 1917, and noted the explanation for this "development of governmental art": "the subordination of private to public interest, the facility in recruitment of the necessary talent when the boycott on government service was lifted, the indifference to established precedent in administrative or other method, the freedom from hairsplitting judicial restraint, the unification of leadership. . . . "—The President's Research Committee on Social Trends, *Recent Social Trends in the United States* (New York and London, 1933), p. 1539. Cf. Max Lerner, "The State in War Time," in Willard Waller (ed.), *War in the Twentieth Century* (New York, 1940), pp. 409–28.

the depression. Daniel Roper, who would soon be Roosevelt's Secretary of Commerce, suggested a few days after the election that the new President "appoint one 'super' secretary with the other secretaries assistant to him and organize under this 'super' secretary the plan of the National Council of Defense composed of, say 21 men working without compensation as they did in War times." [61] Many believed the crisis could be met only by vesting in the President the same arbitrary war powers that Woodrow Wilson had been given.[62] The depression, declared Alfred E. Smith on February 7, 1933, was "doing more damage at home to our own people than the great war of 1917 and 1918 ever did." "And what does a democracy do in a war?" Smith asked. "It becomes a tyrant, a despot, a real monarch. In the World War we took our Constitution, wrapped it up and laid it on the shelf and left it there until it was over." [63] Four days later, Republican Governor Alf Landon of Kansas inquired: "Why not give the President the same powers in this bitter peacetime battle as we would give to him in time of war?" [64]

As early as the spring of 1932, weeks before Roosevelt had even been nominated, his brain trust had requested Joseph D. McGoldrick and Howard L. McBain to prepare a memorandum on presidential war powers, for they anticipated Roosevelt would need them as authority for emergency acts.[65] Early in January, 1933, the President-elect asked Rexford Tugwell to explore the possibility that the Trading with the Enemy Act of 1917 might provide the

61. Daniel Roper to William Dodd, November 16, 1932, Library of Congress, Dodd MSS, Box 41.

62. Key Pittman to Franklin D. Roosevelt, June 16, 1932, Library of Congress, Pittman MSS, Box 16; Henry Morrow Hyde MS Diary, January 4, 1933.

63. *New York Times*, February 8, 1933.

64. Willis Thornton, *The Life of Alfred M. Landon* (New York, 1936), p. 84.

65. Raymond Moley, *After Seven Years* (New York, 1939), pp. 22–23.

basis for an edict embargoing gold exports. Tugwell's research quickly involved him in a comedy of errors in which the New Dealers sought both to obtain the necessary information without letting the Hoover Administration learn what they were up to and at the same time to persuade themselves that a statute that had been amended many times gave them the legal authority to do what they intended to do anyway.[66] Governor Roosevelt's legal aides could not have been more co-operative. Senator Thomas Walsh, Roosevelt's choice to be Attorney General, promised that, if the President-elect found he needed the powers, he would quiet his doubts and rule that the old statute gave him the authority he required. When, after Walsh's death, Roosevelt picked Homer Cummings for the post, he turned over to him the folder on the Trading with the Enemy Act. Cummings obligingly found the statute was still alive.[67]

As the day of Roosevelt's inauguration approached, the epidemic of bank failures drove governors in state after state to proclaim bank holidays and raised fears that the economic system was on the verge of collapse. "A blight has fallen over all American industry," declared the Akron *Beacon-Journal* on March 3. "A foreign invader making easy conquest of our shores could do no worse." [68] As Roosevelt took the oath of office, the atmosphere in Washington, wrote Arthur Krock, was like that "in a beleaguered capital in war time." [69]

Roosevelt's inaugural address on March 4, 1933 reflected the sense of wartime crisis. The nation, he resolved, must

66. Tugwell, "Notes from a New Deal Diary," January 4, 1933, February 27, 1933, Franklin D. Roosevelt Library, Hyde Park, N.Y., Tugwell MSS; Key Pittman to Roosevelt, February 28, 1933, Pittman MSS, Box 16.

67. Ernest K. Lindley, *The Roosevelt Revolution* (New York, 1939), p. 78; Rexford Tugwell, COHC, pp. 37–40.

68. Cited in Ruth McKenney, *Industrial Valley* (New York, 1939), p. 71.

69. *New York Times*, March 5, 1933.

move "as a trained and loyal army willing to sacrifice for the good of a common discipline." He would ask Congress to adopt his legislative program, but if Congress failed to act and the emergency continued, the new President announced: "I shall not evade the clear course of duty that will then confront me. I shall ask the Congress for the one remaining instrument to meet the crisis—broad executive power to wage a war against the emergency, as great as the power that would be given to me if we were in fact invaded by a foreign foe." [70]

During the "Hundred Days," President Roosevelt sought to restore national confidence by evoking the mood of wartime: the feeling of national unity above any claim of partisan or private economic interest because the very existence of the country was imperiled. The opposition press suspended criticism of the President; business corporations, labor unions, and farm organizations pledged their cooperation; and Republican leaders urged the country to rally around the Democratic chief executive. Governor Landon declared: "If there is any way in which a member of that species, thought to be extinct, a Republican Governor of a mid-western state, can aid [the President] in the fight, I now enlist for the duration of the war." [71]

The New Deal hoped to arouse the same sense of devotion to the nation and the same spirit of sacrifice that had been displayed in the war. "It is important," wrote Rexford

70. Roosevelt, *Public Papers*, II, 14–15. The task of putting people to work, the President stated, could be "accomplished in part by direct recruiting by the Government itself, treating the task as we would treat the emergency of a war" (*ibid.*, p. 13).

71. Schlesinger, Jr., *The Coming of the New Deal*, p. 3. One periodical noted: "The country was in an exalted mood. It rose to greet the new President as if to support him in the repulsion of invading armies."—*Review of Reviews and World's Work*, LXXXVII (April, 1933), 10. In April, 1933, a Democratic senator completed a volume which was a sustained use of the war as a parable for the depression (Millard Tydings, *Counter-Attack: A Battle Plan to Defeat the Depression* [Indianapolis, 1933]).

Tugwell, "that we should again explore the possibilities of what William James called 'the moral equivalents' of war." [72] "The ordeal of war," he told Dartmouth students, "brings out the magnificent resources of youth. . . . The ordeal of depression ought to try your mettle in similar ways. . . . The feeling which shook humanity during the War and which after the War reshaped the entire civilization of mighty nations is called for again." [73]

When the planners of the thirties looked back at the war, they were most impressed by how much had been accomplished once the nation had been unified by allegiance to a common purpose. Writers like Rexford Tugwell and George Soule argued that the effective functioning of "a regime of industrial democracy" required the same spirit of "loyalty to larger aims" that the War Industries Board had exploited.[74] Nationalistic to the core, unabashedly patriotic, they believed that if the country could once again give fealty to a transcendent ideal, the depression would be conquered as once the armies of the Kaiser had been. Charles Beard proposed a "heroic national effort" that would leave people "richer in goods—and still more important, in patriotic spirit." [75] Many conceived the New Deal not simply as a new kind of economic mobilization but also, as the war had

72. Rexford G. Tugwell, *The Battle for Democracy* (New York, 1935), p. 75.

73. *Ibid.*, p. 296. Thurman Arnold noted that in war, democracies "achieve unity to an extent which seems extraordinary to one viewing the wartime economy from the tangled confusion of peacetime values." Arnold added: "Thus, in peacetimes, when the lack of coöperation between men is distressingly evident, and when the endless argument about the contradictions involved in our symbols seems to have no hope of ending, we look back to the unity of the time when nations were drawn up in battle lines and we demand a moral substitute for war."—Arnold, *The Symbols of Government* (New Haven, 1935), pp. 243–45.

74. The words are Tugwell's (Tugwell, *The Industrial Discipline and the Governmental Arts* [New York, 1933], p. 100). See, too, George Soule, *A Planned Society*, pp. 196–97.

75. Beard, "A 'Five-Year Plan' for America," p. 11.

been, a venture in "nation-saving."[76] One of the New Deal experiments was later to be lauded because it had led to "a new baptism of patriotism and an increased consciousness of national unity."[77]

Roosevelt's first important official act was to use the authority of the Trading with the Enemy Act of 1917 to proclaim a national bank holiday.[78] When he sent his banking bill to Congress, the House received it with much the same ardor as it had greeted Woodrow Wilson's war legislation. Speaker Rainey said the situation reminded him of the late war when "on both sides of this Chamber the great war measures suggested by the administration were supported with practical unanimity. . . . Today we are engaged in another war, more serious even in its character and presenting greater dangers to the Republic."[79] After only thirty-eight minutes debate, the House passed the Administration's banking bill, sight unseen.[80]

76. George N. Peek, with Samuel Crowther, *Why Quit Our Own* (New York, 1936), p. 123. Raymond Moley, it might be noted, had directed Americanization activities in Ohio under Governor James Cox during World War I.

77. Alfred C. Oliver, Jr., and Harold M. Dudley, *This New America* (London, 1937), p. viii. See, too, the reference to "nation-building" in John L. Christian, "America's Peace Army," *Current History*, XLIX (1939), 43.

78. Roosevelt, *Public Papers*, II, 18. Tugwell, who worked on the banking proclamation, referred to it as "this rather doubtful executive act" (Tugwell, "Notes from a New Deal Diary," March 31, 1933). See, too, Rixey Smith and Norman Beasley, *Carter Glass* (New York, 1939), pp. 341–42.

79. *Congressional Record*, 73d Cong., 1st Sess., LXXVII (March 9, 1933), 70.

80. "It was a grim Congress which met today, the most momentous gathering of the country's legislators since war was declared in 1917. It is trite to say that they declared war, but it is nevertheless true that they hurled against the enemy of depression and despondency a weapon which they hoped would penetrate the subtle armor of an allegorical or Bunyan-like antagonist."—*New York Times*, March 10, 1933. Roosevelt's new banking act was deliberately framed to use the "war power" to overcome possible objections to its constitutionality. The President's extraordinary powers were granted "during time of war or during any other period of national emergency declared

On March 10, Roosevelt sent his second message to Congress, a plea for plenary powers to slash government spending. To the dismay of progressive Republicans and liberal Democrats, Roosevelt proved to be as orthodox on fiscal matters as his predecessor. When Senator Tom Connally of Texas talked to Roosevelt in December, 1932, the President-elect had stressed the importance of balancing the budget by cutting federal spending and had dwelt upon the constitutional limitations of the President. "If it was constitutional to spend forty million dollars in a war," Connally told Roosevelt angrily, "isn't it just as constitutional to spend a little money to relieve the hunger and misery of our citizens?" [81] The President-elect brushed aside such remonstrances and chose instead to heed the counsel of his conservative choice for Budget Director, Lewis Douglas. After studying the wartime authority Congress had granted Woodrow Wilson, Roosevelt decided to ask the new Congress to renew those powers in order to enable the President to balance the budget.[82]

The spirit of war crisis speeded through the economy bill. "It is true this bill grants a great deal of power," conceded Representative John McDuffie of Alabama, "but this country is in a state of war—not against a foreign enemy but war against economic evils that demand some sacrifice on your part and mine." Representative John Young Brown of Kentucky spoke even more bluntly when he scolded fellow Democrats:

> . . . I may say to you that we are at war today, and the veterans of this country do not want you, in their name, to desert the standards of the President of the United States.

---

by the President" (Gustav Cassel, *The Downfall of the Gold Standard* [Oxford, 1936], p. 117).

81. Tom Connally, as told to Alfred Steinberg, *My Name Is Tom Connally* (New York, 1954), p. 148.

82. Schlesinger, Jr., *The Coming of the New Deal*, pp. 9–10.

I had as soon start a mutiny in the face of a foreign foe as start a mutiny today against the program of the President of the United States. [Applause.] And if someone must shoot down, in this hour of battle, the Commander in Chief of our forces, God grant that the assassin's bullet shall not be fired from the Democratic side of this House. [Applause] [83]

Many Congressmen disliked the Administration's economy bill, but feared to oppose the President. When Senator Wallace H. White, Jr., spoke out against the proposal, a Maine constituent warned him that he was "riding out to certain death." He agreed that White's position was logically sound, yet he cautioned that since "a state of war does exist," the Senator would be foolish to sacrifice himself by disregarding the war spirit.[84] After only two days debate, Congress voted the Economy Act. Senator Henry Fountain Ashurst of Arizona explained: "The conditions are as serious as war and we must follow the flag." [85]

There was scarcely a New Deal act or agency that did not owe something to the experience of World War I. The Tennessee Valley Authority—the most ambitious New Deal experiment in regional planning—grew out of the creation of a government-operated nitrate and electric-power project at Muscle Shoals during and after the war. In his message

83. *Congressional Record*, 73d Cong., 1st Sess., pp. 201, 209.

84. Wingate F. Cram to White, March 18, 1933, Library of Congress, Wallace White MSS, Box 1.

85. *New York Times*, March 11, 1933. "The President has been elected as Commander-in-Chief to pull us out of this financial crisis and it is my purpose to stand by him," agreed Rep. Sam McReynolds of Tennessee (McReynolds to George Fort Milton, March 27, 1933, Library of Congress, Milton MSS, Box 13). At a homecoming meeting for the Nevada Congressional delegation, following the historic session of the Hundred Days, Senator Pat McCarran stated: "On March 9 of this year, to the astonishment of many, war was officially declared. . . . The war was against fear, fear that the entire government would go into bankruptcy." Clipping, n.d., Scrapbook 44018, Nevada State Historical Society, Reno, Nev., James Scrugham MSS.

asking for creation of the TVA, President Roosevelt concluded: "In short, this power development of war days
leads logically to national planning. . . . " [86] When the TVA
bill was introduced in April, 1933, it seemed appropriate to
refer it to the House Military Affairs Committee. Although
war considerations played an inconsequential part in the
birth of the Authority, the TVA Act of 1933 stipulated that
in case of war or national emergency, any or all of the
property entrusted to the Authority should be available to
the government for manufacturing explosives or for other
war purposes. The original World War I nitrate plant,
which was turned over to the TVA, was to be held as a
standby which might be needed in a future war.[87] When
foes of the TVA challenged it in the courts, Chief Justice
Charles Evans Hughes found constitutional authority for
the construction of the Wilson Dam by resting his ruling,
in part, on the war power.[88] The TVA was only one of a
number of resources operations—from soil conservation to
public power development—that employed the war rhetoric
or drew from the World War I experience.[89]

86. Roosevelt, *Public Papers*, II, 122. Cf. Sarah Elizabeth Boseley
Winger, "The Genesis of TVA" (Ph.D. dissertation, University of
Wisconsin, 1959), pp. 580–81; Judson King, *The Conservation Fight:
From Theodore Roosevelt to the Tennessee Valley Authority* (Washington, D.C., 1959), chaps. vii–viii; Norman Wengert, "Antecedents of
TVA: The Legislative History of Muscle Shoals," *Agricultural History*,
XXV (1952), 141–47; Kenneth McKellar to George Fort Milton, May
17, 1933, Milton MSS, Box 13. The special form of the TVA—the
government corporation endowed with many of the powers and much
of the flexibility of a business corporation—had first found wide
acceptance in the war.

87. Tennessee Valley Authority, *To Keep the Water in the Rivers
and the Soil on the Land* (Washington, D.C., 1938), p. 44.

88. *Ashwander et al.*, v. *Tennessee Valley Authority et al.*, 297 U. S.
288 (1936); Joseph C. Swidler and Robert H. Marquis, "TVA in Court:
A Study of Constitutional Litigation," *Iowa Law Review*, XXXII
(1947), 296–326.

89. In arguing the case for passage of the Taylor Grazing Act,
a former senator claimed: " . . . The remaining public domain is
vital to the nation from a standpoint of national defense. . . . Without
an adequate supply of meat and wool the nation would be considerably
handicapped in case of war."—Holm Bursum to Charles McNary,

The public-housing movement of the thirties had first
come of age during the war. In World War I, Congress
authorized the Emergency Fleet Corporation and the United
States Housing Corporation to provide housing for war
workers. The war established the principle of federal intervention in housing, and it trained architects like Robert
Kohn, who served as chief of production of the housing division of the U.S. Shipping Board.[90] After the armistice,
Kohn observed: ". . . The war has put housing 'on the map'
in this country."[91] In 1933, President Roosevelt named
Kohn to head the New Deal's first public-housing venture.

Imaginative wartime experiments with garden-city ideas
paved the way for the greenbelt towns of the thirties, while
the rural resettlement and subsistence homestead projects
of the New Deal reaped the harvest of seeds planted by
Elwood Mead and Franklin K. Lane in the war years.[92] Roy
Lubove has pointed out:

April 16, 1934, Bursum MSS, University of New Mexico, Albuquerque,
N. M., Box 1. The public-power reformers of the New Deal were
schooled in wartime agencies like the Power Section of the Emergency
Fleet Corporation (Morris L. Cooke, "Early Days of Rural Electrifi-
cation," *American Political Science Review*, XLII [1948], 437); "U.S.
War Industries Board, 1918," folder, J. D. Ross MSS, University of
Washington, Seattle, Wash. One conservationist commented on his
work on the Mississippi Valley Committee with Morris Cooke: "To all
of us it was a great experience . . . epoch-making. . . . The exper.
was as valuable to me as to you; it was similar to an enriching exper.
I had under the same leadership back in 1917-18, during the war."
Harlow Person to Donald Bower, December 9, 1935, "Quasi Official
and Personal Correspondence of Morris L. Cooke," National Archives,
REA Files (notes of Jean Christie).

90. Timothy L. McDonnell, S. J., *The Wagner Housing Act* (Chicago, 1957), pp. 7–9; Curtice N. Hitchcock, "The War Housing Program and Its Future," *Journal of Political Economy*, XXVII (1919),
241–79; Miles Colean, *Housing for Defense* (New York, 1940), chap. i.

91. Robert D. Kohn, "Housing in a Reconstruction Program,"
Survey, XLII (1919), 341. The most intense interest in government
housing, however, came not so much in the war as in the reconversion
period, although it was triggered by the war experience. (McDonnell,
The Wagner Housing Act, pp. 12–15).

92. Conkin, *Tomorrow a New World*, pp. 50–54, 67; Roy Lubove,
"Homes and 'A Few Well-Placed Fruit Trees': An Object Lesson in
Federal Housing," *Social Research*, XXVII (1960), 469–86.

In such residential communities as Yorkship Village (New Jersey), Union Park Gardens (Delaware) and the Black Rock and Crane Tracts (Bridgeport, Connecticut), the Emergency Fleet Corporation and the United States Housing Corporation offered American architects and planners their first opportunity to apply garden city principles in comprehensive fashion: curvilinear street systems and street sizes adapted to function; park and play facilities; row-house design; the skillful spacing of mass and volume for maximum aesthetic effect and maximum sunlight and ventilation. The memory of the federal war-housing program persisted over the next two decades, a reminder of the potentialities of non-speculative, large-scale site planning for working-class housing.[93]

The New Deal's program of farm price supports owed something to the wartime Food Administration and even more to a decade of proselytization by George Peek, a hard-bitten farm-belt agitator who had served as "a sort of generalissimo of industry" under the War Industries Board.[94] Peek's war experience with the ways government could benefit industry had led him to argue that the government should give the same measure of aid to the distressed farmer.[95] Frustrated in the twenties by Republican presidents in his campaign to win support for McNary-Haugenism, Peek pinned his hopes on the election of Franklin Roosevelt in 1932. "It looks to me as though in the campaign for Roosevelt for President we are in the last line of trenches and if he is not elected that agriculture

93. Roy Lubove, "New Cities for Old: The Urban Reconstruction Program of the 1930's," *Social Studies*, LIII (1962), 205.

94. James Shideler, "Wilson, Hoover, War and Food Control, 1917–1918," paper delivered at the convention of the Mississippi Valley Historical Association, Denver, Colo., April 25, 1959; Grosvenor Clarkson, *Industrial America in the World War* (Boston and New York, 1923), p. 239.

95. Gilbert Fite, *George N. Peek and the Fight for Farm Parity* (Norman, Okla., 1954), p. 32.

is doomed to peasantry," Peek wrote.[96] Roosevelt's victory
touched off a serious debate over how to curb farm sur-
pluses which, after months of wrangling, ended in the
passage of the Agricultural Adjustment Act in the spring
of 1933.[97] To head the new Agricultural Adjustment Administration, Roosevelt named George Peek.[98] "To him, with
his war experience, this whole thing clicks into shape,"
Peek's wife noted, "and some of the fine men of the country
are coming to his call as they did in 1917, and with the same
high purpose." [99]

96. George Peek to Earl Smith, October 18, 1932, Western Historical Manuscripts Collection, University of Missouri, Columbia, Mo.,
Peek MSS.

97. During the debate, Senator Smith Wildman Brookhart of Iowa
advocated a "war emergency" plan in which the surplus would be
"commandeered" by the government (*Jackson* [Miss.] *Daily Clarion-
Ledger*, January 23, 1933). When Roosevelt sent his farm message
to Congress, Secretary of Agriculture Henry Wallace announced: "In
no case will there be any gouging of the consumer. We hope to revive
the Wartime spirit in everyone to put this thing across." *Time*, XXI
(March 27, 1933), 12. A study of Wallace's rhetoric has noted his
fondness for military terminology in his speeches (Robert Gene King,
"The Rhetoric of Henry Agard Wallace" [Ph.D. dissertation, Department of Speech and Drama, Teachers College, Columbia University,
1963]). The farm protest movement employed similar metaphors. One
farmer told an Iowa county agent bluntly that "the World War [had]
its slackers" and that, sixteen years after the war, the country was
plagued by "yellow pups running around in the shape of nincom-poop-
flatheaded County Agents." Jesse Sickler to Milo Reno, April 16,
1933, Reno MSS (privately held).

98. Roosevelt had first offered the post to Peek's "boss," Bernard
Baruch, who, as head of the War Industries Board, was regarded as
the most important of the war administrators. J. F. T. O'Connor MS
Diary, May 13, 1933, Bancroft Library, University of California,
Berkeley, Calif., O'Connor MSS.

99. Georgia Lindsey Peek MS memoir, "Early New Deal," Peek
MSS. For Jerome Frank's first experience with farm issues in the
United States Food Administration, see Jerome Frank, COHC, pp.
52–53. "It was the greatest thing that ever happened when the
government took charge of the wheat situation and told the big and
little barons what price the farmers should get for their wheat," a
Florida newspaper stated that summer. "Everyone knows what the
government was able to do with the price of wheat during the war."
"Why Not Government Control of Citrus Fruit?", *Lakeland* (Fla.)

Consciously devised to provide the moral equivalent to war that men like Tugwell sought, the Civilian Conservation Corps aimed to install martial virtues in the nation's youth.[100] When the CCC enlisted its first recruits, it evoked memories of the mobilization of the AEF. "By the fifteenth of July we shall have 275,000 people all actually at work in the woods," Roosevelt reported a few weeks after Congress adopted the CCC proposal. "It is a pretty good record, one which I think can be compared with the mobilization carried on in 1917." [101] "America has a new army and has sent it to war," observed one writer that summer. "In two brief months 300,000 men have enlisted, been trained, transferred to the front, and have started the attack. The battle is on in earnest." [102]

News, July 1, 1933, clipping in P. K. Yonge Library, University of Florida, Gainesville, Fla., Spessard Holland MSS, Box 52.

100. There had been widespread agitation for offering such an alternative to groups like the "wandering boys of the road" and the bonus marchers (George Rawick, "The New Deal and Youth" [Ph.D. dissertation, University of Wisconsin, 1957], p. 40; Pelham Glassford, "Training Camps for the Unemployed," Institute of Industrial Relations Library, University of California at Los Angeles, Los Angeles, Calif., Glassford MSS, Box 1; James Harvey Rogers, "Sound Inflation," *Economic Forum*, I (1933), 127.

101. Roosevelt, *Public Papers*, II, 238. Schlesinger points out that Louis Howe's original plan for the CCC called for "a large-scale recruiting effort, bands playing and flags flying, leading to a mass exodus of the unemployed to the forests" (Arthur Schlesinger, Jr., *The Coming of the New Deal*, p. 337). See, too, "Memorandum for the Secretary of War: Subject: Civilian Conservation Corps," April 3, 1933, Franklin D. Roosevelt Library, Hyde Park, N. Y., Louis Howe MSS, Box 59. The Third Corps Area, it was observed, enrolled the first recruit in the "peace time army" on the anniversary of America's entrance into World War I (Charles Price Harper, *The Administration of the Civilian Conservation Corps* [Clarksburg, W. Va., 1939], p. 24).

102. Harrison Doty, "Our Forest Army at War," *Review of Reviews and World's Work*, LXXXVIII (July, 1933), 31. "It represented the greatest peacetime demand ever made upon the Army and constituted a task of character and proportions equivalent to emergencies of war," Chief of Staff Douglas MacArthur wrote in a communique to all Army Corps Area Commanders. "It was well done, Army. MacArthur."—Rawick, "The New Deal and Youth," p. 66. See, too, "Extracts from Address of Honorable George H. Dern, Secretary of War," n.d., Library of Congress, Dern MSS, Box 1.

While the agency was under civilian direction, the Army ran the camps.[103] CCC recruits convened at army recruiting stations; traveled to an Army camp where they were out-fitted in World War I clothing; were transported to the woods by troop-train; fell asleep in army tents to the strain of "Taps" and woke to "Reveille." [104] A stanza of a poem by a CCC worker made clear the Army's role:

Uncle, he says to his Army,
"You did a good job before
When you took three million rookies
And polished 'em up for war,
Now if you can handle the civvies
Like the Doughboys and the Gob,
And stiffen their ranks till they're tough as the yanks
I'll give 'em a great big job."[105]

The CCC newspaper, frankly modeled on *Stars and Stripes*, offered a prize for the best nickname for a CCC worker: "You know—some word that has caught on in your camp—the way the word 'doughboy' was used to describe the American soldier in France." [106] *Happy Days* recounted the work of the "Tree Army" in the language of military communiques: "Company 217 at Beachy Bottoms, N.Y. has

103. To quiet fears of military control, Roosevelt named as CCC Director the union leader Robert Fechner whom he had first en-countered when both were engaged in determining war labor policies. The real control of the camps, however, lay with the military (Tucker Smith to Jane Addams, March 8, 1933, Swarthmore College Peace Collection, Swarthmore, Pa., Jane Addams MSS, Box 22; "Unofficial Observer" [John Franklin Carter], *The New Dealers* (New York, 1934), pp. 163–65; Rawick, "The New Deal and Youth," chap. v.

104. Charles W. B. Hurd, "The Forestry Army at the Front," *Literary Digest*, CXVI (September 9, 1933), 5–6; Joseph Cream, "The Genesis of the Civilian Conservation Corps" (Master's thesis, Colum-bia University, 1955), pp. 45 ff.

105. Reprinted in Oliver and Dudley, *This New America*, p. 133.

106. *Happy Days*, I (May 20, 1933), 8. Cf. Levette J. Davidson, "C.C.C. Chatter," *American Speech*, XV (1940), 210–11.

been filled to full Gypsy-moth-fighting strength," or, in
Montana, "Depression Warriors Holding Western Front." [107]
On July 1, *Happy Days* reported:

> The big drive has begun. Uncle Sam has thrown his full C.C.C.
> strength into the front lines of the forest. . . . The entire refores-
> tation army has landed in the woods—and has the situation well
> in hand.
>
> In all sectors the reforestation troops are moving ahead. Battle
> lines of the Gypsy moth are beginning to crack and fall back in
> New York and New England. Yellow pine beetles are retreating
> from the mountains of Colorado and California before the on-
> slaught of the C.C.C. Forest fires . . . are being repulsed on all
> flanks the moment they show their smudgy red heads through
> the trees.[108]

Of all the New Deal agencies, the CCC was probably the
most popular, because it united two objectives: "the conservation of America's natural resources and the conservation
of its young manhood." [109] Many observers believed that
the "forestry army" embodied James's proposal for an army
of youth enlisted in a "warfare against nature," although
Roosevelt himself may not have been directly affected by
James.[110] The Corps, it was claimed, had rescued young
men from meaninglessness, rebuilt bodies and character,

107. *Happy Days*, I (June 3, 1933), 2; (June 24, 1933), 3.

108. *Ibid.*, I (July 1, 1933), 1.

109. Christian, "America's Peace Army," p. 43. Cf. Tulsa *World*,
April 10, 1933, clipping in University of Oklahoma, Norman, Okla.,
W. A. Pat Murphy MSS.

110. Ferdinand Silcox, "Our Adventure in Conservation: The CCC,"
Atlantic Monthly, CLX (1937), 714. Moley recalls that when the
question of James's influence was raised, Roosevelt conceded there
might be a relationship, but he had no conscious awareness of one.
Then the President added: "But look here! I think I'll go ahead with
this—the way I did on beer" (Moley, *After Seven Years*, p. 174).

and given men a soldier's pride of accomplishment.[111] Speaker Rainey wrote: "They are also under military training and as they come out of it they come out improved in health and developed mentally and physically and are more useful citizens and if ever we should become involved in another war they would furnish a very valuable nucleus for our army." [112]

While the CCC, the AAA, the TVA, housing, economy, and banking legislation all shared in the war legacy, it was the National Recovery Administration that was the keystone of the early New Deal, and the NRA rested squarely on the War Industries Board example. The National Industrial Recovery bill, modeled on WIB procedures, wove together a series of schemes for government-business co-ordination of the kind that had prevailed in the war.[113] One of the most influential recovery designs, sponsored by Meyer Jacobstein, a Rochester (New York) banker, and H. G. Moulton, president of the Brookings Institution, recommended the creation of "a National Board for Industrial Recovery, with powers similar to those so effectively utilized during the World War by the War Industries Board." [114] When the President commissioned Raymond Moley to frame legislation for industrial recovery, Moley asked General Hugh Johnson, who in World

111. A *Detroit News* cartoon which bore the title, "The Old Veterans of the Conservation Army Will Have Something Worth Bragging About," showed an elderly man holding a little boy by the hand and pointing with his cane to a great forest. The caption read: "In 1933 I planted all of these in the great war against depression" (Hurd, "The Forestry Army at the Front," p. 6).

112. Henry T. Rainey to K. G. Baur, March 13, 1934, Library of Congress, Rainey MSS, Box 1.

113. *New York Times*, April 29, 1933; Rexford Tugwell, "Notes from a New Deal Diary," May 30, 1933; Jerome Frank, COHC, p. 27. An article which appeared after this essay was written amply demonstrates the importance of the war precedent: Gerald D. Nash, "Experiments in Industrial Mobilizations: WIB and NRA," *Mid-America*, XLV (1963), 157–74.

114. Meyer Jacobstein and H. G. Moulton, "A Plan for Economic Recovery," Wagner MSS.

War I had functioned as a liaison between the Army and the War Industries Board, to take over for him. "Nobody can do it better than you," Moley coaxed. "You're familiar with the only comparable thing that's ever been done—the work of the War Industries Board." [115] The recovery bill, drafted by Johnson and others, won Senate approval by only the narrowest of margins; conservatives foresaw that the measure would enhance the power of the state and progressives believed the proposal would encourage cartelization. Franklin Roosevelt was more sanguine. When the President signed the recovery act of June 16, he commented: "Many good men voted this new charter with misgivings. I do not share these doubts. I had part in the great co-operation of 1917 and 1918 and it is my faith that we can count on our industry once more to join in our general purpose to lift this new threat. . . . " [116]

Before labor would agree to the industrial-recovery program, it insisted on the same degree of government recognition of the right to organize as it had enjoyed in World War I. In December, 1932, shortly after he learned that Frances Perkins would be the new Secretary of Labor, Sidney Hillman sent her a memorandum which urged the government to pursue the kinds of policies the War Labor Board had initiated.[117] In framing the recovery bill, W. Jett Lauck, who had been secretary of the War Labor Board, served as spokesman for John L. Lewis's United Mine Workers. Lauck, who sponsored a plan for "a national board composed of labor modeled after the War Labor Board," played a prominent part in shaping the labor pro-

115. Moley, *After Seven Years*, p. 188.

116. Roosevelt, *Public Papers*, II, 252.

117. Matthew Josephson, *Sidney Hillman: Statesman of American Labor* (Garden City, N.Y., 1952), p. 357. Hillman had been a member of the Board of Control and Labor Standards for Army Clothing during the war.

visions of the legislation.[118] When the national industrial-recovery bill emerged from the drafting room, it incorporated the pivotal section 7(a) which granted labor's demand for recognition of the right of collective bargaining. The essential provisions of 7 (a), noted Edwin Witte, were "but restatements" of principles first recognized by the National War Labor Board.[119]

Franklin Roosevelt had not only had a prominent part in framing World War I labor policies, but had, as Gerald Nash has pointed out, "sketched out the blueprint for the War Labor Policies Board which was modeled on his directive." [120] To staff the National Labor Board of 1933, the President named men he had first encountered in developing war labor programs. William Leiserson, executive secretary of the board, had been Roosevelt's personal adviser on labor affairs in 1918.[121] In formulating labor policy—from interpreting 7(a) through the adoption and administration of the Wagner Act—Roosevelt and his lieutenants drew heavily on war precedents. The war agencies had established the basic principles of the New Deal labor program: that workers had the right to unionize, that they must not be discharged for union activity, and that presidential boards could restrain employers from denying such rights. More than this, they had evolved the procedure of plant elections to determine bargaining representatives which

118. "Docket—Coal & Stabilization," April 24, May 6, May 23, 1933, National Recovery Act file, Alderman Library, University of Virginia, Charlottesville, Va., W. Jett Lauck MSS; *Business Week*, May 24, 1933, pp. 3–4.

119. Edwin E. Witte, "The Background of the Labor Provisions of the N.I.R.A.," *University of Chicago Law Review*, I (1934), 573.

120. Nash, "Franklin D. Roosevelt and Labor: The World War I Origins of Early New Deal Policy," *Labor History*, I (1960), 49. See, too, Frank Freidel, *Franklin D. Roosevelt: The Apprenticeship* (Boston, 1952), pp. 328–32.

121. Nash, "Franklin D. Roosevelt and Labor," p. 51.

was to be the crucial instrumentality employed by Roosevelt's labor boards.[122]

To head the NRA Roosevelt named the fiery General Johnson, who could boast pertinent experience not only with the War Industries Board but in organizing the draft.[123] In mid-July, Johnson launched a national campaign dramatized by the symbol of the Blue Eagle.[124] "In war, in the gloom of night attack, soldiers wear a bright badge on their shoulders to be sure that comrades do not fire on comrades," explained the President. "On that principle, those who cooperate in this program must know each other at a glance. That is why we have provided a badge of honor for this purpose. . . . " [125]

Cabinet members greeted with skepticism Johnson's proposal for a mass movement to enlist the nation behind the NRA. Homer Cummings pointed out that the country was not at war, and it might be difficult to get everyone to sign a pledge. Johnson replied that he felt it could be put over, for the depression was more real than the war had been to

122. Irving Bernstein, *The New Deal Collective Bargaining Policy* (Berkeley and Los Angeles, 1950), pp. 19–20; "Address by Milton Handler, General Counsel of National Labor Board, before the Legal Division of the National Industrial Recovery Administration," n.d., Franklin D. Roosevelt Library, Hyde Park, N.Y., Leon Henderson MSS, Box 6; Robert Wagner to Rep. William Ashbrook, April 24, 1935, Wagner MSS.

123. "Now the battle for recovery has shifted from the stage of map work at GHQ to the firing line of action," wrote Raymond Clapper. Administrators like Peek and Johnson were "the top sergeants of recovery" (Clapper, "Top Sergeants of the New Deal," *Review of Reviews and World's Work*, LXXXVIII [August, 1933], 19).

124. The idea of an NRA insignia had been suggested by Bernard Baruch in a speech in May. Baruch based the proposal on a War Industries Board notion. (Bernard Baruch, *The Public Years* [New York, 1960], pp. 73, 251). In his speech, Baruch had declared: "If it is commonly understood that those who are coöperating are soldiers against the enemy within and those who omit to act are on the other side, there will be little hanging back. The insignia of government approval on doorways, letterheads, and invoices will become a necessity in business. This method was a success in 1918."—Hugh Johnson, *The Blue Eagle from Egg to Earth* (Garden City, N.Y., 1935), p. 251.

125. Roosevelt, *Public Papers*, II, 301.

most Americans. "Almost every individual has either suffered terribly, or knows of friends and relatives who have;
so there is waiting here to be appealed to what I regard
as the most fertile psychology that you could imagine. . . .
I think this has anything that happened during the War
backed off the board." [126]

To enforce the Blue Eagle, Johnson enlisted the housewives of the country. "It is women in homes—and not
soldiers in uniform—who will this time save our country,"
he proclaimed. "They will go over the top to as great a
victory as the Argonne. It is zero hour for housewives.
Their battle cry is 'Buy now under the Blue Eagle!' " [127]
By kindling the spirit of the Liberty Loan drives and the
draft registration of World War I, Johnson kept alive the
intense spirit of the Hundred Days through another season.
"There is a unity in this country," declared Franklin Roosevelt, "which I have not seen and you have not seen since
April, 1917. . . . " [128]

The Recovery Administration conceived of the depression
as, in part, a crisis in character. The New Dealers hoped
that businessmen would place the public weal above their
private interests, just as the copper magnates had responded
to Baruch's appeal in 1917 by supplying metal to the army
and navy at less than half the market price. In 1933, businessmen were asked to accept as a patriotic duty the assign-
ment to raise wages and agree to a "truce" on price-cutting.

126. Schlesinger, Jr., *The Coming of the New Deal*, p. 113.
127. Hugh Johnson, *The Blue Eagle from Egg to Earth*, p. 264.
Johnson, who had planned and directed the draft registration, used
many of the same techniques in administering the NRA (Peek, *Why
Quit Our Own*, pp. 122–23; Russell Owen, "General Johnson Wages a
Peace-Time War," *New York Times Magazine*, July 30, 1933, p. 3;
Division of Press Intelligence, "Memorandum on Editorial Reaction,
Week from April 30 through May 6," May 7, 1935, Louis Howe MSS,
Box 85). Ruth McKenney observed of Akron: "Precisely like the old
draft board, a local N.R.A. Compliance Committee was set up, its
members the very 'best' people in town."—McKenney, *Industrial
Valley*, p. 107.
128. Roosevelt, *Public Papers*, II, 345.

The recovery drive, it was argued, would succeed only if it aroused the same kind of "spiritual" fervor that World War I had awakened. Morris Cooke wrote:

> Conversations with a good many different kinds of people convince me that there is needed to expedite industrial recovery a talk by the President in which he would read into our 57 varieties of effort an ethical and moral quality and call on us individually and collectively to put our shoulders to the wheel just as if we were at war. . . .
>
> Everywhere I get the impression of our people wanting to be told that the main purpose of the Recovery Administration is not exclusively the rehabilitation of our material wellbeing but a reaffirmation of the spiritual values in life.[129]

To man the New Deal agencies, Roosevelt turned to the veterans of the war mobilization.[130] Top NRA officials included Johnson's chief of staff, John Hancock, who had managed the War Industries Board's naval industrial program; Charles F. Horner, the genius of the Liberty Loan drive; Leo Wolman, who had headed the section on production statistics of the War Industries Board; and Major General Clarence Charles Williams, who had been Chief of

129. Cooke to Louis Howe, July 3, 1933, Franklin D. Roosevelt Library, Hyde Park, N.Y., Morris Cooke MSS, Box 51. Russell Leffingwell of the House of Morgan observed later: "Just as the war tore us all up by the roots, and made us seek such opportunity as there might be to serve our country in its need, so every man of good-will, every man of imagination and understanding has been struggling these last four and one-half years to find out how the human agony of the deflation could be stopped."—Leffingwell, "The Gold Problem and Currency Revaluation," Academy of Political Science, March 21, 1934, Franklin D. Roosevelt Library, Hyde Park, N.Y., Franklin D. Roosevelt MSS, President's Personal File 866.

130. Political scientists had been disappointed by Hoover's failure to name social scientists to government agencies. "During the World War," wrote Arthur Holcombe, "economists and sociologists and statisticians were found to be very useful in Washington and were employed in large numbers. They should be used also in times of peace."—Holcombe, "Trench Warfare," *American Political Science Review*, XXV (1931), 916.

Ordnance in charge of the vast war purchasing.[131] Many other New Dealers had had their first taste of government service during the war. The first Administrator for Public Works, Colonel Donald H. Sawyer, had built cantonments; Felix Frankfurter had chaired the War Labor Policies Board; Captain Leon Henderson of Ordnance had served with the War Industries Board; and Senator Joseph Guffey had worked in the War Industries Board on the conservation of oil.[132] For many, the summer of 1933 seemed like old times. "Washington is a hectic place," wrote Isador Lubin in August. "The hotels are filled, and the restaurants remind me very much of war times. One cannot go into the Cosmos Club without meeting half a dozen persons whom he knew during the war." [133]

The commandants of New Deal agencies thought of themselves as soldiers in a war against depression. The young men who came to Washington said they had "volunteered in peacetime." [134] Some even claimed they were conscripts. When Holger Cahill expressed reluctance to accept a bid to head the new Federal Art Project, an associate advised him he had no alternative. "An invitation from the Government to a job like that is tantamount to an order. It's like

131. One commentator noted that General Williams, as "an old army man, could think in terms of the government interest" ("Unofficial Observer" [John Franklin Carter], *The New Dealers*, p. 47). For the high incidence of army officers in New Deal agencies, see John D. Millett, *The Works Progress Administration in New York City* (Chicago, 1938), p. 221.

132. Joseph Guffey, *Seventy Years on the Red-Fire Wagon* (Lebanon, Pa., 1952), p. 46. The New Deal's oil controls as well as the coal agencies Guffey helped establish rested, in part, on the precedent of the wartime Fuel Administration (Carl Brent Swisher, *American Constitutional Development*, p. 661).

133. Lubin to Louis Brandeis, August 25, 1933, University of Louisville Law Library, Louisville, Ky., Brandeis MSS, G5. Lubin, United States Commissioner of Labor Statistics, had served as Thorstein Veblen's assistant in the Food Administration and later under Wesley Mitchell with the War Industries Board.

134. Russell Lord, *The Wallaces of Iowa* (Boston, 1947), p. 346.

being drafted." [135] This theme quickly became commonplace. From his "general headquarters in Washington, D. C.," reported one writer, "General" Harry L. Hopkins had organized the Federal Emergency Relief Administration as "only one division of the 'American Army' in the War on Want."[136] One of Hopkins' "noncoms," a relief worker in northern Michigan, observed: "We were like an army, drafted into service during a war." She wrote of the FERA Field Director: ". . . He had been in the front-line trenches with the rest of us when the battle raged at its worst. . . . " When the FERA gave way to the Works Project Administration late in 1935, her staff was broken up. "At this time," she commented, "I lost the other two members of my shock troops. . . . " [137]

The processes of New Deal government owed much to the war legacy. The war provided a precedent for the concentration of executive authority, for the responsibility of government for the state of the economy, and for the role of Washington as the arbiter among social groups. It originated the practice of shunting aside the regular line agencies and creating new organizations with dramatic alphabetical titles. When the RFC, the first of the new agencies, was established, one periodical reported: "R.F.C., of course, is Reconstruction Finance Corporation, and the

135. Holger Cahill, COHC, p. 340. Roosevelt told Carter Glass it was a "war duty" to accept the post of Secretary of the Treasury (Daniel Roper to Edward House, January 24, 1933, Sterling Memorial Library, Yale University, New Haven, Conn., House MSS). Note, too, his attitude toward Cermak's assassination in Cordell Hull, *The Memoirs of Cordell Hull* (2 vols.; New York, 1948), I, 158. Tugwell commented on his appointment as Assistant Secretary of Agriculture: "F.D.R. marshalled me into service."—Tugwell, "Notes from a New Deal Diary," February 18, 1933. That fall, George Creel pledged his "continued devotion to NRA as soldier in the ranks" (George Creel to Roosevelt, September 23, 1933, Library of Congress, Creel MSS, Box 4).

136. William Dow Boutwell, "The War on Want: How It Is Being Fought—and Won!" *School Life*, XIX (1933), 31.

137. Louise Armstrong, *We Too Are the People* (Boston, 1938), pp. 435, 465.

newspapers have fallen into the war-time habit of using the simple initials instead of the rather cumbersome full name of this anti-hard-times organization."[138] The war offered a precedent, too, for setting up co-ordinating bodies like the National Emergency Council headed by Frank Walker.[139] Not least in importance, the war experience was used to justify the New Deal's emergency legislation in the courts.[140]

The war example saw service too as a way to refute opponents of the President's economic policies. When critics objected that the country could not "afford" New Deal reforms, Roosevelt's supporters responded with the now familiar retort that if the country could spend as it had in war, it could spend in this new emergency. "When people complain to me of the amount of money that the government has been borrowing," commented Thomas Lamont of the House of Morgan, "I always answer it by saying: 'Well, if the country was willing to spend thirty billion dollars in a year's time to try to lick the Germans, I don't see why people should complain about spending five or six billion

138. *Literary Digest*, CXII (February 13, 1932), 9.

139. Leon Henderson noted a meeting with Hugh Johnson: "I asked—'who does your work of tieing into the adm. whole plan.' He said 'I do—but there isn't much done. There is no plan: not like old War Ind. Bd. We've got to have one soon. Walker runs too easy. The super-cabinet is just a lot of prima donnas sitting around—can't please 'em.' "—Henderson MS Diary, February 20, 1934, Henderson MSS.

140. One writer noted that "the New Deal legislation was heavily garlanded with 'emergency clauses' describing the dire national peril. This was because the Court had decided during the World War that war powers were supreme."—"Unofficial Observer" [John Franklin Carter], *The New Dealers* (New York, 1934), p. 394. See, too, Jane Perry Clark, "Emergencies and the Law," *Political Science Quarterly*, XLIX (1934), 268–83. Cf. Justice Sutherland's dissent in *Home Building and Loan Association* v. *Blaisdell*, 290 U.S. 471 (1934). In his press conference after the adverse ruling in the Schechter case, Roosevelt protested the Court's failure to recognize an emergency in view of "those war acts which conferred upon the Executive far greater power over human beings and over property than anything that was done in 1933" (Roosevelt, *Public Papers*, IV, 206).

dollars to keep people from starving.' " [141] By 1936, when Roosevelt returned to Forbes Field in Pittsburgh, where, four years before, he had promised to slash Hoover's reckless spending, the President concluded that the argument now offered the best reply to critics who accused him of a profligate disregard of campaign promises. "National defense and the future of America were involved in 1917. National defense and the future of America were also involved in 1933," Roosevelt asserted. "Don't you believe that the saving of America has been cheap at that price?" [142]

Roosevelt's argument would have been more compelling if he had spent at anywhere near the rate that both he and his conservative foes implied he had. For a time in the winter of 1933–34, the Administration gave a fillip to the economy when it embarked on lavish spending through the Civil Works Administration, but early in 1934, the President, alarmed by mounting deficits, decreed the death of the CWA. Distressed by Roosevelt's verdict, Senator Robert LaFollette, Jr., of Wisconsin inquired: "In 1917, Mr. President, what Senator would have dared to rise on the floor of the Senate and suggest that we could not fight the war against Germany and her allies because it would unbalance the Budget?" [143] *The Nation* voiced a similar protest: "The country is confronted with a vastly greater crisis than it had to meet in the World War but has not yet extended itself financially as it did at that time." [144] Progressives warned that unless the President began to spend at a wartime pace the country might take years to pull out of the depression. The progressive Cassandras proved correct.

141. Schlesinger, Jr., *The Coming of the New Deal*, p. 498.

142. Roosevelt, *Public Papers*, V, 407. Cf. Lewis Kimmel, *Federal Budget and Fiscal Policy*, pp. 190–92.

143. *Congressional Record*, 73d Cong., 2d Sess., LXXVIII (February 8, 1934), 2174.

144. "Not Back to Hoover, Please!" *Nation*, CXXXVIII (1934), 346.

The New Deal mobilization of 1933–34, from which so much had been expected, brought disappointing economic returns.

The crux of the difficulty lay in the fact that the metaphor of war was, in more than one way, inapt. As a model for economic action, World War I was unsatisfactory, for the problems confronting Roosevelt in 1933 were quite unlike those Woodrow Wilson had been called on to meet in 1917. As the Harvard economist Edwin Gay wrote: "War stimulates the full expansion of productive energy, but the deep depression cripples every economic process and discourages even the most sanguine business leaders." [145] Some who recalled the war experience hoped that it could provide a prototype for the same kind of impressive increases in output that had been achieved in 1917–18. But the aims of the New Deal mobilization were not the same as those of the war; General Johnson even called for "an armistice on increasing producing capacity." [146] Frank Freidel has pointed out:

> Unlike wartime measures, the new agencies were to reduce output in most areas rather than raise it, and encourage price increases rather than restrain them. Thus, waging a war on the depression was in some ways the reverse of waging one on a foreign foe.[147]

John M. Clark has made a similar point. The war, Clark noted, provided precedents for emergency controls, deficit spending, and expanded powers for the Federal Reserve System, but the problems of war and of depression "were radically different; in fact, they were in some respects

145. Edwin F. Gay, "The Great Depression," *Foreign Affairs*, X (1932), 529.
146. Johnson, *The Blue Eagle from Egg to Earth*, p. 222.
147. Freidel, *America in the Twentieth Century*, p. 312.

opposite to one another." [148] The question of determining
priorities in a war economy, Clark observed, was not at all
the same as that of reinvigorating sick industries. Clark
concluded:

> All the machinery for allocating limited supplies of essential
> resources among conflicting uses, which played so large a part
> in the wartime controls, had no application to the depression.
> Where the actuating motives of private industry fail and the
> result is partial paralysis, the problem is essentially opposite to
> that of war.[149]

These misgivings were not simply the result of hindsight.
In the midst of the Hundred Days, the economist Paul
Douglas warned that the country did not face the wartime
task of rationing scarce resources but the quite different
problem of stimulating production. "Industry must get
some business before it can proceed to ration it out,"
Douglas gibed. He was disconcerted by the New Deal's
obsession with the menace of overproduction when the
critical question was how to increase purchasing power.
Douglas noted: "Certainly those who are arguing from the
analogy of the War Industries Board miss the point. That
body had behind it the gigantic purchasing power of the
government, and with this weapon it was able to instill some
order in the industrial system. But unless the government
creates such purchasing power in the present emergency,
the regulatory body will be operating in a void." [150]

148. John M. Clark, *Social Control of Business* (New York, 1939),
p. 424. The New Deal theorists were captivated by the idea of
"balance." They sought to redress the imbalances between supply
and demand, just as the war mobilizers had done. But they lacked
the ingredients the war mobilizers could count upon: ample purchasing power and massive federal spending.

149. *Ibid.*, p. 425.

150. Paul H. Douglas, "The New Deal After Ten Weeks," *The
World Tomorrow*, XVI (1933), 419.

The war analogy proved mischievous in an even more significant respect. The Tugwells thought of the war as a time when the intellectuals had exercised unprecedented power over the economy, and when the feasibility of a planned society had been brilliantly demonstrated. Yet, although the intellectuals did wield power, agencies like the War Industries Board had, after all, been run chiefly by business executives. If they learned anything from the war, it was not the virtues of collectivism but the potentialities of trade associations, the usefulness of the state in economic warfare with the traders of other nations, and the good-housekeeping practices of eliminating duplication and waste. The immediate consequence of the war was not a New Jerusalem of the planners but the Whiggery of Herbert Hoover as Secretary of Commerce. While the war mobilization did establish meaningful precedents for New Deal reforms, it was hardly the "war socialism" some theorists thought it to be. Perhaps the outstanding characteristic of the war organization of industry was that it showed how to achieve massive government intervention without making any permanent alteration in the power of corporations.

The confusion over the meaning of the war experience helped conceal the ambiguities of the so-called "First New Deal." The architects of the early New Deal appeared to be in fundamental agreement, since they united in rejecting the New Freedom ideal of a competitive society in favor of business-government co-ordination in the 1917 style. In fact, they differed sharply. Tugwell hoped that the co-ordination authorized by the NRA would enable the Recovery Administration to become an agency for centralized government direction of the economy, a possibility insured in part by the NRA's licensing power. Most of the other "First New Dealers," however, meant by business-government co-ordination an economy in which businessmen would make the crucial decisions. As administrator of the

NRA, General Johnson gave small scope to the government direction Tugwell had envisaged. He never used the licensing power, but relied instead on negotiation with business and on the force of social pressure. Like Moley and Richberg and the President, Johnson placed his faith not in a planned economy but in voluntary business co-operation with government.[151]

The New Deal administrators shared, too, the conviction of the war bureaucrats that progress would be achieved not through worker or farmer rebellions, but through government programs, conceived and executed by agency officials. A month after the armistice, Wesley Mitchell had voiced the need for "intelligent experimenting and detailed planning rather than for agitation or class struggle." [152] The war approach which the New Dealers adopted rejected both mass action and socialist planning, and assumed a community of interest of the managers of business corporations and the directors of government agencies. Roosevelt's lieutenants believed that the great danger to such an experiment lay not in the opposition of the conservatives, who were discredited, but in the menace of antiplutocratic movements. Yet in damping the fires of popular dissent, they also snuffed out support they would need to keep the reform spirit alive.

The New Dealers, distrustful of the policies of group conflict, sought to effect a truce like that of 1917 when class and sectional animosities abated. Perhaps no other approach could have accomplished so much in the spring of 1933, yet it was a tactic which had obvious perils for the

151. It was not merely that Johnson had the temperament of a war administrator who turned naturally to the tactics of social coercion, but that he had well-founded doubts about whether the Supreme Court would sanction government edicts (Schlesinger, Jr., *The Coming of the New Deal*, pp. 108–9). Schlesinger also suggests that Johnson decided on this course because Harold Ickes moved so slowly in spending for public works. This seems unlikely. Johnson made this decision almost as soon as he took office, well before the outlines of Ickes' operation had become clear.

152. Lucy Sprague Mitchell, *Two Lives*, p. 303.

cause of reform. By presenting the depression not as the collapse of a system but as a personalized foreign enemy, Roosevelt as much as Hoover sought to mend the social fabric. In doing so, Roosevelt, like his predecessor, deflected blame away from business leaders whom many thought responsible for hard times, and diverted attention from the fact that the depression was not the consequence of an assault by a foreign foe but evidence of internal breakdown.

Even more important, the New Dealers, in the interest of national solidarity, tried to suppress anti-business expressions of discontent. President Roosevelt warned the AF of L convention in 1933: "The whole of the country has a common enemy; industry, agriculture, capital, labor are all engaged in fighting it. Just as in 1917 we are seeking to pull in harness; just as in 1917, horses that kick over the traces will have to be put in a corral." [153] General Johnson left no doubt of the intent of the President's words: "Labor does not need to strike under the Roosevelt plan. . . . The plain stark truth is that you cannot tolerate strikes. Public opinion . . . will break down and destroy every subversive influence." [154] Far from operating a "labor government," as conservatives charged, the New Dealers in 1933 deeply resented strikes as acts of "aggression" which sabotaged the drive for recovery. Frances Perkins recalls that Johnson believed that "during the period when NRA was attempting to revive industry no stoppage of work could be tolerated under any circumstances.

153. *Report of Proceedings of the Fifty-third Annual Convention of the American Federation of Labor* (Washington, D.C., 1933), p. 307. In the summer of 1933, the President had made a "no strike" appeal. He said of it: "It is a document on a par with Samuel Gompers' memorable war-time demand to preserve the *status quo* in labor disputes. . . . It is an act of economic statesmanship."—Roosevelt, *Public Papers*, II, 318.

154. AF of L, *Proceedings*, 1933, p. 359.

It was like a stoppage of work in war time. Anything had to be done to prevent that." [155]

An administrator who spurned direct government sanctions but who was determined to have his way soon found that he was either resorting to bluster or encouraging vigilantism. Such had been the pattern in World War I.[156] On one occasion, the War Industries Board's price-fixing committee had warned a producer to co-operate, or become "such an object of contempt and scorn in your home town that you will not dare to show your face there." [157] Ray Lyman Wilbur, chief of the conservation division of the Food Administration, recalled: "Indiana I found the best organized state for food conservation that I had yet seen. The people were approaching rapidly the stage where violations of wheatless days, etc., were looked upon as unpatriotic enough to require that inquiries as to the loyalty of the guilty citizen, baker or hotel-keeper be made." [158]

If the New Dealers never ran to such excesses of vigilantism, they were not beyond employing this kind of social coercion, and they matched the war administrators in the technique of bluster. "I have no patience with people who follow a course which in war time would class them as slackers," declared Attorney-General Homer Cummings of the alleged hoarders of gold. "If I have to make an example of some people, I'll do it cheerfully." [159] When Frances

155. Frances Perkins, COHC, VII, 139–40; Roosevelt, *Public Papers*, II, 302.

156. In a capitalist society, bluster frequently serves as a reform government's alternative to institutional rearrangements that would give government a direct share in corporation policy-determination. President Kennedy's role in the 1962 steel-price-hike incident is a case in point.

157. Clarkson, *Industrial America in the World War*, p. 99.

158. Edgar Eugene Robinson and Paul Carroll Edwards (eds.), *The Memoirs of Ray Lyman Wilbur* (Stanford, Calif., 1960), p. 264.

159. *Time*, XXI (June 19, 1933), 12. "Hoarders are at heart cowards," declared Chandler Hovey, senior partner of Kidder, Peabody. "The government should declare that to hoard at this time is

Perkins hit out at the effort of the steel industry to dodge the intent of section 7 (a) by setting up company unions, she denounced these unions as "war bridegrooms," the popular epithet for matrimonial draft-dodging during the war.[160] When the economist Oliver W. M. Sprague resigned in protest at the Administration's gold-buying policy, Hugh Johnson accused him of "deserting with a shot in the flank of the army in which he had enlisted."[161] During the Blue Eagle drive, Donald Richberg insisted that in a time of crisis there could be "no honorable excuse for the slacker who wastes these precious moments with doubting and debate—who palsies the national purpose with legalistic arguments."[162]

Such statements infuriated the conservatives. Senator Carter Glass of Virginia found particularly galling Richberg's denunciation of NRA opponents as "slackers who deserved to have white feathers pinned on them by the women of the country." Glass wrote of Richberg's war record: "He never heard a percussion cap pop; he did not know the smell of gun powder; he did not even reach a training camp to learn the difference between 'Forward March' and 'Parade Rest.' When asked by a responsible newspaperman to give his war record in justification of his vituperative assault on other people, he could do no better than allege he had helped sell some Liberty bonds."[163] Glass's resentment was shared by other conservative critics. "The man who lives well within his income," protested Lewis Douglas,

unpatriotic, destructive and against the public interest."—Clipping in Holy Cross College Library, Worcester, Mass., David I. Walsh MSS.

160. "Unofficial Observer" [John Franklin Carter], *The New Dealers*, p. 178.

161. Hugh Johnson to Carter Glass, Alderman Library, University of Virginia, Charlottesville, Va., December 4, 1933, Glass MSS, Box 4.

162. Richberg, *The Rainbow* (Garden City, N.Y., 1936), pp. 288–89.

163. Carter Glass to Walter Lippmann, August 10, 1933, Glass MSS, Box 4.

"has come to be regarded as unpatriotic and as a slacker in the fight against the depression." [164]

If the rhetoric of coercion disturbed the conservatives, it troubled some of the New Dealers even more. In the summer of 1933, a group of AAA officials protested:

> General Johnson, in picturing the results of his campaign, has frequently used the analogy of the war-time 'gasless Sundays.' Then, General Johnson recalls, if a man drove a car on Sunday, his neighbors pushed the car into the ditch. Popular opinion at that time was so inflamed that it expressed itself by violence.
>
> General Johnson's analogy is profoundly significant and disturbing. If his program is adopted, professional drive organizations will soon reappear in full force. Agitators may take advantage of the possible resulting hysteria to set group against group, such as farmers against wage earners, and thus defeat the real progress toward cooperation already made by the Roosevelt Administration.[165]

Some even thought they detected in Johnson's administration of the NRA the glimmerings of a corporate state.[166]

164. Lewis W. Douglas, "There Is One Way Out," *Atlantic Monthly*, CLVI (1935), 267. Walter Lippmann was troubled by the frequent use the planners made of the war analogy (Lippmann, *The Good Society* [Boston, 1937] pp. 89–105). Cf. John M. Clark, *Social Control of Business*, pp. 463–64.

165. "Memorandum on Proposal for Blanket-Code," July 18, 1933, in George Peek to Frank Walker, July 18, 1933, Peek MSS (letter not sent). The Washington correspondent of the *New Republic* wrote: "What administration officials—half-consciously, half-unconsciously—want to do is to create a war psychosis in which any corporation head attempting to defy Mr. Roosevelt and the N.R.A. will be at once identified by the country with Kaiser Bill, Hindenburg, Ludendorff and Grover Bergdoll."—T.R.B., "Washington Notes," *New Republic*, LXXV (1933), 340.

166. Criticism of the New Deal as fascist was quite common, and not limited to concern over Johnson's predilections. A radical commentary on Tugwell's *The Industrial Discipline and the Governmental Arts* noted: "The really ominous word which Mr. Tugwell has spoken in his volume lies in his assumption that government in a capitalist society may be imbued with an essentially social aim that is *inclusive*,

If such was Johnson's purpose—and the grounds for such a supposition are unsubstantial—the General received no encouragement from the President. Roosevelt moved quickly to squelch signs of militarism. When Harry Woodring, Assistant Secretary of War, wrote early in 1934 that the Army stood prepared to organize the CCC, veterans of World War I, and reliefers into a corps of "economic storm troops," the White House reprimanded him.[167] In late 1934, the authoritarian-minded Johnson was let go. That same year, Henry Wallace, seeking to pursue a "middle course," wrote: "There is something wooden and inhuman about the government interfering in a definite, precise way with the details of our private and business lives. It suggests a time of war with generals and captains telling every individual exactly what he must do each day and hour." [168]

Most of all, the Brandeisian faction of the New Dealers objected to the crisis spirit. Felix Frankfurter wrote Louis Brandeis: "Much too much of 'slacker' talk & old coercions." [169] For the Brandeisians, the "enemy" was not "depression" but "business." They welcomed the breakup of the nation in 1934 and 1935 from the national interest into class and group interests. The early New Dealers had emphasized the war spirit of cooperation, co-ordination, and exhortation, because they feared that the bonds that held society together might be snapped. By 1935, it was clear that the crisis had been weathered, and the mood of war seemed inappropriate. Brandeisians felt free to assault

---

and may, therefore, in a grave emergency find it necessary to 'compel or persuade a higher co-operation for a national purpose.' The analysis is *liberal;* the solution is essentially *fascist.*"—J. B. Matthews and R. E. Shallcross, "Must America Go Fascist?" *Harper's,* CLXIX (June, 1934), 12.

167. Schlesinger, Jr., *The Coming of the New Deal,* p. 339; H. H. Woodring, "The American Army Stands Ready," *Liberty,* January 6, 1934.

168. Henry Wallace, *New Frontiers* (New York, 1934), p. 21.

169. Frankfurter to Brandeis, August 2, 1933, Brandeis MSS, G6.

business interests, other New Dealers lost faith in their ability to convert businessmen, and business groups increasingly viewed Roosevelt as their enemy. As in wartime, the first enthusiasm as the troops paraded to the front had given way to the realization that the army was not invincible, the casualty lists would be long, and the prospect of early victory was no longer promising.[170] Yet the danger of annihilation had been averted too, and as the sense of urgency lessened, the spirit of national solidarity slackened. "The enemies who began to emerge in the eyes or the imagination of men," Paul Conkin has observed of the end of the "wartime effort" in 1935, "were not such as could demand the hostility of all Americans, for these enemies were not natural, or providential, or foreign, but human and native. A class and group consciousness was forming." [171]

Yet the rhetoric of war persisted, even when such agencies of mobilization as NRA died. In the summer of 1935, Representative Robert L. Doughton of North Carolina observed: "Of course in every War, if it has a chance at all to be successful, there must be a leader, and this Administration and the Congress have been engaged in a war on hunger, destitute [sic], unemployment, bankruptcy and every evil incident to the economic life of our people." [172] In his 1936 campaign, Franklin Roosevelt told a Massachusetts crowd that, like Marshal Joffre at the First Battle of the Marne, he bore the blame for victory or defeat in war. "Three and a half years ago we declared war on the depression," the President asserted. "You and I know today that that war is being won." But he was quick to point out that the war had not yet been won. The country still needed

170. "The Crisis of the N.R.A.," *New Republic*, LXXVI (1933), 349.
171. Conkin, *Tomorrow a New World*, p. 130. Cf. Arthur Schlesinger, Jr., *The Politics of Upheaval* (Boston, 1960), pp. 395–98.
172. Doughton to Henry Baker, July 15, 1935, University of North Carolina, Chapel Hill, N.C., Doughton MSS, Drawer 7.

the services of its commander-in-chief.[173]   In his Franklin
Field address, when he accepted renomination in June, 1936,
Roosevelt declared: "I accept the commission you have
tendered me. I join with you. I am enlisted for the duration
of the war." [174] But by then references to war had become
purely rhetorical.[175] When, that very year, the Administration explored the possibility of using the war power, and
especially the precedent of Wilson's War Labor Policies
Board, to justify federal regulation of the hours of labor,
it concluded that the idea was not feasible.[176]
Only the New Dealers committed to a planned economy
held fast to the earlier vision. As late as the summer of
1939, Rexford Tugwell looked back wistfully toward the
war collectivism. Tugwell pleaded for a reorientation of
progressive thought away from the traditional emphases
on freedom for business, a change that only a crisis like
that of 1917 or 1929 would produce. Of the two, Tugwell
thought that war offered the best hope, for 1929 had yielded
only "atomistic reforms" while 1917 had resulted in "national organization on a unitary scheme." "How different
it was in 1917!" Tugwell wrote. "It was possible . . . to
make immense advances toward industrial unity. . . . That
great wartime release of energy was achieved by freeing
men's minds. Quantities and qualities could be thought of
rather than profits." No sane person would wish a war in

173. Roosevelt, *Public Papers*, V, 522–23.

174. *Ibid.*, p. 236.

175. Among countless examples of war rhetoric, see Roosevelt,
Public Papers, V, 207, 475, and VII, 228, 545; Address of Governor
George H. Earle, Wilkes Barre, Pa., March 16, 1935, Speech and News
File No. 68, Earle MSS, Bryn Mawr, Pa. (privately held); Donald
McCoy, *Angry Voices: Left-of Center Politics in the New Deal Era*
(Lawrence, Kan., 1938), p. 166.

176. Victor E. Cappa, "Two Studies of Certain Constitutional
Powers as Possible Bases for Federal Regulation of Employer-
Employee Relations," Office of National Recovery Administration
Division of Review, *Work Materials No. 68* (Washington, D.C., March,
1936). Mimeographed. Copy in Leon Henderson MSS, Box 17.

order to bring about a "purposive national organization," he observed. "Yet the fact is that only war has up to now proved to be such a transcending objective that doctrine is willingly sacrificed for efficiency in its service." [177]

If the references to war in the later Roosevelt years were largely rhetorical, the rhetoric was often revealing. In his Franklin Field speech, Roosevelt insisted that the nation was waging "not alone a war against want and destitution and economic demoralization" but "a war for the survival of democracy." "We are fighting to save a great and precious form of government for ourselves and for the world," the President declared.[178] With each passing year, the challenge of the Fascist powers was more defiant, and the demands of foreign affairs came to supersede the claims of domestic issues. New Deal agencies increasingly directed their attention to preparing for the eventuality of war with the Axis. In 1938, the TVA boasted it was "developing the power necessary for the large-scale operation of war industries in this well-protected strategic area." The furnaces at Muscle Shoals, the Authority reported, were being utilized to turn out phosphorus, a material "used in war for smoke screens and incendiary shells," and the TVA's electric furnaces, the agency foresaw, "might be converted to the electrolytic manufacture of aluminum or of chlorine—used in war gases. . . ." [179]

Henry Wallace had long believed that the AAA was an "adjustment" program whose machinery could be used to

---

177. R. G. Tugwell, "After the New Deal," *New Republic*, XCIX (1939), 324. Three years later, Stuart Chase wrote: "Nothing in the agenda of the New Deal was as radical as the war agenda of 1917 in respect to the government control of economic activity."—Chase, *The Road We Are Traveling 1914–1942* (New York, 1942), p. 42.

178. Roosevelt, *Public Papers*, V, 236.

179. Tennessee Valley Authority, *To Keep the Water in the Rivers and the Soil on the Land*, pp. 43–44. After the war, Judson King claimed: "TVA and the Columbia River dams 'saved our lives' in World War II. They made possible production of phosphorus, nitrates, light metals and other war materials, including materials for the atom bomb."—King, *The Conservation Fight*, pp. 280–81.

increase output as well as to limit it. If there were a conflict beyond the ocean, a prospect he dreaded, the United States, he observed in 1934, could, through the Triple A, "provision a war . . . with far less of that plunging, uninformed and altogether unorganized overplanting which got us into so much trouble during and after the last great war." [180] A week before the outbreak of the European war in September, 1939, Wallace wrote the President that if war came the government might consider developing plans modeled on the Food Administration with which Wallace had worked in World War I. "When we set up County Committees in AAA in 1933, I couldn't help thinking what a splendid mechanism we would have, if we ever got into a war, to meet the food problem. . . . Again when we set up the Ever Normal Granary System, I thought how marvelously this mechanism with its reserve supplies would help the country in case of war." [181]

In 1939, James V. Forrestal tried to persuade New Dealers that the way to put across their program was to sell it as preparedness rather than reform; after all, the TVA had had its start in the Defense Act of 1916.[182] He won few con-

180. *New York Times*, August 19, 1934.
181. Wallace to Roosevelt, August 26, 1939, Franklin D. Roosevelt MSS, President's Secretary's File 27. Such observations may suggest that, from the beginning, the New Deal was bent on war, and that the intervention in World War II was a logical culmination of Roosevelt's policies, or that there was a symbiotic relationship between war and the New Deal species of reform. Nothing I have found in my own research would support the conclusion that the New Dealers conspired to involve the nation in war, and very little would suggest an inevitable marriage of New Deal reform with war. Yet the relationship between progressivism and war in the twentieth-century state, it should be added, is a subject which is imperfectly understood and one which deserves more exploration and illumination.
182. Eliot Janeway, *The Struggle for Survival* (New Haven, 1951), p. 20. Although proud of the achievements of the New Deal, Morris Cooke nonetheless believed that what had been done was still inadequate. "I am convinced," he wrote in 1938, "that we have to arouse something akin to a war psychology if we are really to make this a permanent country."—Cooke to W. C. Lowdermilk, June 30, 1938, cited in Jean Christie, "Morris L. Cooke" (draft of Ph.D. dissertation, Columbia University, 1963).

verts—most liberals refused to adopt a stratagem that surrendered the theology of liberalism—but when the war in Europe led to a new emphasis on defense, the New Dealers were quick enough to adapt themselves. A month after war began in Europe, Roosevelt phoned Wallace to call all bureau chiefs and ask what their experience had been in World War I, and how the new emergency would affect their present position.[183] Many soon found themselves running the new defense agencies. Leon Henderson controlled prices, AAA Administrator Chester Davis coordinated agriculture with defense requirements, and Brehon Somervell, who had directed the WPA in New York, took charge of military construction.

The NYA began to train aircraft mechanics; CCC workers developed target ranges and airports for the Army; TVA dams produced the power for aluminum needed in bomber production; and the REA turned out the electricity for army camps and naval installations.[184] New Dealers charged with developing defense and war labor policies turned repeatedly to the War Labor Board's precedents.[185] When war came, Schlesinger writes, it "almost seemed an NRA reunion. The child of the War Industries Board, NRA was the father of the War Production Board. Leon Henderson, Donald Nelson, Sidney Hillman, Averell Harriman, William H. Davis,

183. Harry Slattery, Administrator of the Rural Electrification Administration, reported: "I told the Secretary that I was special assistant to Secretary Lane during the war period when he was Vice Counsel of the National Defense Council; . . . and that finally I was assigned to handle a plan for granting of land for returning soldiers, and had that especially under me."—"Memorandum of conference with Secretary Henry Wallace, October 11, 1939," Duke University, Durham, N.C., Slattery MSS.

184. Kenneth Holland and Frank Ernest Hill, *Youth in the CCC* (Washington, D.C., 1942), p. 184; H. S. Person, "The Rural Electrification Administration in Perspective," *Agricultural History*, XXIV (1950), 79–80; Harold Ickes, *Autobiography of a Curmudgeon* (New York, 1943), chap. xv.

185. Frances Perkins, COHC, VII, 776 ff.; Eliot Janeway, *The Struggle for Survival*, p. 161; Matthew Woll to W. Jett Lauck, December 20, 1940, Lauck MSS, Correspondence.

Isador Lubin, Edward R. Stettinius, Jr.—all had their
training in national mobilization in the breathless days of
1933 and 1934." [186] Many of these men, it might be added,
had first entered government service in World War I.

Precisely as the Keynesians had foreseen, defense and
war demands sparked an economic boom. In the summer
of 1940, Keynes noted that the United States had failed to
achieve recovery, because the volume of investment had
been "hopelessly inadequate." The "dreadful experience"
of war might teach the United States what it had failed to
learn in peacetime. He predicted: "Your war preparation,
so far from requiring a sacrifice, will be the stimulus, which
neither the victory nor the defeat of the New Deal could
give you, to greater individual consumption and a higher
standard of life." Keynes observed sadly: "It is, it seems,
politically impossible for a capitalistic democracy to organize expenditure on the scale necessary to make the grand
experiment which would prove my case—except in war
conditions." [187]

186. Schlesinger, Jr., *The Coming of the New Deal*, p. 176. Tugwell
wrote later: "New agencies were multiplying as they had not since
1933; and in a way this period was much like that of the earlier one
when the enemy had been the impalpable but terrifying depression.
Franklin had, indeed, used the analogy of war at that time."—Tugwell, *The Democratic Roosevelt* (Garden City, N.Y., 1957), p. 600.
"The New Deal was some preparation for this upheaval," observed
Marquis Childs. "It was a kind of war."—Childs, *I Write from
Washington* (New York and London, 1942), p. 3. Frances Perkins
reflected that the New Deal had, unconsciously, prepared the nation
to meet the demands of war (Perkins, *The Roosevelt I Knew* [New
York, 1946], pp. 349–51). From the very beginning, however, Roosevelt, who wished to maintain personal control of the mobilization,
shied away from proposals to reconstitute a War Industries Board
("Meeting with the Business Advisory Council," May 23, 1940, Franklin D. Roosevelt MSS, President's Secretary's File 17). But there were
numerous observations on how World War I could serve as a useful
precedent. See, e.g., Maxcy R. Dickson, "The Food Administration–
Educator," *Agricultural History*, XVI (1942), 91–96.

187. Keynes, "The United States and the Keynes Plan," *New
Republic*, CIII (1940), 156–59. Morris Cooke, writing in the same
issue that he did not think war orders as such would necessarily end
unemployment, added: "But I do feel that in executing billions in war

Keynes's remark was to the point. The "grand experiment" of the New Deal had achieved much. But it had not created, or indeed in any serious sense even attempted to create, a new model for American society. The New Dealers resorted to the analogue of war, because in America the sense of community is weak, the distrust of the state strong. Up to a point, the metaphor of war and the precedent of World War I proved invaluable. They helped provide a feeling of national solidarity which made possible the New Deal's greatest achievement: its success in "nation-saving," in mending the social fabric. The heritage of World War I justified the New Deal's claim to represent an overarching national interest to which business and other parochial interests must conform. The war proved that, at a time of crisis, the power of private individuals with money to turn the nation's resources to their own benefit could be limited by the prior claim of providing a "social minimum." [188] Since the war mobilization had brought to fruition much of progressivism, it offered a useful example for the New Dealers, and since the wartime control of industry went much further than earlier efforts in recognizing the place

orders we may learn a technique for deploying American manpower in such a way as to change, radically and permanently, our unemployment outlook."—Cooke, "Can We Afford the New Deal?" *New Republic*, CIII (1940), 165. Even before the United States entered the war, writers were predicting that the defense program would provide a precedent for new government intervention to secure full employment in the postwar era. *Business Week* commented: "It is inconceivable that, when the defense program ends, . . . the government will stand idly by in the midst of a great unemployment crisis born of nationwide demobilization. . . . The operation of the profit motive will be limited by the dominant requirement of full employment for the people."—*Business Week*, August 16, 1941, pp. 36–37, cited in Stuart Chase, *The Road We Are Traveling, 1914–1942*, p. 98. See, too, Arthur Feiler, "Economic Impacts of the War," *Social Research*, VIII (1941), 297–309. As World War I provided a precedent for the New Deal planners, so World War II taught lessons in "full employment" to the liberals of the Truman era.

188. John M. Clark, *Social Control of Business*, pp. 782–85.

of the twentieth-century state, it was especially pertinent for some of the problems the New Deal confronted.

Yet in other respects the war analogue proved either treacherous or inadequate. The very need to employ imagery which was so often inappropriate revealed both an impoverished tradition of reform and the reluctance of the nation to come to terms with the leviathan state. Only in war or in a crisis likened to war was it possible to put aside inhibiting doctrines, create a sense of national homogeneity, and permit the government to act in the national interest. But once the war ended, or the sense of crisis dissipated, traditional doctrines once again prevailed. The country had yet to find a way to organize collective action save in war or its surrogate. Nor had it faced up to the real problems of the relation of order to liberty which the power of the twentieth-century state creates.

World War II rescued the New Deal from some of its dilemmas and obscured others. In the war years, many of the New Deal programs were set aside—the WPA, Roosevelt said, had earned an "honorable discharge." [189] The New Dealers turned their talents to "manning the production line." The AAA helped increase farm production instead of restricting crops; the new industrial agencies sought to speed factory output rather than curtail it. Perhaps the greatest irony of the New Deal is the most familiar. Only in war was recovery achieved. Only in war did the country finally rescue that one-third of a nation ill-housed, ill-clad and ill-nourished. Only in war was the "army of the unemployed" disbanded.

189. Malcolm Cowley, "The End of the New Deal," *New Republic,* CVIII (1943), 729.

The Great Depression: Another Watershed in American History?

RICHARD S. KIRKENDALL

THE DECADE of the 1890's, according to Henry Steel Commager, is "the watershed of American history," [1] but a few historians point to the 1930's, with its Great Depression and New Deal, as a major watershed. When applied to history, the term is used in its British sense as synonomous with "divide" and amounts to an attempt to suggest that points or periods in history resemble geographical features such as continental divides, the lines separating drainage basins. Although not many historians employ this concept in their interpretations of the depression decade, several of them use similar terms and at times identify them with "watershed." In a major essay interpreting the New Deal as a revolution, Carl N. Degler writes: "as the Civil War constituted a watershed in American thought, so the depression and its New Deal marked the crossing of a divide from which, it would seem, there could be no turning back." [2]

1. *The American Mind: An Interpretation of American Thought and Character since the 1880's* (New Haven, 1950), p. 41.

2. *Out of Our Past: The Forces that Shaped Modern America* (New York, 1959), p. 416. See also Mario Einaudi, *The Roosevelt Revolution* (New York, 1959), p. 230.

The idea of a watershed renders a distorted view of the flow of history in the 1930's for it exaggerates the role of change in the period and neglects the importance of continuity. While significant changes took place during those years, the decade also had important ties with the past. The concept of continuity as well as of change needs to be employed in an analysis of the Great Depression and the New Deal. The chief significance of the latter lay in its major contributions to a development that had been under way since the third quarter of the nineteenth century: the rise of a collectivistic or organizational type of capitalism.

Those interpreters of the 1930's who use concepts that stress breaks with the past usually begin with emphasis on the great expansion of government that took place during the period. "Buffeted and bewildered by the economic debacle, the American people in the course of the 1930's abandoned, once and for all, the doctrine of laissez faire." "The state had previously been a passive or impartial force. . . . Now it became the interventionist state." In these words, two leading historians, Louis M. Hacker and Carl N. Degler, describe what they call "the Third American Revolution." [3]

In pinning the laissez faire label on the pre-New Deal period, these historians accept a myth, for long before the 1930's Americans had come to expect the government to deal with economic affairs in many important ways.[4] General aspects of the New Deal can, in fact, be traced to late nineteenth- and early twentieth-century critics of laissez faire theories. The New Deal's pragmatic approach to the use of state power, its rejection of both socialism and the

3. Hacker, "The Third American Revolution," reprinted in Edwin C. Rozwenc (ed.), *The New Deal: Revolution or Evolution?* (Boston, 1959), p. 2; Degler, *Out of our Past*, p. 384.

4. Robert A. Lively, "The American System: A Review Article," *Business History Review*, XXIX (1955), 81–95.

negative state, its efforts to strengthen the free-enterprise system by introducing essential reforms and by equalizing opportunity, its belief that liberal democratic values could be attained in a complex industrial society only by practical state action—all of these ideas had been developed by theorists of an earlier day, men such as Lester Ward, Henry George, Richard T. Ely, John R. Commons, Herbert Croly, and Louis Brandeis.[5] Richard Hofstadter, in a famous essay emphasizing discontinuity in the New Deal, notes that it failed to produce a significant body of political writing comparable to that produced in the Progressive period. A perceptive critic, Andrew M. Scott, maintains that the New Deal did not need to do this:

> the task of criticizing the old ideas and shaping the new had largely been completed *during the Progressive Era*. It was because the basic thinking had already been done that the general approach to the crisis . . . could be agreed upon so quickly and with so little need for agonizing reappraisal.[6]

Specific programs of the New Deal as well as its theoretical approach to problems had been worked out in the past. Franklin Roosevelt's administration employed both types of programs that the Progressives had developed to deal with big business. The emphasis upon acceptance and regulation of it that Theodore Roosevelt had called for in the New Nationalism reappeared in the National Industrial Recovery Act, while the anti-bigness point of view of the Sherman Anti-Trust Act of 1890 and Woodrow Wilson's New Freedom of 1912 came to the fore again in such fea-

5. Sidney Fine, *Laissez Faire and the General-Welfare State: A Study of Conflict in American Thought, 1865–1901* (Ann Arbor, Mich., 1956), chap. xi; Commager, *The American Mind*, chaps. x, xii, xvi.
6. Hofstadter, *The Age of Reform: From Bryan to F.D.R.* (New York, 1955), pp. 316–17; Scott, "The Progressive Era in Perspective," *Journal of Politics*, XXI (1959), 696–98.

tures of the New Deal as the Public Utilities Holding Company Act and the Temporary National Economic Committee. In other words, both of the leading Progressive philosophies figured in the New Deal's enlargement of government.[7]

To support his thesis that the New Deal marked a "drastic new departure . . . in the history of American reformism," Hofstadter calls attention to the "many men" who had endorsed the Progressive movement but "found in the New Deal an outrageous departure from everything they had known and valued. . . ."[8] It is true that Newton Baker, for example, lashed out at the increase in power of the national government occurring under the New Deal. Baker's reputation as a progressive, however, rested chiefly on his activities on the municipal level, in Cleveland, from 1901 to 1916. Another survivor of the Wilson administration, on the other hand, Josephus Daniels, applauded the New Deal enthusiastically.[9] Idaho's Senator Borah, another carryover from the Progressive era, criticized the New Deal on the grounds that it did not do enough to restore the old competitive economic system of small units, a system that he assumed would require only a small government. Borah, however, represented but one type of Progressive, the type labeled "traditionalist" by John Braeman and opposed to the "moderns" who looked to Theodore Roosevelt for poli-

7. *Ibid.*, 692–93; Eric Goldman, *Rendezvous with Destiny: A History of Modern American Reform* (New York 1953), chaps. xiv–xv; Arthur M. Schlesinger, Jr., *The Coming of the New Deal* (*The Age of Roosevelt* [Boston, 1959]), chaps. vi–x, xxvii, xxix; Schlesinger, *The Politics of Upheaval* (*The Age of Roosevelt* [Boston, 1960]), chaps. xiii, xv, xvii, xxi; Rexford G. Tugwell, *The Democratic Roosevelt: A Biography of Franklin D. Roosevelt* (Garden City, N.Y,. 1957), chaps. xiv–xxii.

8. *The Age of Reform*, pp. 301–2.

9. C. H. Cramer, *Newton D. Baker: A Biography* (Cleveland, 1961), pp. 7, 8, 260, 267, 276, 277; E. David Cronon, "A Southern Progressive Looks at the New Deal," *Journal of Southern History*, XXIV (1958), 151–76.

tical leadership. Three former followers of T.R., William Allen White, Peter Norbeck, and Gifford Pinchot, looked upon the New Deal as a revival of the Progressive movement.[10] In short, since that movement contained conflicting groups and the New Deal contained more than one part, old Progressives surviving in the 1930's responded in varied ways to the programs of that decade: as Progressives, all of them rejected laissez faire; they disagreed, however, about the types of government action they desired.

The Hacker-Degler interpretation is somewhat confusing in regard to early rejections of laissez faire in theory and practice. Hacker, although aware of government intervention before the 1930's, seems to suggest that prior to the New Deal Americans had a "laissez faire, or passive, state." Degler, while admitting that "the rejection of laissez faire had a long history" and that the Progressives "limited business" and "assisted agriculture," implies that earlier departures had been temporary while "with the depression the nation at large accepted the government as a permanent influence in the economy"; thus, the New Deal was not "repudiated by the Eisenhower administration, the first Republican government since the reforms were instituted."

Of crucial significance here are distinctions that these historians make between types of state action. For example, they argue that prior to the New Deal the state "had refused to interfere significantly in the interests of the security and the welfare of its laboring peoples," that the "progressive impulse . . . continued to conceive of the state as policeman or judge and nothing more," and that the New Deal's

---

10. Marian McKenna, *Borah* (Ann Arbor, Mich., 1961), pp. 308, 313, 317, 318, 320–22, 376–77; John Braeman, "Seven Progressives: A Review Article," *Business History Review*, XXXV (1961), 582; Walter Johnson, *William Allen White's America* (New York, 1947), pp. 8, 432; Gilbert C. Fite, *Peter Norbeck: Prairie Statesman* (Columbia, Mo., 1948), pp. 192–206; M. Nelson McGeary, *Gifford Pinchot: Forester–Politician* (Princeton, N.J., 1960), pp. 393, 424.

"primary and general innovation was the guaranteeing of a minimum standard of welfare for the people of the nation." Hacker refers to New Deal government as "the social-welfare state" while Degler calls it "the guarantor state." [11]

Related to this is one of Hofstadter's important distinctions between the Progressive movement and the New Deal. The latter, he suggests, had "a social-democratic tinge that had never before been present in American reform movements." Earlier movements had been "concerned very largely with reforms of an essentially entrepreneurial sort and only marginally with social legislation," while from the 1930's on "American political reformism" took "responsibility on a large scale for social security, unemployment insurance, wages and hours, and housing." [12]

In the depression crisis, the federal government did take on vast new responsibilities in the social-welfare field and make new efforts to reduce economic inequalities. Note the relief programs, labor provisions of the National Recovery Administration codes, and legislation dealing with social security, housing, labor standards, and taxation. These responsibilities and efforts, however, grew out of the past; and they included certain features of the Progressive movement, especially the ideas and activities of the social workers, a group that played an important, not a marginal, role in that movement. "Without minimizing the importance of the social-reform measures inaugurated during the 1930's," Robert H. Bremner writes, "it may be said that the measures then adopted were largely implementations, amplifications, and—in some instances—but partial fulfillments of the preventive social work formulated before World War I." "By standing firm in the old progressive faith, by ex-

11. Hacker, "The Third American Revolution," 2, 19; Degler, *Out of Our Past*, pp. 384, 393, 414–15.
12. *Age of Reform*, p. 306.

ploring new lines of theory and practice," Clarke A. Chambers points out, "the partnership of social reformer and social worker anticipated [during the 1920's] in broad concept and often in intimate detail the welfare consensus which marked the New Deal." [13] In this connection, attention should be paid to pre-New Deal reform movements in Wisconsin, New York, and Massachusetts; Theodore Roosevelt's proposals; the Progressive party platform of 1912; Woodrow Wilson's suggestions in the same year, his programs a few years later; and the work of such groups as the National Child Labor Committee, the National Consumers' League, and the American Association for Labor Legislation. Furthermore, individuals who contributed in major ways to the development of New Deal social-welfare programs, including Frances Perkins, Robert F. Wagner, David I. Walsh, Edwin E. Witte, and Arthur J. Altmeyer, had developed their basic ideas in this field back in the Progressive era.[14] In short, Arthur Link's conclusion that "the Second New Deal" represented "the full flowering of social-justice progressivism" provides a more adequate view than Hofstadter's of the relations between this aspect of the New Deal and the past.[15]

13. Bremner, *From the Depths: The Discovery of Poverty in America* (New York, 1956), 261; Chambers, "Creative Effort in an Age of Normalcy, 1918–1933," *The Social Welfare Forum* (1961), 271.

14. Scott, "The Progressive Era in Perspective," 693–95; J. Joseph Huthmacher, "Urban Liberalism and the Age of Reform," *Mississippi Valley Historical Review*, XLIX (1962), 231–41; Bremner, *American Philanthropy* (Chicago, 1960), 149–55; Arthur J. Altmeyer, "The Wisconsin Idea and Social Security," *Wisconsin Magazine of History*, XLII (1958), 19–25; Timothy L. McDonnell, S.J., *The Wagner Housing Act: A Case Study of the Legislative Process* (Chicago, 1957), chap. i; Elizabeth Brandeis, "Organized Labor and Protective Labor Legislation," in Milton Derber and Edwin Young (eds.), *Labor and the New Deal* (Madison, Wis., 1957), pp. 197–98, 230–31; Sidney Ratner, *American Taxation, Its History as a Social Force in Democracy* (New York, 1942), 510–11; Robert J. Lampman, *Changes in the Share of Wealth Held by Top Wealth-Holders, 1922–1956* (New York, 1960), pp. 30–32.

15. *American Epoch: A History of the United States since the 1890's* (New York, 1955), p. 400.

Hofstadter's emphasis upon the depression in his inter-pretation of the relations between the New Deal and the Progressive movement should also be questioned. He argues that the former was different "because its central problem was unlike the problems of Progressivism" and maintains that the central problem was the depression.[16] Of course, the Progressives of the early twentieth century had oper-ated in a period of prosperity, and Herbert Hoover was the first President to insist that the central government was obliged to combat dips in the business cycle.[17] On the other hand, the anti-depression efforts of the New Deal repre-sented its major failure: millions remained unemployed when war provided the stimulus the economy needed.[18] Most of the ideas that New Dealers hoped to put into action had been formed to deal with other problems. This suggests that New Dealers did not believe that the problem of depres-sion should monopolize the center of the stage. They were vitally interested in the more general problems of an urban industrial civilization. Like the Progressives before them, they sought ways to realize liberal democratic values in an America that had been changed radically by the rise of in-dustry and the city, and they found opportunities in the depression situation to enact laws embodying ideas that had been developing for more than half a century.[19]

16. *Age of Reform*, pp. 301–4.

17. Harris Gaylord Warren, *Herbert Hoover and the Great De-pression* (New York, 1959).

18. Broadus Mitchell, *Depression Decade: From New Era through New Deal, 1929–1941* (New York, 1947), pp. 21–24, 371–72, 396–98.

19. Scott concludes: "To a very considerable extent the history of American political thought and controversy since the Civil War is the history of efforts to effect a satisfactory adjustment of men's ideas and the changing social, economic, and political realities. When the Progressive Era is examined in this light, its pivotal position stands out in clear relief. It opened the door to the present. The Progressives blazed the trail; the New Dealers turned it into a thoroughfare."— "The Progressive Era in Perspective," 701.

Furthermore, the major anti-depression formula that emerged from the new experiences, the "Keynesian" emphasis upon deficit financing, had ties with the Progressives' fundamental assumptions concerning the role of government. While the formula enlarged somewhat the economic responsibilities and significance of government, making it "the indispensable partner of business," [20] Keynesianism employed well-established powers of government, the taxing and spending powers; attempted to make capitalism work rather than to substitute another system for it; and reflected confidence in the ability of an active government to deal with economic problems.[21]

This stressing of the New Deal's links with the past does not deny that significant changes took place in American political practices during the 1930's. Washington, D.C. became a much more important place; the number of federal employees increased more than in any earlier decade, with the executive branch growing from slightly less than six hundred thousand persons in 1933 to well over nine hundred thousand by 1939. One historian of American cities, however, notes that Washington had been emerging "as the political center of national affairs" for a number of years; that as early as World War I state authority "had dwindled to a shadow of its former importance. Boston's and Albany's, Denver's and Sacramento's loss was Washington's gain." And a student employing a statistical approach to the trend of government activity in the United States, while recognizing that the depression and the New Deal played important parts in producing the great increase

20. John Kenneth Galbraith, *American Capitalism: The Concept of Countervailing Power* (Sentry Edition; Boston, 1962), p. 80; see also pp. 68–83, 177–81.

21. Lawrence R. Klein, *The Keynesian Revolution* (New York, 1947), pp. 167, 184; Harlan L. McCracken, *Keynesian Economics in the Stream of Economic Thought* (Baton Rouge, La., 1961), pp. 126–28.

during the twentieth century in the size of government, rejects the hypothesis that this increase is to be explained by "a changed concept of government's functions brought into being under the New Deal." Instead, he suggests, the development was "part of a trend already established before the great depression." [22]

When looking, then, at the enlargement of government that took place during the 1930's, there seems no good reason to reject the conclusion that Henry Steele Commager reached nearly twenty years ago. Writing in 1945, he insisted that "the Roosevelt revolution was no revolution, but rather the culmination of half a century of historical development. . . ." [23] The depression provided the climate in which ideas that had been taking shape for a number of years could become more widely accepted by the public and more firmly fixed in government practices. As a consequence, Americans came out of the decade with many new and permanent national programs and with what could justifiably be labeled a "big government." This matched the earlier rise of "bigness" in the business world.

Turning away from the central government and looking at the impact of the depression and the New Deal on a significant group, the farmers, we again find both continuity and change. Government became more important in their lives and was used to make them more like the lives of urban people, especially like those of businessmen. American agriculture, however, had been moving in these directions for a number of years.

22. Constance McLaughlin Green, *American Cities in the Growth of the Nation* (London, 1957), p. 238; Solomon Fabricant, *The Trend of Government Activity in the United States since 1900* (New York, 1952), pp. 3, 28–29, 32, 40, 83, 141–48; Andrew Jackson Wann, "Franklin D. Roosevelt and the Administrative Organization of the Executive Branch" (Ph.D. dissertation, University of Missouri, 1961), p. 353.

23. "Twelve Years of Roosevelt," reprinted in Rozwenc (ed.), *The New Deal*, p. 20.

Leading the list of New Deal farm legislation was the Agricultural Adjustment Act of 1933, a clear-cut expression of the idea that government had major responsibilities to the nation's farmers. Yet, much nineteenth-century land legislation, the establishment of educational and research facilities for agriculture, and the farm-credit legislation of the Wilson administration had been based on this idea. The 1933 law, though, had a different focus—farm prices—and sought actively to change price relationships so that farmers would obtain purchasing power equal to that obtained in an earlier and prosperous period. This focus, however, grew out of more than a decade of preparation and agitation, beginning after the price-break of 1920 and continuing beyond the passage of the Agricultural Marketing Act of 1929. During those years, the battle to get the federal government to accept responsibility was fought by farm groups, chiefly in the Middle West and South; leaders in the United States Department of Agriculture, especially its Bureau of Agricultural Economics, and in the land-grant colleges, including M. L. Wilson and his Montana colleagues; and even a few urban businessmen, led by George N. Peek with his McNary-Haugen plan. These people took progressivism's positive attitude toward government action for economic purposes, translated it into specific programs for the farmer, and reinterpreted old ideas about his importance, placing a new emphasis upon farm purchasing power and its relation to national prosperity. These intellectual and political activities laid the groundwork for changes in government practices during the 1930's.[24]

24. Arthur S. Link, "What Happened to the Progressive Movement in the 1920's?" *American Historical Review*, LXIV (1959), 845–46; Murray R. Benedict, *Farm Policies of the United States, 1790–1950: A Study of their Origins and Development* (New York, 1953), pp. xii, 238, 516; Theodore Saloutos and John D. Hicks, *Agricultural Discontent in the Middle West, 1900–1939* (Madison, Wis., 1951), 539–40, 562; Saloutos, *Farmer Movements in the South, 1865–1933* (Berkeley, Calif., 1960), 281, 284–87; James H. Shideler, *Farm Crisis, 1919–1923* (Berkeley, Calif., 1957); Gilbert C. Fite, *George N. Peek and the*

By calling upon farmers to regulate their production as a means of getting higher prices, the Agricultural Adjustment Administration rejected romantic conceptions of the farmer as a self-sufficient yeoman and the old agrarian emphasis on trust-busting as the solution to the ills of agriculture. Instead, the farm program looked upon farming as another business and urged farmers to imitate the practices of successful urban businessmen, the industrialists who used their power to balance supply with demand at a profitable level. Crop control, however, was not a new idea. Farmers, especially in the South, had been considering it seriously for a generation before the New Deal came to power. Furthermore, New Dealers were not the first important people to suggest that farmers should look upon themselves as businessmen and imitate urban businessmen, rather than attempt to force them to change their ways. Since the end of the nineteenth century, at least, farm journals, farm organizations, and urban businessmen—the latter disturbed by the anti–big business slant of the Populist Revolt and aware of the importance, for them, of farm purchasing power—had been urging farmers to think of themselves as businessmen and to copy business methods so as to make profits.[25]

In its basic farm legislation, the New Deal was, in effect, urging the farmer to participate in, rather than resist, the development of a collectivistic or organizational type of

---

Fight for Farm Parity (Norman, Okla., 1954); Roy E. Huffman, "Montana's Contributions to New Deal Farm Policy," *Agricultural History*, XXXIII (1959), 164–67; Clifford B. Anderson, "The Metamorphosis of American Agrarian Idealism in the 1920's and 1930's," *Agricultural History*, XXXV (1961), 184–85.

25. Richard S. Kirkendall, "A Professor in Farm Politics," *Mid-America*, XLI (1959), 212–14, 217; Kirkendall, "Four Economists in Political Process," *Journal of Farm Economics*, XLI (1959), 204–5; Hofstadter, *Age of Reform*, pp. 120–26; Anderson, "The Metamorphosis of American Agrarian Idealism in the 1920's and 1930's," 186; Benedict, *Farm Policies of the United States*, pp. 514–15; Saloutos and Hicks, *Agricultural Discontent in the Middle West*, pp. 539–40, 562; Saloutos, *Farmer Movements in the South*, pp. 281, 284–87.

capitalism, a development that had started in the urban
business world in the nineteenth century. One feature of
this type of capitalism was the pressure group, and the
New Deal helped the farmers, at least a large number of
them, to develop a powerful pressure group. Here again,
the development had started before the advent of the New
Deal and a number of farm groups of this kind, led by the
Grange, the National Farmers Union, and the American
Farm Bureau Federation, were already active in the early
1930's. The Farm Bureau organization however, grew
amazingly during New Deal years. Formed shortly after
World War I, it had declined in size after its early years
of growth, reaching an all-time low in 1933, with only one-
third the membership of 1921. By 1941, however, membership had climbed above the previous high of 466,000.
In this growth, government agencies, especially the extension services and the AAA, played important promotional
roles. In the late 1930's, friction developed between the
Roosevelt administration and the Farm Bureau, and in
the early 1940's the latter battled successfully against several reform and planning programs that seemed to threaten
its interests and power. In short, a large number of commercial farmers, located chiefly in the Midwest and the
South, emerged from the 1930's with a powerful organization capable of dealing with the newly enlarged national
government. Like other businessmen, these farmers had
formed an effective pressure group, and now this representative of rural businessmen co-operated politically with
organized urban business.[26]

26. Christiana McFadyen Campbell, *The Farm Bureau and the
New Deal: A Study of the Making of a National Farm Policy, 1933–
1940* (Urbana, Ill., 1962), pp. 102, 186, 194–95; Grant McConnell,
The Decline of Agrarian Democracy (Berkeley, Calif., 1953), pp. 77,
79, 126, 175, 180; William J. Block, *The Separation of the Farm
Bureau and the Extension Service: Political Issue in a Federal System*
(Urbana, Ill., 1960), pp. 16, 19–21; Kirkendall, "A Professor in Farm
Politics," 214–17.

In addition to efforts to promote a business orientation
in rural America, some of the New Dealers sought also to
make farming more scientific. They encouraged farmers
and government officials to call upon scientists, including
social scientists, for advice as to the best ways to use the
land. The AAA, for example, encouraged Southern farmers,
with some success, to shift some of their lands out of cotton,
convert them to other uses, rotate their crops, improve their
plowing methods, and apply more lime and fertilizer to the
soil.[27] The Taylor grazing program, based on legislation
passed in 1934, provides another illustration of this approach. Among other aims, the program attempted, by
regulating grazing on the public domain, to stop injury to
those lands and to improve them. Lands found to be valuable chiefly for grazing were restricted to that purpose, and
cattlemen were issued permits which allowed them to graze
only as many animals as the range could safely carry.
Although these men blocked effective regulation, the program at least diminished the rate of injury, lessened over-
grazing and soil deterioration, improved the range somewhat, and prevented further homesteading, a practice that
had resulted in destruction of the range as well as failure
for farmers.[28]

This closing of the public domain to the homesteader
dramatized a major theme of New Deal farm policy: a
determination to break with the tradition of agricultural

27. John Leonard Fulmer, *Agricultural Progress in the Cotton
Belt since 1920* (Chapel Hill, N.C., 1950), pp. 3, 5, 16, 169, 173–74;
James H. Street, *The New Revolution in the Cotton Economy:
Mechanization and its Consequences* (Chapel Hill, N.C., 1957), pp.
48–49; Thomas D. Clark, *The Emerging South* (New York, 1961), pp.
51–52, 66, 96.

28. Phillip O. Foss, *Politics and Grass: The Administration of
Grazing on the Public Domain* (Seattle, Wash., 1960), pp. 196, 203–04;
E. Louise Peffer, *The Closing of the Public Domain: Disposal and
Reservation Policies, 1900–1950* (Stanford, Calif., 1951), pp. 5, 326,
330, 339, 341; Roy M. Robbins, *Our Landed Heritage: The Public
Domain, 1776–1936* (Princeton, N.J., 1942), p. 423.

expansion, a tradition that assumed an abundance of farm land and "family farmers" was important for social and political as well as for economic reasons. A belief that too much land lay behind farmer's fences dominated the thinking about land policy in Roosevelt's Department of Agriculture. This break with tradition in the Taylor Grazing Act and other New Deal programs designed to improve the ways in which the nation used its land had roots in the conservation movement of the Progressive period; and it also grew out of the long-standing efforts of agricultural societies and journals, the Department of Agriculture, and the land-grant colleges to get farmers to operate more scientifically. Hoover's Secretary of Agriculture, reflecting ideas that had been developing in his Bureau of Agricultural Economics for a decade, had announced before Roosevelt came to power: "We have laid aside the expansionist philosophy carried forward from the pioneer epoch. We are now turning to sound economic planning for agriculture." [29]

Efforts to bring the ways of business and science into rural America involved attempts to reduce differences between urban and rural life. The Rural Electrification Administration worked in the same direction. When it went into operation in 1935, only 10 per cent of the nation's farms were tied to power lines; twenty years later the percentage had jumped to well over ninety. In that period, over four million farms were connected to electrical systems; the REA served 60 per cent of them. This change enabled rural folk to enjoy many of the features of modern life previously reserved for city people: electric lights, radios, washing machines, mechanical refrigerators, electric ranges, television sets, deep freezes, and so on. REA, however, did not represent the first effort by government

29. Kirkendall, "L. C. Gray and the Supply of Agricultural Land," *Agricultural History*, XXXVII (1963), 206–14; Kirkendall, "A Professor in Farm Politics," 215; Kirkendall, "Four Economists in the Political Process," 206.

to "urbanize" rural America. Before this electrical program came rural mail deliveries, parcel post, the building of farm-to-market roads, and the like. REA, in other words, formed a major part of a long-term attempt by government, in addition to many private groups, to promote on various levels "a social and cultural 'equality' for farmers," to shatter "the old isolation and social barrenness of rural living. . . ." [30]

The 1930's, then, formed a significant segment of a long period of major changes in rural America. Nevertheless, farmers and farm spokesmen of the decade did not discard Jefferson completely. Ancient ways of thought still found expression. Jeffersonian democracy influenced the efforts to bring farmers into the planning and administration of farm programs, organizing them into committees on the state and local levels. Some farm spokesmen continued to speak of farming as a way of life, not a business; of the farmer, living close to nature and God, as morally superior to urban businessmen and laborers; and of the urbanization of America as bound to lead to national ruin. [31] The family farm remained the characteristic unit of farming, with the Department of Agriculture insisting that one of its continuing major objectives was "the establishment and maintenance of such farms as the predominating operating farm unit in the United States"; and the Farm Bureau looked upon the farm program as designed to preserve free American farmers from a descent into a European-like peas-

30. Lemont Kingsford Richardson, *Wisconsin REA: The Struggle to Extend Electricity to Rural Wisconsin, 1935–1955* (Madison, Wis., 1961), pp. 144, 147, 149; Clark, *The Emerging South*, pp. 97–100.

31. Kirkendall, "A Professor in Farm Politics," 213–17; Anderson, "The Metamorphosis of American Agrarian Idealism in the 1920's and 1930's," 185, 187. For an excellent study of the mixture of old and new ideas on rural America see Paul K. Conkin, *Tomorrow a New World: The New Deal Community Program* (Ithaca, N.Y., 1959).

antry.[32] The Farm Security Administration and its New
Deal predecessors represented something quite new in farm
policy: a concern for the rural poor comparable to that
shown the urban poor in the social-welfare programs. The
old philosophy, however, exerted a large influence on the
operations of FSA, for under the Bankhead-Jones Act the
ideal of the family farm became an explicit goal of the
agency. The Act represented, A. Whitney Griswold has
written, "a decision not to let economic and technological
trends run their course, as the British had done, but to
resist them in defense of the agrarian way of life and the
family farm." [33]

While Jefferson's philosophy continued to be heard and to
have some influence on policy, his idealized rural American
operated in a far from self-sufficient fashion and was involved in an elaborate system of government controls. The
latter was somewhat unpopular. "It is clear," Gilbert C.
Fite has concluded, "that the farmers would not voluntarily
have reduced their acreage without attractive cash induce-
ments. They learned to live with acreage controls . . . but
it was like accepting an unwanted child." [34] Nevertheless,
farmers did not accept the advice of the Farmers' Independence Council, a "propaganda organ for industry, the
meat packers, and some large cattle interests" that preached
an individualistic philosophy. The Council worked hard but
unsuccessfully in the mid-1930's to turn the farmer against
the New Deal. Clearly, he was no longer the self-reliant
individual idealized by Jefferson.[35] The farmer had become

32. A. Whitney Griswold, *Farming and Democracy* (New York,
1948), p. 15; Campbell, *The Farm Bureau and the New Deal*, p. 29.

33. Griswold, *Farming and Democracy*, pp. 163–65; McConnell, *The
Decline of Agrarian Democracy*, pp. 84–85, 94; Benedict, *Farm
Policies of the United States*, p. 256.

34. "Farmer Opinion and the Agricultural Adjustment Act, 1933,"
Mississippi Valley Historical Review, XLVIII (1962), 673.

35. James C. Carey, "The Farmers' Independence Council of America, 1935–1938," *Agricultural History*, XXXV (1961), 77.

part of the larger world of business, science, and the city, had joined a large organization, and had increased his demands upon the government for help. He was moving, at times reluctantly, with, rather than against, the development of a collectivistic type of capitalism.

No area of American life experienced more change in the 1930's than the labor movement. Labor leaders, for example, faced with massive unemployment and declining unions, changed their attitude toward government, discarding Samuel Gompers' concept of "voluntarism," the idea that the worker should depend upon his union, not upon the state, and that the union should depend upon itself. Late in 1932, The American Federation of Labor reversed its earlier stand and endorsed a government program of unemployment insurance. From that point on, organized labor became increasingly active in support of social security and stopped demanding that workers depend solely on the union in their quest for a larger share of the material benefits of the economic system.[36]

Not only did organized labor change its attitude toward government, but the national government developed a much more positive view of unions and began to encourage and protect their growth and operations. In a series of laws passed from 1932 to 1935 and topped by the National Labor Relations (or Wagner) Act of the latter year, the national government insisted that workers should be free to associate and select representatives for collective bargaining, that their employers should not interfere in the exercise of these rights, that employees could elect their own representatives with the choice of the majority governing all, and that

36. Irving Bernstein, *The Lean Years: A History of the American Worker 1920–1933* (Boston, 1960), pp. 345, 347, 351, 353–54; Philip Taft, *The A.F. of L. from the Death of Gompers to the Merger* (New York, 1959), pp. 281–82, 284, 287, 293, 294; Edwin E. Witte, "Organized Labor and Social Security," in Derber and Young (eds.), *Labor and the New Deal*, pp. 271–72.

employers should recognize and deal with these spokesmen. By accepting this government protection in the organizing process, labor leaders departed still further from voluntarism, accepting the assumption of the sponsors of the laws that only government could overcome the obstacles in the organizer's path, especially the antiunion practices of management.[37] To some disciples of Gompers the new developments seemed deplorable. One of them complained that "under Mr. Gompers' regime, the trade union movement stood upon its own feet; now it must depend, to a large extent, upon the support of State and Federal administration." [38]

In the 1930's, government did become much more active in this area. Under the Wagner Act, the administrators did not simply prohibit interference with the right to organize and encourage collective bargaining; they established the procedures that workers employed to elect their bargaining units, determined those units, and influenced the negotiating processes and the nature and content of the contracts accepted by labor and management. With government playing such a large role in the lives of unions, the next logical step would be government regulation of unions to match government promotion of them, a sequence that had characterized relations between the railroads and the national government in the second half of the nineteenth century. In 1947, the federal government would take this second step in the labor field.[39]

37. Irving Bernstein, *The New Deal Collective Bargaining Policy* (Berkeley, Calif., 1950), pp. ix, 129–30; Harry A. Millis and Emily Clark Brown, *From the Wagner Act to Taft-Hartley: A Study of National Labor Policy and Labor Relations* (Chicago, 1950), pp. 3–4, 13–15, 29–30; Bernstein, *Lean Years,* pp. 391, 415.

38. James O. Morris, *Conflict within the AFL: A Study of Craft versus Industrial Unionism, 1901–1938* (Ithaca, N.Y., 1958), p. 290. Quoting John P. Frey.

39. Bernstein, *The New Deal Collective Bargaining Policy*, pp. 148–49; Taft, *The A.F. of L. from the Death of Gompers to the Merger,* pp. 127, 130–35; R. W. Fleming, "The Significance of the

During those years of government promotion, the labor movement grew at a rapid pace. With only three million members in 1933, unions grew slowly in the uncertain situation of the next three years; and then, from 1936 to 1941, membership doubled, jumping to well over eight million. Furthermore, much of this growth took place in strategic sectors of the economy previously closed to unions. In 1935 unionism was confined largely to the needle trades, coal-mining, printing, public utilities, the railroads, and the building trades. Significantly absent from this list was heavy industry. By 1941, the centers of heavy industry had been successfully invaded; cities such as Pittsburgh, Detroit, and Akron, and industrial giants like United States Steel, General Motors, Chrysler, General Electric, Ford, Republic Steel, Bethlehem Steel, and Westinghouse, all formerly anti-union, had been transformed into union strongholds. A new labor group, the Congress of Industrial Organizations, had entrenched itself "in vital centers of American industrial might." To one student of American labor, this seemed "a fundamental, almost revolutionary change in the power relationships of American society." [40] Certainly the labor movement had become "a major force in American life." [41]

Even more than big government, big labor was a development of the 1930's. In the years following that decade membership doubled once more. Almost all of these gains, however, were made by unions that had achieved substan-

Wagner Act," in Derber and Young (eds.), *Labor and the New Deal*, pp. 148–52; Doris E. Pullman and L. Reed Tripp, "Collective Bargaining Developments," in *ibid.*, pp. 356–58; Millis and Brown, *From the Wagner Act to Taft-Hartley*, pp. 272, 317, 329–30, 332–34, 345, 655–56; Walter Galenson, *The CIO Challenge to the AFL: A History of the American Labor Movement, 1935–1941*, (Cambridge, 1960), p. 640.

40. Galenson, *The CIO Challenge to the AFL*, pp. xvii, 587–92, 642–44.

41. Milton Derber, "Growth and Expansion," in Derber and Young (eds.), *Labor and the New Deal*, p. 42.

tial growth by 1939. As Milton Derber has pointed out, "the biggest unions of 1939 in both the AFL and CIO were, with only a few exceptions, the biggest unions of the 1950's. . . ."[42]

The move into heavy industry constituted a victory for critics of the Gompers' group that dominated the AF of L. Representing largely the industrial-type unions, especially those in the mining and clothing industries, these critics had been demanding for many years that workers be organized along industrial, rather than craft, lines. Unfortunately, the craft unions that controlled the AF of L refused to accept the view of the critics. Consequently, as industrialism moved forward, creating mass-production industries and multiplying the number of unskilled and semiskilled workers, millions of workers remained outside the labor movement. Given the inflexibility of the leadership of the AF of L, a new organization had to take shape and give expression to the views of the critics if the majority of workers were to be drawn into the labor movement. Late in 1935, the CIO emerged under the leadership of John L. Lewis, "perhaps the greatest entrepreneur of American labor organization. . . ."[43]

While organizing the unorganized into industrial unions, the CIO also accepted the critics' demand that organized labor champion a comprehensive program of social-welfare legislation and place greater emphasis upon political action in order to get it enacted. The new organization established permanent (rather than temporary, election-year) political machinery, committed a far greater proportion of its time, personnel, and money to politics and tied itself more closely

42. *Ibid.*, p. 42.

43. Galenson, *The CIO Challenge to the AFL*, pp. 641–42; Morris, *Conflict within the AFL*, pp. 2–3; Edwin Young, "The Split in the Labor Movement," in Derber and Young (eds.), *Labor and the New Deal*, pp. 69–70; Taft, *The A.F. of L. from the Death of Gompers to the Merger*, pp. 155–56, 166.

to one political party—the Democratic—than unions had in pre-New Deal days. Following the passage of the Taft-Hartley Act in 1947, the AF of L imitated its rival, establishing Labor's League for Political Education and explicitly endorsing a presidential candidate. With government playing big roles in the lives of workers and their unions, large-scale political action by the labor movement had become a necessity.[44]

The labor movement had changed its relations with government and politics, its size, and its power. Nevertheless, it had not broken all ties with the past. As has already been suggested, the establishment of the CIO with its industrial and political orientation represented the triumph of ideas that had been developing in the labor movement for a number of years. Furthermore, such a movement did exist at the beginning of the 1930's. Even though it was weak by comparison with the situation a decade later (and also a decade earlier), the movement was strong enough to provide one basis for the organizing success of the 1930's, efforts that were led by men who had been nurtured in the old organizations. In addition, the largest labor organization at the beginning of the decade—the AF of L—remained the largest after the great activities of the 1930's. By 1933, its membership had dropped lower than any point since 1916, but by 1936 the Federation had more than recouped its depression losses. Then, stimulated largely by the rise of a rival, the AF of L made strenuous and successful efforts to enlarge itself, developing in the process a greater interest in organizing the unskilled into industrial unions.[45]

44. Morris, *Conflict within the AFL*, pp. 271–75; Galenson, *The CIO Challenge to the AFL*, pp. 605–6, 609–10, 643; Taft, *The A.F.of L. from the Death of Gompers to the Merger*, pp. 311–13, 322–23.

45. *Ibid.*, pp. 199–200, 202, 450; Derber, "Growth and Expansion," in Derber and Young, *Labor and the New Deal*, pp. 38–40; Morris, *Conflict within the AFL*, pp. 289–90; Galenson, *The CIO Challenge to the AFL*, pp. 643–44.

The new as well as the transformed old organization adhered to the pro-capitalist philosophy that Gompers had preached for half a century. Labor power continued to be valued by most labor leaders chiefly as a means of obtaining for wage earners a larger share of the benefits of a highly industrialized capitalistic system, not as a means of overthrowing it. Although those leaders increased their political activity, they continued, like Gompers before them, to operate within the established party system and to oppose the formation of a labor party.[46]

The growth of the labor movement in the 1930's formed a highly significant part of the long-term alteration of American capitalism. Organization of the labor sector took a great leap forward in the decade, giving the wage earners more power to deal with previously established business organizations. The rise of the latter had meant new controls over the workers' lives, often by bureaucracies centered in some metropolis outside of the workers' communities. Now wage earners turned to political and labor organizations with their bureaucracies which were frequently centered in Washington, D.C. The workers made this move to find security and a chance to "get ahead," not to create a radically new social and economic system. They hoped to discover means of fulfilling old desires to acquire mass-produced goods, desires that had been frustrated by the depression and seemed now to depend for their fulfillment on new institutional developments.[47]

Closely related to the changes in the labor movement was the change that took place in the relative status of the two major political parties. During the 1930's, the Democrats

46. Selig Perlman, "Labor and the New Deal in Historical Perspective," in Derber and Young (eds), *Labor and the New Deal*, pp. 366–69.

47. Maurice R. Stein, *The Eclipse of Community: An Interpretation of American Studies* (Princeton, N.J., 1960), pp. 56–68, 92–93, 106–7, 281; W. Lloyd Warner, *The Corporation in the Emergent American Society*, (New York, 1962).

replaced the Republicans as the nation's majority party, largely as a consequence of changes in the political behavior of the urban working classes. Roosevelt's victories, just like the repeal of prohibition at the start of his regime, depended heavily upon discontent in the cities.[48]

The discontent appeared in the election of 1932. Roosevelt devoted most of his energies then to efforts to capture the West and South, especially the rural progressives who disliked the power of business groups in the Republican party and the Southerners who had voted against Alfred E. Smith in 1928. (Professor Schlesinger argues that "the essence of the Democratic problem was to bring these rural Democrats back into the party." [49] Nevertheless, although the only states and most of the cities that he failed to carry were in the Northeast, Roosevelt increased the strength his party had in urban areas, especially among the wage-earners, carrying thirty-two of the thirty-six leading cities and receiving over 17 per cent more votes in those places than Smith had. Coal miners also deserted the Republican party. In 1928, Hoover had carried thirty-six of the forty-five coal-mining counties; in 1932, Roosevelt captured thirty-nine of them. "Labor voted overwhelmingly against joblessness and Hoover's failure to deal with it," a leading student of labor concluded. "Workers who had voted for Smith in 1928 cast their ballots for Roosevelt in 1932; many who had voted for Hoover four years earlier switched to Roosevelt; and a great number who had not voted at all in 1928 came out to support Roosevelt in 1932." [50]

48. Andrew Sinclair, *Prohibition: The Era of Excess* (Boston, 1962).

49. Arthur M. Schlesinger, Jr., *The Crisis of the Old Order, 1919–1933 (The Age of Roosevelt* [Boston, 1957]), p. 237. See also chaps. xxvii, xxviii, xxxiii.

50. Bernstein, *The Lean Years,* pp. 508–12; Frank Freidel, *Franklin D. Roosevelt: The Triumph* (Boston, 1956), pp. 8, 95–98, 240, 255, 268–75, 285, 337, 341–51; Oscar Handlin, *Al Smith and His America* (Boston, 1958), chaps. vi–vii, pp. 167–70; Samuel Lubell, *The Future of American Politics* (2d ed.; Garden City, N.Y., 1956), p. 46.

These urban groups became increasingly important to Roosevelt after his program went into operation. "Between 1932 and 1936," according to Samuel Lubell, "the Democratic plurality in the cities leaped 80 per cent, the biggest change in any single election." [51] Twelve cities of over one hundred thousand people had not supported Roosevelt in 1932, but each one moved behind him four years later. Ten states contained the twelve cities of half a million people or more that could provide enough strength for a candidate to capture the electoral votes of the states, nearly everything he needed for victory. Although most of these states had supported the G.O.P. from the Civil War to the Great Depression, their cities now switched to the Democratic party to make it the majority party for the first time since 1860. In 1940 and 1944, the size of the urban majorities was especially important for it enabled Roosevelt to win while his support was declining in rural areas and small towns.[52]

Important in this urban support for Roosevelt were the numerous children of the millions of immigrants who had poured into the country, chiefly from southern and eastern Europe, late in the nineteenth and early in the twentieth century. Their experiences in slums and factories made them interested in many of the programs that Roosevelt championed. The depression, striking these insecure and ambitious groups, strengthened their belief that they should turn to government for help in their quest for security and social mobility. They also applauded Roosevelt's appointment policies, which recognized that people of "new immigrant" stock could make important contributions; and they appreciated the equalitarian ideology of many New Dealers,

51. *Ibid.*, p. 36, See also pp. 46, 54.

52. Walter Johnson, *1600 Pennsylvania Avenue: Presidents and the People, 1929–1959* (Boston, 1960), pp. 80, 92. For analyses of one state see Samuel T. McSeveney, "The Michigan Gubernatorial Campaign of 1938," *Michigan History,* XLV (1961), 97–127 and Stephen B. and Vera H. Sarasohn, *Political Party Patterns in Michigan* (Detroit, 1957), pp. 25–26.

which rejected the racist assumptions of many old-stock Americans that were implicit in immigration policy and other areas of American life. As these ethnic groups rallied behind Roosevelt, they also became more "Americanized" for they were turning for help to the national government, rather than to their own organizations, including the local political machines; and they and other members of the working class thought less in terms of the cultural differences that once had kept them apart and more in terms of the interests they shared as members of a class. Both immigrant and native workers joined forces in the CIO as well as in the "Roosevelt Coalition." For a time, the coalition also contained farmers who had battled against urban groups in the 1920's.[53]

Negro voters formed another significant element in this coalition. Here, too, population movements were important for since early in the twentieth century Negroes had been moving out of southern agriculture in large numbers and locating chiefly in northern cities, thus shifting from areas in which their political activity was discouraged to places where politicians urged them to vote. They deserted the Republican party and in 1936 gave a majority of their votes for the first time to a Democratic presidential candidate. (Most of the southern Negroes who voted joined in the change.) They did this partly out of disgust for Republicans who had been taking the Negro vote for granted for a number of years. Even more important, with most Negroes in the lowest income groups and millions of them unemployed, they derived great benefits from the New Deal.

53. Lubell, *The Future of American Politics*, pp. 29–31, 53–54; J. Joseph Huthmacher, *Massachusetts People and Politics, 1919–1933* (Cambridge, 1959), pp. 265–67; Maldwyn Allen Jones, *American Immigration* (Chicago, 1960), pp. 299–300; Johnson, *1600 Pennsylvania Avenue*, pp. 77, 79–80; Oscar Handlin, *Adventures in Freedom: Three Hundred Years of Jewish Life in America* (New York, 1954), pp. 213–15. For a discussion of all of the groups in the coalition in 1936 see Schlesinger, *The Politics of Upheaval*, chaps. xxii, xxiii, xxxii.

They also appreciated the New Deal's ideology and its appointment policy, which placed more Negroes in important government jobs than Roosevelt's predecessors had. The New Deal marked an early stage in what C. Vann Woodward calls the "New" or "Second" Reconstruction, the period of improvement in race relations in which the nation has been involved for the past thirty years.[54] "Somewhere in the mid-1930's there was a turn," Oscar Handlin has written, " . . . discrimination increasingly took on the aspect of an anachronistic survival from the past rather than a pattern valid for the future." [55]

Working-class support for reform expanded along with the increase in working-class support for the Democratic party. In the border states, for example, the votes of wage earners in the cities and the mining regions had been controlled by pro-business groups, but under the impact of the depression and the New Deal, these workers switched their political allegiance to labor leaders and reformers.[56]

Samuel Lubell labels the "toppling of the dominance held by the Republicans for nearly three-fourths of a century" the "Third American Revolution." ". . . The distinctive

54. C. Vann Woodward, *The Strange Career of Jim Crow* (rev. ed.; New York, 1957), chap. iii; Elbert Lee Tatum, *The Changed Political Thought of the Negro, 1915–1940* (New York, 1951), pp. 139, 147–61, 180–81; John Hope Franklin, *From Slavery to Freedom: A History of American Negroes* (2d ed.; New York, 1956) 512–33; V. O. Key, Jr., *Southern Politics in State and Nation* (New York, 1949), pp. 74, 286, 290–91, 645; Alexander Heard, *A Two-Party South?* (Chapel Hill, N.C., 1952), pp. 225–28; Edwin D. Hoffman, "The Genesis of the Modern Movement for Equal Rights in South Carolina, 1930–1939," *Journal of Negro History*, XIV (1959), 360–64; Johnson, *1600 Pennsylvania Avenue*, pp. 81–82; Theodore White, *The Making of the President, 1960* (Cardinal Edition; New York, 1961), pp. 276–78.

55. *Race and Nationality in American Life* (New York, 1957), p. 141.

56. John H. Fenton, *Politics of the Border States: A Study of Political Organization and Political Change Common to the Border States—Maryland, West Virginia, Kentucky and Missouri* (New Orleans, 1957), pp. 206, 209, 211, 213, 215, 216.

feature of the political revolution which Franklin D. Roosevelt began and Truman inherited lies," he suggests, "not in its resemblance to the political wars of Andrew Jackson or Thomas Jefferson, but in its abrupt break with the continuity of the past." Although he makes this bold statement, Lubell also points out that "the Republican hold on the cities was broken not by Roosevelt but by Alfred E. Smith," and goes so far as to suggest that "before the Roosevelt Revolution there was an Al Smith Revolution." [57] Perhaps he needs a term that recognizes that the change in the relationships between the major parties was evolutionary in character.

Urban discontent with Republican rule had been growing for some time before the rise of Franklin Roosevelt. During the 1920's, and especially in the Smith-Hoover campaign of 1928, "new immigrant" groups and Negroes expressed their growing unhappiness with Republican policies that seemed to be dominated by old-stock, white, and upper-income points of view. Although a Republican, Congressman Fiorello LaGuardia represented some of the discontent of lower-class urban groups in the 1920's.[58] In this situation, and before the Great Depression, the Democrats made gains in urban areas such as Massachusetts, which, as Professor Huthmacher points out, "stood in the forefront of the states most permeated by the Newer American culture of cities, factories, and new-stock citizens." [59] Consequently, Roosevelt simply carried much farther a development that started before he had his chance to acquire the votes and deal with the problems of urban groups that had supported Al Smith.[60]

57. *The Future of American Politics*, pp. 3, 35, 36.

58. Tatum, *The Changed Political Thought of the Negro*, pp. 65–72, 101–8, 137, 142–43, 146, 178–79; Arthur Mann, *LaGuardia: A Fighter against His Times, 1882–1933* (Philadelphia, 1959); Howard Zinn, *LaGuardia in Congress* (Ithaca, N.Y., 1959).

59. *Massachusetts People and Politics*, p. ix. See also pp. 260–62, 265–66 and Robert A. Dahl, *Who Governs? Democracy and Power in an American City* (New Haven, 1961), pp. 49–50.

60. Handlin, *Al Smith and His America*, pp. 179, 181.

Furthermore, questions should be raised about the significance of the rise of the Democrats to majority status. Certainly the Roosevelt coalition was a very unstable arrangement, unable to produce a majority vote for a Democratic presidential candidate after Roosevelt passed from the scene.[61] A major element in the coalition with great power in Congress—the southern Democrats—contained many anti–New Dealers, unhappy with the new relations between Democrats and Negroes and with many of the economic policies that seemed to threaten important economic interests in the South. At least as early as 1936, some southern voters—those in North Carolina, for example—when given a choice between pro- and anti–New Deal Democrats chose the latter and sent to Congress men who recognized that their political futures did not demand that they follow the lead of the President. Throughout the late 1930's and beyond many southern Democrats openly rebelled against Democratic presidents, looking upon their domestic programs as betraying the traditions of the party.

The unstable character of the Democracy presented a situation that Republicans could and did exploit by accepting New Deal policies and practices that were attractive to northern urban groups and, at the same time, appealing to southern resentments and other anti–New Deal sentiments. Although a difficult game, the Republicans played it with some success. From 1940 on, some of Roosevelt's urban supporters switched to the Republican party. As time passed, Republicans also made impressive gains in the South.[62]

61. See White, *The Making of the President, 1960.* p. 435.

62. *Ibid.*, pp. 243–44, 274, 287, 425, 430, 431, 434; Lubell, *The Future of American Politics*, pp. 239, 256, 263–64; Johnson *1600 Pennsylvania Avenue*, p. 83; Elmer L. Puryear, *Democratic Party Dissension in North Carolina* (Chapel Hill, N.C., 1962), chap. ix; Key, *Southern Politics in State and Nation*, pp. 255, 259, 329, 330, 361–62, 367, 472; Heard, *A Two-Party South?* pp. 18–19, 64–65, 151–53; Dewey W. Grantham, Jr., "An American Politics for the South," in Charles Grier Sellers, Jr. (ed.), *The Southerner as American* (Chapel

Finally, attention should be called to Lubell's suggestion about the class orientation of American politics. Although a revolution supposedly took place under Roosevelt, American politics maintained its middle-class character. The people who flocked to Roosevelt's colors did so in hopes of acquiring a middle-class standard of living. His programs helped many of them realize their ambitions and much of their political activity in the prosperous days after World War II sought to protect what they had gained. As the groups achieved middle-class status, they produced their own economic resources for political campaigns and their own middle-class men to lead them.[63] The New Deal expanded the middle class as it enlarged organizations.

As the 1930's moved forward, business leaders found themselves operating in a rapidly altering situation. The depression challenged their prestige; the rise of big government and big labor threatened their profits, power, and status. A half century earlier, business had initiated the development of collectivist capitalism. Now the great promoters of change were working in other sectors of American life, bringing them into conformity with the "bigness" that had earlier become a characteristic of so much of the business world and thereby affecting the position of businessmen in major ways.

Perhaps business leaders could have avoided the changes in their relations with the government and with their workers if they could have avoided the sharp decline in their

---

Hill, N.C., 1960), pp. 162–67; Dahl, *Who Governs?* pp. 45, 50–51, 57–59, 110; Tatum, *The Changed Political Thought of the Negro*, pp. 138–41, 163–65, 180, 182, 184–85. For the beginnings of "modern" Republicanism see Donald R. McCoy, "Alfred M. Landon and the Presidential Campaign of 1936," *Mid-America*, XLII (1960), 195–218; McSeveney, "The Michigan Gubernatorial Campaign of 1938," 126–27 and Donald Bruce Johnson, *The Republican Party and Wendell Willkie* (Urbana, Ill., 1960).

63. Lubell, *The Future of American Politics*, pp. 85, 232–34; Johnson, *1600 Pennsylvania Avenue*, pp. 77–80.

prestige. "In 1929 business, particularly big business," writes Thomas C. Cochran, "enjoyed a degree of public approval unique in American history." Then came the crash and the depression and the growth of "an attitude of greater distrust of both business honesty and ability than had characterized any previous period. . . ." The public relations of one industry—electrical utilities—declined "to a lower level, with the possible exception of the railroads in the 1880's and 1890's, than any other industry experienced at any time in American history." [64] To businessmen, this cataclysmic change in their status was bewildering. "We did not make the depression," they protested. To be distrusted and to be forced on the defensive were puzzling experiences for men who were confident that they had been giving good service to the public and their employees and that only a few businessmen deserved criticism.[65] Now they found the public and their employees convinced that the old leaders were unreliable and that government and unions must therefore become more important.

In the new situation the government played a competitive role. Banks and insurance companies interested in making loans and investments faced competition from government agencies, especially the large and active Reconstruction Finance Corporation. (Some compensation was provided by the great increase in government bonds, available chiefly as a consequence of New Deal spending. Insurance companies added heavily to their holdings of these secure, tax exempt, but low-yield, papers.)[66] Many executives in the

64. Thomas C. Cochran, *The American Business System: A Historical Perspective, 1900–1955* (Cambridge, 1957), p. 140; Forrest McDonald, *Let There be Light: The Electric Utility Industry in Wisconsin, 1881–1955* (Madison, Wis., 1957), p. 305.

65. Raymond C. Miller, *Killowatts at Work: A History of the Detroit Edison Co.* (Detroit, 1957), pp. 333, 353–54.

66. N. S. B. Gras, *Business and Capitalism: An Introduction to Business History* (New York, 1939), pp. 323, 325; Shepard B. Clough, *A Century of Life Insurance: A History of the Mutual Life Insurance Company of New York, 1843–1943* (New York, 1946), pp. 253–54,

insurance industry complained bitterly about social security. "The old idea of individual responsibility is being slowly undermined by those who have little of the world's goods," an economist for the Travelers company maintained. He wished that everyone was obliged to read William Graham Sumner's "What Social Classes Owe Each Other." (A few companies, however, recognized quickly that the government's program could help them sell insurance.)[67] Electrical power companies encountered government producers, like the Tennessee Valley Authority, and co-operatives subsidized by the REA. To one utility executive, the building of a co-operative in his area seemed one of those irrational things that human beings sometimes did, a form of behavior he distrusted and could not understand. He looked upon the co-operative not only as an economic and engineering monstrosity, doomed to fail, but as a blemish on the landscape, a highly conspicuous suggestion that somewhere his company had been remiss in its duty. In Nebraska, the private companies were driven completely from the field, replaced throughout the state by public power after Nebraskans concluded that their principal private enterprise—agriculture—could be helped if, in the matter of electricity, public enterprise were substituted for private.[68]

302–4, 308–9, 311, 314, 316–17; Marquis James, *The Metropolitan Life: A Study in Business Growth* (New York, 1947), pp. 287–88, 298, 305, 306, 312, 318; J. Carlyle Buley, *The American Life Convention, 1906–1952: A Study in the History of Life Insurance* (New York, 1953), pp. 783–84, 789, 808; Harold F. Williamson and Orange A. Smalley, *Northwestern Mutual Life: A Century of Trusteeship* (Evanston, Ill., 1957), p. 258. On the RFC's operations under Roosevelt see Schlesinger, *The Coming of the New Deal*, chap. xxvi.

67. Buley, *The American Life Convention*, pp. 709–10, 787, 793, 818; James, *Metropolitan Life*, pp. 337–38; Clough, *A Century of Life Insurance*, pp. 283, 285. See "The Birth of Social Security" in Schlesinger, *The Coming of the New Deal*, chap. xviii.

68. McDonald, *Let There be Light*, pp. 319–20, 358–59; Miller, *Kilowatts at Work*, pp. 240–42; W. Stewart Nelson, "The Private Companies and a Public Power Paradox," *Business History Review* XXXV (1961), 532–49. On TVA and REA see Schlesinger, *The Coming of the New Deal*, chap. xix and *The Politics of Upheaval*, chap. xx.

The new situation also brought more government regulations. The New Deal, for example, imposed federal controls on the investment process, forced reductions in the size of public-utility holding companies, and employed old regulatory powers more rigorously. Such actions as these compelled business firms to alter their behavior in a number of ways: henceforth, they provided more information for investors, enlarged and improved their accounting methods, expanded their legal departments, changed their depreciation and dividend policies, participated more actively in business associations, sent new representatives to Washington, severed ties with other firms, and the like.[69] Following 1935, new and effective federal regulations for the rapidly growing trucking business promoted stability for they limited competition by controlling rates and entry into the industry. A similar tale can be told for oil where leading firms demanded regulations, triumphed over the opponents of "monopoly" and government "interference," and obtained programs that promoted stability and efficiency.[70]

The enlargement of government plus the efforts to base taxation on the ability-to-pay principle forced business firms

69. McDonald, *Let There be Light*, pp. 318–20; Miller, *Kilowatts at Work*, pp. 230, 360–61; Henrietta Larson and Kenneth Wiggins Porter, *History of Humble Oil and Refining Company: A Study in Industrial Growth* (New York, 1959), pp. 337, 340, 525, 551–52; Williamson and Smalley, *Northwestern Mutual Life*, pp. 247–55; John L. Loos, *Oil on Stream: A History of Interstate Oil Pipe Line Company, 1909–1959* (Baton Rouge, La., 1959), pp. 318, 351; Gertrude G. Schroeder, *The Growth of Major Steel Companies* (Baltimore, 1953), p. 27; James Don Edwards, "Public Accounting in the United States from 1928 to 1951," *Business History Review*, XXX (1956), 470. On various New Deal regulatory programs see Schlesinger, *The Coming of the New Deal*, chaps. xxvii, xxix and *The Politics of Upheaval*, chap. xvii.

70. Merrill J. Roberts, "The Motor Transportation Revolution," *Business History Review*, XXX (1956), 78, 84, 85; Wayne G. Broehl, Jr., *Trucks . . . Trouble . . . and Triumph: The Norwalk Truck Line Company* (New York, 1954), pp. 38–41, 52–54; Larson and Porter, *History of Humble Oil and Refining Company*, pp. 455–56, 478, 487, 511, 668–71; Paul H. Giddens, *Standard Oil Company (Indiana): Oil Pioneers in the Middle West* (New York, 1955), chap. xx.

to pay higher taxes. In 1931, Humble Pipe Line Company, to take one example, paid no federal corporation and income taxes, while in 1941 it paid well over $3,000,000 for these purposes. In 1925, the tax bill for Sears, Roebuck and Company amounted to something more than $4,000,000, 17 per cent of the Company's net income before taxes. In 1947, the bill exceeded $100,000,000, 49 per cent of net income before taxes. In the steel industry, the relative proportion of income absorbed by income and profits taxes, after falling gradually during the 1920's, rose sharply during the 1930's.[71] Writing of the new situation, W. Lloyd Warner suggests that

> if the entrepreneur succeeds in making a profit, an increasing share is taken from him. The income, excess profit, and many other taxes now take a large part of what the enterpriser makes, to be used for the collectivity and to make it possible for his powerful rival, the huge hierarchical government structure, to be financed.[72]

For many firms, the 1930's also brought new and often effective challenges from the rapidly growing labor movement. Most managers still looked upon unions as threats to their "right" to control their firms and insisted that management alone should decide who was to be paid how much, who was to be promoted, demoted, hired, or fired, how much was to be produced, and what methods and machines were to be used. While some companies avoided organization of their workers by national unions and others adjusted easily to the new organizations, most business leaders found the rise of the labor movement highly per-

71. Larson and Porter, *History of Humble Oil and Pipe Line Company*, p. 525; Boris Emmet and John E. Jeuck, *Catalogues and Counters: A History of Sears, Roebuck and Company* (Chicago, 1950), p. 661; Schroeder, *The Growth of Major Steel Companies*, pp. 183–86. On the new taxes of 1935 see Schlesinger, *The Politics of Upheaval*, pp. 325–34.

72. *The Corporation in the Emergent American Society*, p. 31.

plexing and undesirable, a challenge to their belief that they had always taken good care of their employees. For workers to turn to "outsiders" seemed an act of disloyalty and ingratitude. Some executives looked upon Labor Relations Board elections as tests of loyalty and of confidence in management; thus, elections that favored unions were painful and distressing as well as surprising experiences, difficult to explain. Often the only explanation that satisfied was that the workers had been led astray by the organizers and had switched the type of leadership on which they were dependent. Forced increasingly after 1937 to discard old antiunion practices and accept collective bargaining, some managers attempted to build constructive and harmonious relationships with organized labor while others remained unreconciled, bargaining, when necessary, at arm's length. By the end of the decade, few businessmen had concluded that unions were good for business; most of them attempted to limit the scope of bargaining, to bargain with local rather than national unions, and to bring union activities under government control; and many hoped that collective bargaining would soon pass from the scene. Management's acceptance of the practice as necessary and good lay some distance in the future.[73]

73. John S. Ewing and Nancy P. Norton, *Broadlooms and Businessmen: A History of the Bigelow-Sanford Carpet Company* (Cambridge, 1955), pp. 271–73, 291–94; Thomas R. Navin, *The Whitin Machine Works since 1851: A Textile Machinery Company in an Industrial Village* (Cambridge, 1950), pp. 438, 444, 445, 465–67; Harold F. Williamson and Kenneth H. Meyers, II, *Designed for Digging: The First 75 Years of Bucyrus-Erie Company* (Evanston, Ill., 1955), pp. 237–44, 277–83; Howard F. Bennett, *Precision Power: The First Half Century of Bodine Electric Company* (New York, 1959), p. 294; Giddens, *Standard Oil Company*, pp. 567–71; Loos, *Oil on Stream*, pp. 171–73, 189–95, 269–72, 349; Larson and Porter, *History of Humble Oil and Refining Company*, pp. 362–63, 367–68, 375–76; Miller, *Kilowatts at Work*, pp. 385–90; Wayne G. Broehl, Jr., *Precision Valley: The Machine Tool Companies of Springfield, Vermont* (Englewood Cliffs, N.J., 1959), pp. 140–41, 186–88; 205; Richard C. Wilcock, "Industrial Management's Policies toward Unionism," in Derber and Young (eds.), *Labor and the New Deal*, pp. 311–13; Millis and Brown, *From the Wagner Act to Taft-Hartley*, pp. 252–54.

A few business leaders both welcomed the New Deal and maintained rather friendly attitudes toward it. Although noting that "a powerful section of business" stopped supporting Roosevelt, and seeing the New Deal by the end of 1935 as "a coalition of the non-business groups, mobilized to prevent the domination of the country by the business community," Arthur Schlesinger, Jr. calls attention to certain "dissident businessmen" in this coalition. These businessmen "felt themselves handicapped by Wall Street domination of the money market," and they included "some of the ablest entrepreneurs in the country . . . like Joseph P. Kennedy who invested in both new regions and new industries and was willing to bet on the nation's capacity to resume economic growth." [74] Robert E. Wood of Sears, Roebuck and Co. applauded the NRA and government aid to the unemployed and the farmer. Wood was convinced that the New Deal was helping the country and thus was benefiting his company. "I am one of the businessmen who, selfishly perhaps (because my business is greatly dependent on the welfare of the farmer) but nevertheless, consistently, has supported the Agricultural Adjustment Act," he informed Roosevelt late in 1934. Henry I. Harriman, president of the United States Chamber of Commerce during the early days of the New Deal and a key promoter then of such programs as production control for agriculture, praised Roosevelt as late as 1940 for providing the nation "for the first time" with "a wise and constructive farm policy."

Even these men, however, had doubts. Wood complained especially about tax and labor policies and advisers who seemed dangerously radical, and Harriman criticized Roosevelt for lacking "the strong conviction that a sound but venturesome business is essential to the proper development

74. *The Politics of Upheaval,* pp. 411, 443, 586.

of America." [75] To these friendly eyes, the New Deal seemed something less than the perfect servant of American business.

Some business leaders opposed the New Deal from the very beginning. Henry Ford resisted the NRA's efforts to produce a variety of changes and received praise from businessmen who saw him as a symbol of opposition to big government.[76] More typical were the businessmen who at first welcomed the NRA, viewing it chiefly as a way to escape the price-depressing competition of the early 1930's, and then became disillusioned with it, some because it favored big over small business and others because they believed it exalted non-business groups. The United States Chamber of Commerce, an early supporter, soon became quite critical of the NRA for giving too much power to government and unions. This business group wanted a program that would allow each of the trade associations to control its industry.[77] Obviously, the depression had not effected major changes in the thought of most business leaders. They remained highly critical of government and labor power and simply wanted help in their efforts to control the economy, or at least their own firms.[78]

With the majority of Americans rejecting such business theories, most business leaders from 1934 on turned to an American tradition, embraced it passionately, insisted

75. Richard S. Kirkendall, "The New Deal Professors and the Politics of Agriculture" (Ph.D. dissertation, University of Wisconsin, 1958), pp. 145–49, 217, 392–93. Emmet and Jeuck, *Catalogues and Counters*, pp. 333, 334, 569–70, 615–16.

76. Sidney Fine, "The Ford Motor Company and the N.R.A.," *Business History Review*, XXXII (1958), 354–57, 363, 385.

77. William H. Wilson, "How the Chamber of Commerce Viewed the NRA: A Reexamination," *Mid-America*, XLIV (1962), 95–108; Schlesinger, *The Coming of the New Deal*, chaps. vi–x and *The Politics of Upheaval*, chap. xv; Bennett, *Precision Power*, p. 125; Broehl, *Precision Valley*, pp. 138–40.

78. James Warren Prothro, *The Dollar Decade: Business Ideas in the 1920's* (Baton Rouge, La., 1954), pp. 212 ff.

that the New Deal was "un-American," and worked to convert their fellow citizens to this point of view. The tradition was a form of conservatism that had taken shape late in the nineteenth century and had been used to combat challenges from reform and labor movements in the days of the Populists, the Progressives, and Samuel Gompers. Now, working through various organizations led by the Liberty League, business leaders and their political allies spelled out and publicized the nineteenth-century philosophy that stressed the free individual, limited government, natural laws of economics, property rights, business success, and the importance of "practical experience." Not only was the philosophy an old one and an authentic American tradition, but the behavior of its advocates harmonized with traditional political methods. The Liberty League was not a secret conspiracy of men of great wealth seeking a strong man to protect their property but simply a well-financed pressure group that preached to the American people, failed in its mission, and quietly collapsed.

Although the philosophy and methods were not new, there was a novel feature in the activities of the social groups comprising the Liberty League. In the past these groups had been the objects of attack by protest elements; now they themselves formed the loudest protest movement. This difference pointed to a more significant one. Earlier, the major advocates of change had been the builders of American business; now those roles were being played by the builders of big government and big labor, and their activities implied that the American people could no longer depend so heavily on the old leaders. Their prestige, profits, and power—all three were affected by the changes taking place, and all three were defended by a philosophy that attacked "bigness" in government and labor, although not in business.[79]

79. Frederick Rudolph, "The American Liberty League, 1933–1940," *American Historical Review*, LVI (1950), 21, 32–33; Morton

Business leaders by no means devoted themselves exclusively to efforts to propagate an individualistic philosophy, a creed contradicted by the corporate nature of the economic life of many of its proponents. Taking steps that were more in line with the corporate aspect, they improved techniques designed to convince their workers and the public that they could rely on businessmen. Personnel programs were developed which aimed in part at convincing workers that they had no need to turn to other organizations. Public relations programs were expanded to show the ways in which the system of private enterprise and particular industries and firms served the nation. Early in the 1930's, a leading student of the corporation insisted that the powerful managers of the giant corporations should develop a broader conception of their responsibilities and suggested that government should provide some of the pressure needed to force that development.[80] Now, under the pressures of the decade, corporate leaders more readily proclaimed that they had responsibilities to the whole community.

Improvement and enlargement of personnel and public-relations programs were important and permanent changes in the business community during the 1930's. Even here, however, the degree of change should not be exaggerated. The programs were not completely new nor simply responses to the depression and the New Deal; the programs had been developing for a generation. After all, managers before the 1930's had had to face up to reform and labor movements as well as the internal problems involved in

---

Keller, *In Defense of Yesterday: James M. Beck and the Politics of Conservatism, 1861–1936* (New York, 1958); Schlesinger, *The Coming of the New Deal*, chap. xxx; George Wolfskill, *The Revolt of the Conservatives: A History of the American Liberty League, 1934–1940* (Boston, 1962); Galbraith, *American Capitalism*, pp. 80–81, 136, 151; Clinton Rossiter, *Conservatism in America: The Thankless Persuasion* (2d ed.; New York, 1962), p. 161.

80. Richard S. Kirkendall, "A. A. Berle, Jr.: Student of the Corporation, 1917–1932," *Business History Review*, XXXV (1961), 56–58.

operating large-scale organizations; and these managers had developed a body of ideas and techniques on which they could draw to deal with the changes of the 1930's. The pressures of that decade formed a very important part, but only a part, of an extensive and long-term series of pressures which forced corporate executives to think in terms of broad responsibilities, a significant feature of a collectivistic type of capitalism.[81]

And what should be said of the central figure in American history during the 1930's? Franklin D. Roosevelt provides a major illustration of the need to consider both continuity and change in an interpretation of the decade. First of all, he was a product of the Progressive movement. As such, he believed in promoting change and in using government for that purpose. At the same time, as a progressive, he also believed in maintaining ties with the past. He valued reform as a means not only for bringing about improvements but also for preventing radical developments.

Entering politics in 1910 as a successful candidate for the New York Senate, Roosevelt's reform notions then

81. Morrell Heald, "Management's Responsibility to Society: The Growth of an Idea," *ibid.*, XXXI (1957), 375–84; Norman J. Wood, "Industrial Relations Practices of American Management, 1900–1933," *ibid.*, XXXIV (1960), 404, 418, 420; Henry Eilbirt, "The Development of Personnel Management in the United States," *ibid.*, XXXIII (1959), 345–64; Eilbirt, "Twentieth Century Beginnings in Employee Counseling," *ibid.*, XXXI (1957), 311–22; Heald, "Business Thought in the Twenties: Social Responsibility," *American Quarterly*, XIII (1961), 126–39; Loren Baritz, *The Servants of Power: A History of the Use of Social Science in American Industry* (Middletown, Conn., 1960), esp. chap. vii; Cochran, *The American Business System*, pp. 67–78, 154–57, 162–63, 184–87, 194–201; Otis Pease, *The Responsibilities of American Advertising: Private Control and Public Influence, 1920–1940* (New Haven, 1958), pp. 32–33, 115–16, 139–41; Emmet and Jeuck, *Catalogues and Counters*, pp. 587–601; Larson and Porter, *History of Humble Oil and Refining Company*, pp. 344–45; Bennett, *Precision Power* pp. 136–39, 160; Evelyn H. Knowlton, *Pepperell's Progress: History of a Cotton Textile Company, 1844–1945* (Cambridge, 1948), pp. 363 ff. Ralph M. Hower, *The History of an Advertising Agency: N. W. Ayer and Son at Work, 1869–1949* (Cambridge, 1949), pp. 152, 175–76.

were limited to suggestions concerning political changes, although at Harvard he had been exposed to other varieties of progressivism. During the next decade, under the impact of his experiences in the New York legislature and the Wilson administration and his contact with Theodore Roosevelt, Gifford Pinchot, and other Progressives, Franklin D. Roosevelt's position expanded. Quite naturally, in view of his life at the family estate in Hyde Park, he first developed an active and strong interest in conservation and measures that would benefit the farmer. A concern about the problems of urban workers developed more slowly, but his job as Assistant Secretary of Navy, which brought him into contact with business and labor leaders, helped him shape ideas about urban groups. By the end of the Progressive era, Roosevelt was advocating the use of government to reform social and economic conditions.[82] During the 1920's, he tried to impose progressive orientation as well as unity upon the badly divided Democratic party, developed a strong interest in public power and farm relief, maintained an interest in such matters as social-welfare legislation, and continued to reject the conservative notion that businessmen should make the essential decisions in America and that government should not "interfere" with the operations of the business system.[83]

From 1929 to 1933, while he served as governor of New York and campaigned for the presidency, Roosevelt's progressivism grew even though, like most progressives as

82. Frank Freidel, *Franklin D. Roosevelt: The Apprenticeship* (Boston, 1952), chaps. iv–xii; Daniel R. Fusfeld, *The Economic Thought of Franklin D. Roosevelt and the Origins of the New Deal* (New York, 1956), chaps. ii–v; Schlesinger, *The Crisis of the Old Order*, pp. 331–67; Freidel, *Franklin D. Roosevelt: The Ordeal* (Boston, 1954), chap. v.

83. *Ibid.*, chaps. ix, xii–xvi; Schlesinger, *The Crisis of the Old Order*, pp. 373–85; Fusfeld, *The Economic Thought of Franklin D. Roosevelt and the Origins of the New Deal*, chaps. vi–viii; James MacGregor Burns, *Roosevelt: The Lion and the Fox* (New York, 1956), pp. 83–89.

well as the conservatives, he could not accept the "Keynesian" ideas about government spending that would later be associated with his administration.[84] During these years he battled for measures that Progressives had advocated for a generation and that would become a part of the New Deal: conservation, government regulation of the economy, and social-welfare legislation. He also experimented with methods, such as the use of "service intellectuals" to develop and administer programs, that reformers like Robert M. La Follette had employed earlier and that Roosevelt would use in Washington.[85] In addition, he championed more recent additions to the progressive agenda that would be involved in the New Deal, such as public power, land-planning, farm relief, old-age pensions, and unemployment insurance. He took a step toward the relief programs of the New Deal by calling for state aid to the unemployed, a clear denial of individual and local responsibility that represented an application of progressivism's faith in government to the special problems of a depression. And he revealed the same confusion concerning the best way to deal with big business that had been present in the days of Theodore Roosevelt and Woodrow Wilson and would form a part of the Washington scene after 1932.[86] By that time, Roosevelt believed that the private enterprise—private profit system should be retained, that "its operations were not always benevolent

84. Fusfeld, *The Economic Thought of Franklin D. Roosevelt and the Origins of the New Deal*, pp. 4, 36–37, 180–82, 203, 205–6, 222, 254.

85. Richard S. Kirkendall, "Franklin D. Roosevelt and the Service Intellectual," *Mississippi Valley Historical Review*, XLIX (1962) 456–71.

86. Freidel, *The Triumph;* Bernard Bellush, *Franklin D. Roosevelt as Governor of New York* (New York, 1955); Schlesinger, *The Crisis of the Old Order*, pp. 386–403, 413–55; Tugwell, *The Democratic Roosevelt*, pp. 214 ff., 221, 230–31, 246–47; Fusfeld, *The Economic Thought of Franklin D. Roosevelt and the Origins of the New Deal*, chaps. ix–xvi; Gertrude Almy Slichter, "Franklin D. Roosevelt's Farm Policy as Governor of New York State, 1928–1932," *Agricultural History*, XXXIII (1959), 168–76; Slichter, "Franklin D. Roosevelt and the Farm Problem, 1929–1932," *Mississippi Valley Historical Review*, XLIII (1956), 238–58.

and did not always promote the general welfare," and, thus, that those operations should "be improved and supplemented by state and Federal government efforts whenever the need arose." [87]

Throughout the pre-1933 period, Roosevelt combined pragmatic methods with guiding ideals much as he did during his presidential years. He worked with as many groups as possible, seeking their support as well as their ideas; tested suggestions to see if they worked in practice; and rejected the doctrines that advocated the country's relying exclusively on either private or public enterprise.[88] At the same time, the basic ideals that had long been a part of American reform thought influenced him. In his use of government he respected the dignity of the human personality and sought to protect and enlarge freedom and opportunity for individuals.[89]

The intellectual position that Roosevelt brought to Washington placed a high value on continuity as well as on change. Eager to avoid a revolution and convinced, as Theodore Roosevelt had also been, that radical changes could grow out of situations like the depression, F.D.R. insisted that reform could prevent such changes from taking place—that reform had a conservative function. To preserve capitalism and democracy in a world in which both were being rejected, statesmen needed to reform capitalism in ways that would persuade Americans that they had no need to turn to other systems.[90]

87. Fusfeld, *The Economic Thought of Franklin D. Roosevelt and the Origins of the New Deal*, p. 251.

88. Schlesinger, "Sources of the New Deal," reprinted in Abraham S. Eisenstadt (ed.), *American History: Recent Interpretations; Book II: Since 1865* (New York, 1962), pp. 344–50; Kirkendall, "Franklin D. Roosevelt and the Service Intellectual," 459–62.

89. Clarke A. Chambers, "F.D.R., Pragmatist-Idealist: An Essay in Historiography," *Pacific Northwest Quarterly*, LII (1961), 53–55.

90. Thomas H. Greer, *What Roosevelt Thought: The Social and Political Ideas of Franklin D. Roosevelt* (East Lansing, Mich., 1958), pp. 207–12; Burns, *Roosevelt*, chap. xii; Einaudi, *The Roosevelt Revolution*, pp. 96–97, 269–71, 340–42, 360.

The failure of the Socialist party, the leading radical organization in America, testified to the success of Roosevelt's methods. It is ironical that, as the historian of that party has pointed out, "the party of Debs which had predicted the collapse of American capitalism, itself collapsed during the worst crisis American capitalism ever had." When called upon to explain this, the party's leader, Norman Thomas, suggested: "What cut the ground out pretty completely from under us was this. It was Roosevelt in a word. You don't need anything more." And Professor Shannon agrees that Roosevelt "did undercut most of their actual and potential support. The story of the decline of the Socialist party since 1933 is, for the most part, the story of the political success of the New Deal." [91] In short, Roosevelt both changed and preserved American capitalism. In the process, he strengthened faith in American democracy by promoting reform programs that encouraged Americans to believe that their political system could make their economic system serve their interests.[92]

The watershed concept, as well as others that emphasize breaks with the past, should be avoided in interpretations of the 1930's. The Great Depression and the New Deal created major changes in American life but also maintained important connections with an earlier America. The leading developments of the depression decade which are associated with the New Deal should not be viewed as radical new beginnings in American history but chiefly as significant parts of a large-scale transformation of American

91. David A. Shannon, *The Socialist Party of America: A History* (New York, 1955), pp. 229, 235, 250. See also Murray B. Seidler, *Norman Thomas: Respectable Rebel* (Syracuse, 1961), p. 119 and Donald R. McCoy, *Angry Voices: Left-of-Center Politics in the New Deal Era* (Lawrence, Kan., 1958), pp. 191–93.

92. For a quite different view of Roosevelt's relations with democracy see Edgar Eugene Robinson, *The Roosevelt Leadership, 1933–1945* (Philadelphia, 1955).

capitalism that had been under way for at least half a century before the 1930's. During those pre-New Deal years, American business lost its individualistic character and, although some unsuccessful attempts were made to restore that, somewhat more successful efforts sought to bring government and various economic groups into harmony with the collectivistic trends. Then in the years of the depression and the New Deal, big government became firmly established, promoted the rise of big labor, and conducted similar, fairly successful efforts designed to get the farmer to conform to the new type of capitalism. Big business lost some of its power but little of its size, and so Americans emerged from the decade with an economy dominated by the interplay among large public and private organizations and with lower-income groups hoping and expecting to improve their status within the system, not to destroy the system—which, in later years, became even more firmly established.[93]

93. For discussions related to the main thesis of this essay see Galbraith, *American Capitalism*; Kenneth E. Boulding, *The Organizational Revolution: A Study in the Ethics of Economic Organization* (New York, 1953); Calvin B. Hoover, "The American Organizational Economy," reprinted in Eisenstadt (ed.), *American History*, pp. 480–90; Rowland Berthoff, "The American Social Order: A Conservative Hypothesis," *American Historical Review*, LXV (1960), 495–514 and Warner, *The Corporation in the Emergent American Society*.

Continuity and Change in Government-Business Relations

ARTHUR M. JOHNSON

ADJUSTMENT of public and private economic interests lies at the very heart of much of American history, especially since the turn of the century. The results have given the economy and the society many of their distinctive characteristics and have produced a unique amalgam of government and business functions and responsibilities. The task of identifying and explaining the key elements of continuity and change in these relationships is a difficult one, and many paths are open. Here, we shall look at government and business in terms of decision-making that affects the economic life of the nation, seeking to differentiate between the establishment of principles, which constitute the framework of the basic relationship, and their implementation, which determines specific relationships and their consequences. The analysis will be in terms of the federal government and large-scale, corporate enterprise, while stressing that the results of adjustment between the two have had major implications for private decision-making in all kinds of business, large and small, which in the aggregate can be conveniently called the "business system."

Given the rapidity and complexity of technological advances, the size and power of business units engaged in mass production and distribution, the increased demands of non-business groups on government, the interrelatedness and interdependence of national and international economic activity, and the economic and military crises of this century, the maintenance of a tolerable balance between government and business decision-making for the economy is a tribute to the processes that have facilitated change. Despite a marked increase in governmental powers and functions, the business decision-maker has remained a key figure in the economy. A remarkably complex set of governmental processes—political, legislative, administrative, and legal—and equally complex processes of manipulation and adaptation by business have provided continuity while accommodating major changes in government-business relations. The purpose of this essay is to examine some of these processes, particularly as they have been revealed in adjustments made to three major challenges to business decision-making in the economy: the decline of price competition and the concentration of economic power associated with large-scale production; the collapse of the economy under the impact of business depression; and the challenge of global war and continued defense preparedness based on fast-moving technology.

At the beginning of the twentieth century, the American businessman was at the height of his power. His decisions, made free from governmental restraints or with positive governmental aid and encouragement, had revolutionized the economy and with it the society. As an industrial power, the United States had risen in a few short decades to challenge and then overtake the leaders of the Old World. Large aggregations of capital had begun to characterize key sectors of the economy such as oil, steel, meat-packing, and railroads. At the end of the nineteenth century, a great wave of mergers had begun to concentrate control of far-flung enterprises, and the movement was continuing unabated.[1] Through concentration of control, business sought by its own devices to achieve a measure of stability and certainty that competition in the classical sense would not permit. Overproduction, excessive competition, and the heavy capital investment in fixed facilities contributed to this movement, which was replacing the entrepreneur with the financier as the leading figure in big business.

As business units had become larger and their ownership more concentrated, governmental functions had remained static or had atrophied. The heads of major enterprises seemingly possessed resources that challenged those of the head of the federal government. The reversal of their respective roles in the years that followed was a triumph of pragmatic processes that confirmed the principle of government's supremacy without destroying the business system.

Change was in the air in 1900, but the direction that change would take was not yet clear. Reviewing the work of the Fifty-sixth Congress, the *Commercial and Financial Chronicle* took some pleasure in noting the lack of accomplishment. While regretting that nothing had been done to reform the consular service or to reduce war-revenue measures, the *Chronicle* was pleased that such "ill-judged or half-considered measures" as the ship-subsidy bill, antitrust legislation, a bill for a new cabinet-rank Department of Commerce, and the Nicaraguan Canal bill had been left to their just deserts. Some of these, the *Chronicle* felt, represented serious departures from traditional policy and reflected the restlessness and agitation of the times.[2] *Iron Age,* journal of the iron and steel industry, lamented the

1. An analysis of the turn-of-the-century merger movement and its successors is in Ralph L. Nelson, *Merger Movements in American Industry, 1895–1956* (Princeton, N.J., 1959).

2. *Commercial and Financial Chronicle,* June 9, 1900, p. 1121.

trend toward paternalism and nationalization seen in various proposals or enactments affecting railroads, telephone and telegraph, savings banks, and in aids to labor, such as workmen's compensation and old-age assistance. As practiced abroad and advocated by American economists, reformers, and even government reports, such measures were denounced by *Iron Age* as representing a "pronounced shift to socialism" and the first step toward "demoralization of the individual." [3] These views of leading business publications, which were not atypical, suggest the range of problems that confronted a newly industrialized nation and the position of many businessmen with respect to them.

The basic question was how the gains of large-scale enterprise could be preserved without the abuse of private economic power. Or, in different terms, how could concentration of ownership and control in basic industries be reconciled with traditional American values associated with decentralized business decision-making and economic opportunity for the individual?

More than a decade earlier the nation had adopted two basic approaches to this problem: regulation of railroads as an answer to the absence of competition or the presence of uneconomic competition, and punitive action for restraints on competition. In the interim, however, the triumph of the political and legislative processes represented by the Act to Regulate Interstate Commerce (1887) and the Sherman Antitrust Act (1890) had been rendered largely impotent. The former was incapacitated by court decisions depriving the Interstate Commerce Commission of power over rail rates. [4] The latter was hamstrung by the ruling in the E. C.

3. "Paternalism and Industrial Development," *Iron Age*, June 28, 1900, p. 17.

4. Following a series of reverses at the hands of the Supreme Court, the ICC announced in its 1897 annual report: "The people should no longer look to this commission for a protection which it is powerless to extend."

Knight case (1895) that deprived the antitrust law of effect with respect to "close" combinations or mergers, though they could suppress competition just as readily as "loose" combinations or overt conspiracies in restraint of trade with which the courts dealt harshly.[5]

The establishment of a principle through legislation and the watering-down of it in implementation has been a key characteristic of changing government-business relations. At the moment a major statute affecting business is signed, and perhaps for a time thereafter, it may seem to the public, and to businessmen, that a significant change in government-business relations has occurred. Frequently, however, the results are long in coming, and then they may come in quite unanticipated ways. Thus, businessmen are often more alarmed at the prospect of change involving new governmental functions than the results warrant. For example, Charles E. Perkins, president of the Chicago, Burlington & Quincy Railroad, had been greatly alarmed about the passage and potential consequences of the Interstate Commerce Act, which he believed violated management's decision-making prerogatives. He communicated these feelings to stockholders through the medium of the railroad's annual reports and, apparently, directly to corporation lawyer Richard Olney. Writing to Perkins in 1892, Olney had advised against any move to abolish the ICC. With real insight into the nature of the pragmatic governmental process, he wrote:

> The Commission, as its functions have now been limited by the Courts, is, or can be made of great use to the railroads. It satisfies the popular clamor for government supervision of railroads at the same time that the supervision is almost entirely nominal.

5. Merle Fainsod, Lincoln Gordon, and Joseph C. Palamountain, Jr., *Government and the American Economy* (3d ed.; New York, 1959), pp. 451–52.

Further, the older such a commission gets to be, the more inclined it will be found to be to take the business and railroad view of things. It thus becomes a sort of barrier between the railroad corporations and the people and a sort of protection against hasty and crude legislation hostile to railroad interests.[6]

Many critics of the administrative process would find little difficulty, though small comfort, in agreeing with Olney's statement of its weaknesses.

Business adaptation to the Supreme Court's interpretation of the Sherman Act was equally pragmatic and challenged the very purposes for which the Act had been adopted. The alliance between government and business was so close during this period that the same Olney as Attorney General, after the government's setback in the Knight case, declared that the outcome only demonstrated the futility of initiating such cases.[7] Building on this attitude and the Supreme Court's position on "close" combinations, businessmen and financiers moved into a great merger movement free from the fear of antitrust prosecution.[8]

The rising public demand that government demonstrate its supremacy over, rather than subservience to, business found a receptive response in Theodore Roosevelt, who entered the White House by accident in 1901. No enemy of big business as such, he recognized that failure to meet this demand for government action could result in big business

6. Quoted in James M. Smith and Paul L. Murphy (eds.), *Liberty and Justice, a Historical Record of American Constitutional Development* (New York, 1958), pp. 292–93.

7. Asserting that he had anticipated the decision (which in part reflected poor handling of the government's case), Olney wrote that he had "taken the responsibility of not prosecuting under a law I believed to be no good" (quoted in Fainsod, Gordon, and Palamountain, *Government and the American Economy* [3d ed.], p. 450).

8. Noting that the Sherman Act had been deliberately allowed to become a "dead letter," the *United States Investor* (March 1, 1902, p. 381) declared: "Great industries have been built up in alleged contravention of dead letter laws, and upon the stability of these industries depends the welfare of thousands and millions of the people in the United States."

undermining the very system of private decision-making that had given it power. Thus he began early to talk about national control of corporations and revision of the tariff, without actively promoting legislation to accomplish either objective. On the other hand, by focusing public attention on specific issues of governmental versus business power, he created a favorable environment for executive, legislative, and judicial actions with respect to business. His task was to steer a middle course between pressures for drastic action and no action at all.

Roosevelt's basic strategy was to revive the antitrust law as a source of uncertainty for business and to strengthen the powers of the ICC. The former was accomplished when, on his initiative, the government launched a successful action against the Northern Securities Company, a railroad holding company in which J. P. Morgan, James J. Hill, E. H. Harriman, and other leading business and financial figures were prominent. The incredulity with which this attack was received by Morgan is reflected in the story that he suggested that his lawyer and Roosevelt's attorney general, Philander C. Knox, get together and settle the problem. Whether the story is apocryphal or not, it is in keeping with the comfortable relationship that had existed up to that time between business and government.[9]

In 1904 the Supreme Court sustained the government's contention that mere possession of power to suppress competition was sufficient to place the Northern Securities Company in violation of the Sherman Act.[10] This decision in conjunction with one rendered the following year against the meat-packers,[11] was sufficient to establish the new potency of the antitrust statute.

9. Morgan himself went to Washington to discuss the prosecution with Roosevelt. According to one report, "Mr. Morgan is a very sore man indeed. The attack on the Northern Securities Company has cut him to the quick."—*Ibid.*, March 29, 1902, pp. 574–75.

10. *Northern Securities Company* v. *U.S.*, 193 U.S. 197 (1904).

11. *Swift & Co.* v. *U.S.*, 196 U.S. 375 (1905).

Meantime, the administration had sought and obtained additional powers for the ICC. The Elkins Act of 1903 strengthened the rebating section of the Interstate Commerce Act, and in 1906 the Hepburn Amendment to the basic statute not only expanded the jurisdiction of the Commission but added to its powers, especially those relating to railroad rates. These legislative victories gave new importance to the administrative process as a means of exercising governmental supervision over business, thus setting a precedent that in subsequent decades became an increasingly important factor in government-business relations.[12] After the excitement engendered among railroad leaders and the public by the build-up to these measures was dissipated in legislative action, however, the process of adjustment settled down to the relative anonymity that characterizes the implementation of much legislation affecting business.

Having vindicated the antitrust principle, Roosevelt had no desire to implement it indiscriminately to destroy big business. Frankly contemptuous of the courts and fearful of their willingness to apply the statute literally to *"every combination"* in restraint of trade, whether meritorious (i. e., reasonable) or not (i. e., unreasonable), he sought to modify the law to place this discretion in the hands of an administrative body. His endeavor to shift power from one branch of the government to another ran into congressional opposition and popular allegiance to the Sherman Act as a statement of the nation's dedication to competition. Meanwhile, Roosevelt drew his own distinctions between "good" and "bad" trusts in selecting targets for prosecution. Thus Standard Oil found itself in the courts while United States

12. The most perceptive study of the Roosevelt strategy is John M. Blum, "Theodore Roosevelt and the Hepburn Act: Toward an Orderly System of Control," Elting E. Morison *et al.* (eds.), *The Letters of Theodore Roosevelt* (8 vols.; Cambridge, 1951-54), VI, pp. 1558-71.

Steel and International Harvester received the presidential blessing.[13] Undoubtedly the co-operation extended by top officials of the latter concerns in connection with Roosevelt's attempt to change the Sherman Act stood them in good stead. But even the managers of the steel corporation had acknowledged the new element of uncertainty under the antitrust law by consulting the President in advance on their proposed acquisition of the Tennessee Coal, Iron & Railroad Company.

Other legislation of this period, such as the Pure Food and Drug Act, and other presidential activity, such as intervention in the anthracite-coal strike, had implications for government-business relations; but Roosevelt's lasting contribution in this area was his emphasis on the *principle* of government's right and capacity to curb business. The assertion and illustration of the principle, even if the results were of a limited short-run nature, were sufficient to alert businessmen to a new form of uncertainty and to satisfy the public that government possessed the means to curb abuses of private economic power.[14] In this way, a difficult transitional period was bridged; the traditions of private decision-making in a competitive economy associated with small-scale units were preserved while the perpetuation of large-scale enterprise in important sectors of the economy

13. See Arthur M. Johnson, "Theodore Roosevelt and the Bureau of Corporations," *Mississippi Valley Historical Review*, XLV (March, 1959), 571–90.

14. The thesis of this essay was succinctly expressed by investment banker Jacob H. Schiff in his comment on the lower court's decision in the Northern Securities case. In April, 1903, he wrote that this decision might prove a "blessing in disguise," for "promotion" had been overdone. Also, he had great faith in the country's adaptability. In his words, "The American people have a particular faculty for adapting themselves to conditions as they exist, and in due time the effects and results of even the conditions now created will wear off."— Cyrus Adler, *Jacob H. Schiff: His Life and Letters* (2 vols.; New York, 1928), I, p. 112.

was assured. To make the transition complete, however, it was necessary first for the judicial process and then for the electorate formally to confirm it.

Certainty that the antitrust law had teeth and uncertainty about the way that it would be interpreted were important elements in its effectiveness as an indirect restraint on business decision-making. The United States Supreme Court's decisions in the Standard Oil and American Tobacco cases (1911), which had been initiated before Roosevelt left office, succeeded in maintaining this delicate balance. While finding each of the combinations guilty of violating the Sherman Act and ordering their dissolution, the Court also announced the so-called "Rule of Reason." In effect, the judiciary claimed for itself the right to exercise discretion as to the reasonableness or unreasonableness of a given combination, thus performing the function that Roosevelt had advocated for an administrative body.[15] While the announcement of the Rule of Reason was hailed with enthusiasm by some leading businessmen, it did not completely replace uncertainty with certainty. The mere fact of combination was now clearly no offense under the law, as at one time during this period it appeared that it might be. On the other hand, the general language of the Sherman Act and the procedural requirement that it be spelled out in case-by-case development still left for businessmen a large area of uncertainty as to what constituted actionable offenses. Again, this was in the pragmatic tradition of government-business relations.[16]

15. A concise and rewarding review of the Rule of Reason is in Milton Handler, *Antitrust in Perspective, the Complementary Roles of Rule and Discretion* (New York, 1957), chap. i.

16. Addressing a luncheon meeting of the Iron and Steel Manufacturers at the Metropolitan Club in New York, May 29, 1911, Judge E. H. Gary of the United States Steel Corporation cautioned his audience against interpreting the recent decisions as permitting business to make its own rules of conduct. If such an interpretation were adopted, he said, "We shall find that as a result and in the long

While the major antitrust prosecutions initiated by the Republican Roosevelt eventuated in satisfactory legal decisions, the changes wrought by them were less impressive. In the Northern Securities case, the dissolution of the holding company and the distribution of its railroad stocks to their original owners left control where it had been.[17] The dissolution of the Standard Oil and American Tobacco combinations took place on the same basis. Ironically, in the case of Standard Oil, the public disclosure of the combination's financial picture as a result of the antitrust proceedings skyrocketed the value of its stocks and resulted in windfall profits for those fortunate enough to own or acquire an interest in the constituent companies. Co-ordination of the activities of these companies continued through common ownership and by virtue of long-established relationships which no legal decree could destroy overnight. Here, as elsewhere, the pragmatism of the governmental process and of businessmen in adjusting to the requirements of public policy made the change gradual. Eventually, of course, ownership became widely dispersed and rival Standard Oil companies dwarfed the combination from which they were separated in 1911. While the appearance of change resulting from the court's decision was greater than the reality, the seeds of long-range change had been sown, governmental action had vindicated public expectations, and the specific enterprises had ample scope to adapt to their altered situation.

---

run we will suffer by reason of such an attitude." His fears were justified, his prophecy correct, but the "long run" proved to be a period of twenty years—a perspective few businessmen, including Gary, could be expected to keep in focus.

17. Justice White, who had dissented from the decision, noted the inconsistency of the remedy. "If the conspiracy and combination existed and was illegal," he wrote, "my mind fails to perceive why it should be left to produce its full force and effect in the hands of the individuals by whom it was charged the conspiracy was entered into." —*Northern Securities Company* v. *U.S.*, 193 U.S. 197 at 373.

The presidential election of 1912 took the form of a popular referendum on the acceptability of the principle of governmental supervision of business and ways of implementing it in the future. Running on the Progressive ticket, Roosevelt pitched his campaign to the familiar theme that large-scale enterprise and co-operation were inevitable in many sectors of the economy and that the task was to keep business in line through governmental supervision. Democrat Woodrow Wilson paid obeisance to popular concern for the small businessman, but he did not oppose big business that played "fair." Whether one adopted this approach or Roosevelt's, it called for increased governmental intervention in business decision-making. Eugene V. Debs, the Socialist candidate, called for a substitution of governmental for business decision-making in key areas of the economy, while William Howard Taft placed primary emphasis on the efficacy of the legal process in dealing with business.

The election of Wilson gave final confirmation to the *principle* of government supremacy over business and set the stage for its legislative implementation through the addition of new government functions. Creation of a central banking system combining public and private elements and adoption of the Sixteenth Amendment, providing for an income tax, were fraught with major long-run implications for business decision-making because of their potential impact on the cost and productivity of capital, which go to the heart of the business system. However, these implications were, once again typically, decades in working themselves out.

Of more immediate importance was confirmation of the principle that governmental regulation involving continuous administrative relationships with business was to be a cornerstone of public policy in areas other than public utilities. Implementation of the principle was to be limited and primarily in the interest of small business. Maintenance of "fair competition" was to be the objective, and reliance was to be placed on a supposedly expert body that could gradually define it. In the words of the conference report on the Federal Trade Commission bill: "The most certain way to stop monopoly at the threshold is to prevent unfair competition. This can be best accomplished through the action of an administrative body of practical men thoroughly informed in regard to business, who will be able to apply the rule enacted by Congress to particular business situations, so as to eradicate evils with the least risk of interfering with legitimate business operations." Authority to proceed in this direction was contained in Section 5 of the FTC Act which declared that "unfair methods of competition in commerce are hereby declared unlawful."

Typical of the multifaceted congressional approach to problems involving business, the FTC Act was accompanied by another statute, the Clayton Act, which attempted to be relatively specific where the former was vague. Thus it prohibited price discrimination, exclusive dealing leases, sales, contracts, discounts, and rebates where any of these practices resulted in substantially lessening competition or tended to create a monopoly in any line of commerce. Other sections of the statute prohibited certain interlocking directorates or acquisition of stock in one corporation by another where the results in terms of competition or monopoly were similar to those of price discrimination outlawed in the Act. Such provisions were intended to provide the businessman with somewhat greater certainty as to the nature of antitrust offenses while organized labor was recognized in its exemption from the antitrust law. Enforcement was to be shared between the FTC and the Justice Department.

Substantively, this legislation added little that was new, but the concept and the procedures specified for implementing it were important in confirming the course laid out for government-business relations during the first decade of the century. They were an affirmation that prevention of business abuses through continuing governmental supervision, publicity, and the exercise of administrative discretion was as important as punishment. The new statutes potentially thrust government further into the areas of managerial decision-making, but primarily in the marketing area. The loopholes in the law, the philosophy of the FTC, and the time-consuming character of administrative and legal processes delayed—where it did not negate—the impact of this legislation on business decision-making.[18]

It has been the thesis of the preceding pages that the pragmatic character of governmental processes and business response to them had, by 1914, brought about a workable adjustment between public and private interests while laying the foundations for future significant changes in government-business relations. Above all, the process had been gradual. The principle that government could supervise and punish business to protect society's interest in private decision-making was firmly established. Although the principle was far from fully implemented, its existence was recognized by businessmen and it met the requirements for action demanded by the electorate. The unique characteristics of its expression lay in the flexibility, multiplicity, and adaptability of the individual processes that were involved. As a result, even though the potential for rapid and drastic change in government-business relations had been suggested, the degree of effective change in the parameters of business decision-making was relatively small.

The adjustment achieved between government and business in the years 1901–14 did not seriously encroach on

18. The long process of giving meaning and effect to Section 7 of the Clayton Act is traced in David D. Martin, *Mergers and the Clayton Act* (Berkeley and Los Angeles, 1959).

business decision-making, and it gained for businessmen one more opportuniity to determine the pace and direction of economic activity with little or no governmental intervention. In a far more complex economy than that of the nineteenth century, business achieved some notable triumphs, especially in fields that were basically scientific, technological, or engineering in nature. Meanwhile, changes in the economy invalidated the premises on which some earlier restrictive legislation, such as the Interstate Commerce Act, was based, and governmental functions intended to restrain business were put to business uses.

Co-operation between business and government was a hallmark of the World War I era, and the lessons of co-operation were carried over into the organization of industry-wide trade associations which played an increasingly important role in business relations with government. In the postwar decade, government was once more subordinated to business. The political and legislative processes offered few threats to the freedom of business decision-making. The judicial process frustrated or modified the limited efforts of government administrators to apply restraints, and the administrators themselves turned to aiding business. The new era for the FTC began when W. E. Humphrey was appointed to the Commission in 1925 and denounced its use as an "instrument of oppression and disturbance and injury instead of a help to business." [19] Thenceforth the Commission took a leading role in encouraging self-regulation of business and, in co-operation with the Department of Commerce, helped trade associations to develop codes governing trade practices.

In this favorable environment, a new merger movement unfolded with the same immunity from governmental restraint as the great similar movement at the turn of the

19. Quoted in Arthur M. Schlesinger, Jr., *The Crisis of the Old Order, 1919–1933 (The Age of Roosevelt)*, (Boston, 1957), p. 65.

century. By 1930 the corporate ownership of business had been impressively concentrated, while management had become further separted from ownership. The famous Berle and Means study of the nation's 200 largest non-financial corporations as of January 1, 1930, showed that they controlled 49.2 per cent of non-banking corporate wealth, received 43.2 per cent of the income in that category, and represented about 38 per cent of all the business wealth in the country.[20] Forecasting still further developments in the same direction, the authors of this study saw a need "for the claims of the community to be put forward with clarity and force." [21]

Meanwhile, the collapse of the economy under the onslaught of depression raised the question of the way in which these claims would be put forward. The economic catastrophe that overtook the country had revealed the weaknesses of a business system allowed too much freedom to regulate itself. "The danger in our situation," declared Dean Wallace Donham of the Harvard Business School, "lies not in radical propaganda, but in lack of effective business leadership." [22] A demoralized business community, like the rest of the electorate, turned to government for answers.

President Franklin D. Roosevelt radiated confidence, but he had no master plan for recovery. As Dexter Perkins has

20. Adolf A. Berle, Jr., and Gardiner C. Means, *The Modern Corporation and Private Property* (New York, 1933), pp. 28–31.

21. In the view of Berle and Means it seemed "almost essential" to the survival of the corporate system that those exercising control of major corporations act to balance the claims of the various groups in the community and assign to each a part of the income stream "on the basis of public policy rather than private cupidity" (*ibid.*, p. 356). For Berle's later views, see *The 20th Century Capitalist Revolution* (New York, 1954). For the other views on the contemporary corporation and its significance, see Edward S. Mason (ed.), *The Corporation in Modern Society* (Cambridge, 1959).

22. Quoted in Arthur M. Schlesinger, Jr., *The Crisis of the Old Order*, p. 181.

observed, "he was experimental rather than revolutionary." [23] Therefore, in the pragmatic tradition, multiple
approaches to the nation's economic problems were adopted.
Many of them had their roots in the past, and they were
frequently contradictory. For example, the type of business
co-operation fostered by trade associations in the 1920's
was given governmental support and exemption from the
antitrust laws in the National Industrial Recovery Act of
1933. Later the same or similar practices were attacked
under the leadership of Assistant Attorney General Thurman Arnold, spurred by the findings of the Temporary
National Economic Committee. The principle of direct
governmental supervision of business established in the
period 1901–14 was given new vitality and meaning as the
statutes of that era were strengthened, and the administrative process assumed a new importance. The principle of
government competition with private enterprise, recognized
during the Wilson administration in the "yardstick" operation of naval shipyards as a check on private naval con-
tractors, was revived—most notably in the Tennessee Valley
Authority. Statutes such as the Securities and Exchange
Act, the Natural Gas Act, and the Public Utility Holding
Company Act imposed restraints on specific types of business activity.[24]

Once again the impact of change was absorbed, though
less completely than before, by the frictions and discon-
tinuities of governmental processes. Although the legislative process was speeded up in the early days of the New
Deal to cope with the emergency, the judicial process re-

23. Dexter Perkins, *The New Age of Franklin Roosevelt, 1932–1945*
(Chicago, 1957), p. 74.

24. The Securities and Exchange Act as a regulatory device placed
major reliance on publicity and afforded the investor some protection
against misleading information but not against errors in investment
judgment. The Natural Gas Act, on the other hand, as the result
of judicial interpretation (*Phillips Petroleum Co.* v. *State of Wisconsin*, 346 U.S. 934 [1954]) brought the Federal Power Commission
into problems of direct price control.

sulted in the invalidation of one major measure after another until 1937. A bitter battle developed between the President and the Supreme Court, but both Congressional and popular allegiance to the traditional interrelationship of governmental processes defeated Roosevelt's plan to "pack" the Court. Nevertheless, in 1937, that tribunal finally abandoned its oft-asserted right to invalidate legislative acts for conflicting with its interpretation of substantive due process of law. Furthermore, it began to show increased reluctance to review administrative acts for compliance with procedural due process.

The change in the Supreme Court's position weakened an important element in the chain of governmental processes which up to 1937 had helped business to alter, deflect, or absorb the impact of change in government-business relations. While the courts still remained open to businessmen challenging the constitutionality of restrictive legislation or the legality of specific administrative determinations, this avenue of relief became considerably less important than it had been previously.

Although the reforming zeal of the New Deal was on the wane by 1938 and businessmen's confidence in their ability to cope with economic problems had revived, some important changes in government-business relationships had occurred. The administrative process took on a new significance for many businesses. Organized labor received the sanction and support of government, thereby imposing a direct and immediate restraint both on business influence in government and on managerial decisions with respect to the human element in production. And, finally, government assumed, on an experimental basis, a new responsibility for performance of the economy through deficit spending and the use of fiscal and monetary controls to affect the environment of entrepreneurial decisions on the allocation of capital.

These changes in government-business relations had a potential for replacing private with public decisions that had not existed previously; yet they still left businessmen with room to adapt. Thus the labor relations expert, the tax expert, and the legal expert assumed a new prominence in business management. While business had always softened the impact of change in its relations with government by adaptation, this process became increasingly important as exploitation of time-consuming governmental processes proved less rewarding.

Despite some fundamental changes in the environment and conditions of business decision-making under the New Deal, government did not replace business as the primary mechanism for allocating resources in the economy.[25] Business had by no means lost all its influence in government, and numerous measures, such as the Buy American Act of 1933 and the Merchant Marine Act of 1936, reflected this fact. Government support of stabilizing devices—in the oil and sugar industries, to mention only two—removed some elements of uncertainty in business decision-making and revealed government as an ally as well as antagonist of business.

Whether additional governmental intervention in the economy might have occurred as a result of continued depression is an academic question since the coming of World War II, and then its aftermath, wrought further basic changes in government-business relationships that have reversed and modified, as well as strengthened, the developments of the 1930's.

The war emergency not only ended the problems arising from depression but brought about a new era of government-business co-operation. The productive capacity of the nation was strained to the limit, while government added

25. In 1940, federal expenditures on goods and services accounted for only about 6.2 per cent of all goods and services produced in that year. U.S. Bureau of Census, *Historical Statistics of the United States, 1789–1945* (Washington, D.C., 1949), p. 12.

to industrial facilities operated by business for the war effort. In the mobilization of these resources, businessmen became bureaucrats. The co-operative and compulsory devices developed during World War I were refurbished and supplemented. The conflicts of the preceding decade between business and government were submerged, if not forgotten, in the common effort for the nation's survival.

The situation was well illustrated by the petroleum industry. As the nation balanced on the brink of war, the major oil companies selling gasoline in the Midwest were smarting under the verdict of the Supreme Court that they had violated the antitrust law in following practices that the companies claimed had been sanctioned under the National Recovery Administration and subsequently.[26] Thurman Arnold's Antitrust Division was preparing a suit against the major oil companies and the industry's leading trade association, the American Petroleum Institute. Pipeline affiliates of these companies faced prosecution for alleged violation of the Elkins Act. With the United States involvement in the world conflict, however, these proceedings were quickly suspended. The industry turned to meeting war's demands; oilmen took government posts; pipeliners accepted a consent decree and, with government authority and funds, went to work on the problem of building emergency pipelines to take the place of tankers lost to German submarines.

Some old controversies died harder than others. Charges and countercharges flew back and forth between some public officials and Standard Oil Company (New Jersey) executives in connection with the synthetic rubber program. The company's president was hailed before a Senate committee to explain prewar agreements with I. G. Farben in con-

26. *U.S.* v. *Socony-Vacuum Oil Co.,* 310 U.S. 150 (1940). Frank Freidel has suggested that the antitrust drive was encouraged by Roosevelt to forestall drastic Congressional action (*The New Deal in Historical Perspective* [Washington, D.C., 1959], pp. 18–19).

nection with synthetic rubber patents, but once this ritual was performed Jersey Standard settled down to producing the essential commodity in facilities financed by the government.

Technological and managerial proficiencies developed in business were applied to other fields important to the war effort. For example, large companies like DuPont, General Electric, and Union Carbide were asked to share in pioneering the development and operation of nuclear facilities, with government providing the capital and exercising overall planning and control. It has been charged that big business profited unduly from such wartime relationships. Benefits were said to have ranged from quick tax write-offs and acquisition of government-built plants at a fraction of their cost to patents and know-how derived from war work at government expense.[27] But if big business benefited from war contracts and war work, small business also made effective claims on government. The Small Defense Plants legislation of World War II provided specific recognition of these interests and was the forerunner of the Small Business Act of 1953, which has made government the guardian and financial backer of the entrepreneur conducting a business "independently owned and operated . . . and not dominant in its field of operation." [28]

Perhaps the most remarkable aspect of the war experience was the speed with which direct government controls on labor, business, and consumer were abandoned after the war. Government allocation of resources and wage, price, and credit controls had centralized wartime decision-making for the economy, but within a year of V-J Day most of these restraints had been abandoned. The responsiveness of the

27. See Walter Adams and Horace M. Gray, *Monopoly in America: The Government as Promoter* (New York, 1955).

28. The way in which small business sought and received government aid and encouragement is told in Harmon Ziegler, *The Politics of Small Business* (Washington, D.C., 1961).

political and legislative processes to major groups in the economy had not been deadened by war.

In the transition to more normal operations, government undertook to affect directly the postwar environment of competition in certain industries by the terms on which it disposed of defense facilities. The Reynolds and Kaiser companies, for example, had government aid in challenging Alcoa's long-time monopoly in the aluminum industry, while the latter company found itself the loser in a landmark antitrust case that repudiated the Supreme Court's earlier stand that unexercised monopoly was no offense under the Sherman Act. On the other hand, the pragmatic and contradictory character of governmental processes was illustrated by the fact that the Attorney General found no objection in 1946 to the sale of the government's Geneva, Utah, steel plant to U.S. Steel, which thus gained some 50 per cent of the Pacific Coast's ingot capacity.

During the war, government began to assume the financial risks of innovation in many areas at the frontiers of science. The continuation of world crisis after the end of active hostilities appears to have confirmed this governmental function. Federal funds, for example, have underpinned the development of commercial jet transportation as well as electronics and rocketry. The large military research-and-development budget underlies the health of many a business, large and small.

Political and military decisions, directly or indirectly, affect many private entrepreneurial decisions. In its normal operations, government is a major customer for many businesses. In connection with defense activities, governmental decisions on what to buy for national stockpiles of strategic materials, as well as what weapons system to emphasize or de-emphasize, have repercussions on firms only partially devoted to government business. Business strategy and profits may well hinge on the perceptiveness with which managers evaluate the government market for goods and services. A direct link between such public and private decision-making is provided by the interchange of personnel between government and business, whereby generals and admirals have been lured to private concerns while business-men have been called to top government posts, especially in the defense establishment.

The latter development suggests that the problems of management and control in government have increasingly paralleled those in business, and the similarities have even extended to the form in which government activities are organized. A corporate form characterizes many government financial and business-type activities. Although this form was tried by government during World War I, it did not come into prominence until the 1930's. Perhaps the most notable example was the Reconstruction Finance Corporation, organized in 1932 to provide financial aid to business and active until 1953. The RFC was followed by an impressive number of other public corporations, including the TVA, the Production Credit Corporation, and the Federal Deposit Insurance Corporation.

Business-type agencies of the government have also entered into business relationships with one another and with private corporations. For example, while the TVA displaced private electrical utilities in its area and the allocation of its costs has been the subject of continuing controversy, it has developed working relationships with private power companies and has even gone into the money market with its own securities. Privately owned companies of various types have profited from markets opened up or supplied by the TVA. Such intermingling of activities could only be the product of a pragmatic system of government-business relations given time to work itself out.

In this tradition, the experimentation of the New Deal was followed by formal adoption of the *principle* of governmental responsibility for full employment and the increased use of monetary and fiscal controls in shaping the environment of private business decision-making. The significant Employment Act of 1946 asserted government's responsibility "to promote maximum employment, production, and purchasing power," though it was to do so "in a manner calculated to foster and promote free competitive enterprise and the general welfare." The wording of section 2 of the Act, from which these quotations are taken, reflects the compromises forced in the legislative process by the conflict between labor and liberal groups, who wished to see fiscal policy made the primary means of insuring full employment, and business and conservative groups, who were unprepared to make this the sole objective of the legislation or fiscal policy the only means to achieve it.[29]

The 1946 Employment Act is based on the concept of countercyclical activity (i.e., government spending more than it taxes to offset economic contraction and reversing the process to check inflationary pressures) aided by Federal Reserve and Treasury policies affecting the cost and availability of credit. "Built-in stabilizers" such as income taxes and unemployment insurance, which are geared to the level of income, supplement the countercyclical devices. Like other major principles mentioned in this chapter, that of governmental responsibility for full employment has undergone a slow process of testing and development. Defense and foreign-policy spending, plus a high level of domestic economic activity, have prevented major crises that would require full implementation of the principle. Fiscal action in 1949 and operation of built-in stabilizers in 1957–58 dampened recession, but monetary policy failed to check postwar inflation.

29. An excellent study of the pragmatic approach to this legislation is contained in Stephen K. Bailey, *Congress Makes a Law, the Story Behind the Employment Act of 1946* (New York, 1950).

These devices for combining stability with growth in the economy rely heavily on business response to the financial environment created by government. The level and type of taxation, for example, affect the profitability of business and, therefore, the incentives for private investment. A businessman-entrepreneur is taxed differently from one who conducts his enterprise in corporate form, and a corporation with income of less than $25,000 a year is taxed differently from one that earns more. The entire structure and financial strategy of a business today may be significantly related to such statutory tax provisions and their administrative interpretation. While government thus conditions the environment for financial decision-making, it does not control most specific decisions. Each businessman is free to adapt to his environment in the manner he thinks best. Similarly, he is free to attempt to change the environment as it affects him specifically or as it affects the whole business system. As a result of the developments of the last sixty years, however, the contemporary businessman is considerably less free than his counterpart in 1900 to make decisions, financial or otherwise, without reference to the framework of government-business relations.

No matter how the impact of change has been absorbed, the steady growth of governmental power to affect business for better or for worse is a phenomenon of major importance to business management. Under these pressures, deliberate flouting of government or public opinion does not characterize most business decision-making. Professional managers of American business today realize that arbitrary use of power can provoke unfavorable public reactions that will be reflected in or through government, bringing new restraints on their freedom of decision-making. The lesson of government-business relations in this century, and particularly in the last thirty years, is quite clear in this respect. Inadequate acceptance of it has brought well-deserved obloquy to a few leading concerns and businessmen in the past few years.[30] Their difficulties have emphasized anew that however pressing the business requirements for a certain line of action, if the possibility of directly affronting governmental authority or public opinion is involved, the *manner* of meeting these requirements is an important ingredient of the results.

If one reviews developments in government-business relations during the past sixty years, the following major changes stand out. First, the role of business in the economy has been made conditional on performance and business acceptance of government as the vehicle through which the public's wants and needs can be effectively expressed. Second, along with this change, businessmen have found that both managerial and entrepreneurial decisions are affected and limited by government, both directly and indirectly. Accordingly, the implications of these decisions have had increasingly to be considered in this light. Third, while other groups have looked to government to curb business, business has also sought and found answers to some of its problems through government, thus inviting further control. Fourth, government has been forced by circumstances, such as war, to rely more than ever before on business. Furthermore, government has utilized business forms and procedures in conducting its business. The interchange between the two has been reflected by the transmigration of public officials into business and, in times of emergency,

30. For an account of one such episode, see John Herling, *The Great Price Conspiracy, the Story of the Antitrust Violations in the Electrical Industry* (Washington, D.C., 1962). For a general indictment of big business, see Theodore K. Quinn, *Unconscious Public Enemies* (New York, 1962). For an analysis and rebuttal of such charges, see John D. Glover, *The Attack on Big Business* (Boston, 1954).

businessmen into government. As a result, government and business have become linked in complex relationships that defy precise description.

Underlying the changes in relations has been the continuity provided by the processes involved. Their common characteristic has been a basic pragmatism which has encouraged flexibility, variety, and specificity in the relationships. The political and legislative processes have offered avenues for the establishment of new principles governing basic relationships and have provided an outlet for the popular emotions and economic pressures that accompany conflicts of group interests. The implementation of the results has involved administrative and legal processes, where the time-lag has frequently been great. In the past these processes, because of their change-absorbing characteristics, have generally given business ample time to adapt to new governmental restraints and, though sometimes abused, have helped to preserve private decision-making in the economy. On the other hand, the history of government-business relations since 1900 shows that over-all change has itself been a long-run process consisting of experimentation, establishment of a principle, and implementation on a gradual basis. Therefore, by the time implementation becomes meaningful, the economy may have changed to the extent that the principle involved needs to be revised or discarded. Again, time-consuming governmental processes retard change and tend to confirm rigidities that limit adjustments to new conditions, whether by business or government. The problems confronting the nation's transportation system stem in part from such rigidity in both the principles and implementation of regulation. As President Kennedy pointed out in his transportation message of April, 1962: "A chaotic patchwork of inconsistent and often obsolete legislation and regulation has evolved from a history of specific actions addressed to specific problems of specific industries at specific times. This patchwork does not fully reflect either the dramatic changes in technology of the past half century, or the parallel changes in the structure of competition." [31] Such are the costs of reliance on a pragmatic process of achieving and cushioning change in government-business relations.

Since the turn of the century there has been remarkable continuity in Congressional approval of broad grants of power to executive departments and semi-autonomous agencies. They have made the government administrator a partner in many business decisions, even if *in absentia.* Especially since the mid-1930's this development has begun to limit the range of managerial adaptation to changing economic conditions and has rendered the legal process, once a bulwark of business against government, a less rewarding avenue for challenging basic principles of government-business relations or their implementation.[32] The latter process has become so continuous and direct that the possible business benefits to be derived by appealing from it are often lost in the time consumed. Resort to the political and legislative processes has the same drawbacks. Thus, an increasingly higher premium has been placed on the businessman's ability to anticipate, avoid, or adapt to administrative expressions of governmental power. The task is not necessarily a difficult one; co-operation as well as combat marks many of these relationships. Still, the time, money, and skills devoted to such matters increase the cost of doing business, which is ultimately borne by the consumer.

31. Message from the President of the United States, "The Transportation System of Our Nation," 87th Cong., 2nd Sess., *House Doc. 384* (1962), p. 2.

32. Justice Jackson, a decade ago, noted that "the rise of administrative bodies probably has been the most significant legal trend of the last century and perhaps more values today are affected by their decisions than by those of all the courts, review of administrative decisions apart."—*FTC* v. *Ruberoid Co.,* 343 U.S. 470, at 487 (1952).

The most recent principle of direct governmental responsibility for the performance of the economy has not yet been fully implemented or tested. Business still exercises the primary, if conditional, role in guiding the nation's economic affairs. The extent of public aid to business, direct and indirect, is testimony to business influence in government and to government's reliance on business. More importantly, perhaps, it reveals the electorate's continuing allegiance to private-business decision-making, even in cases where business has to be publicly supported or controlled. No better illustration of the pragmatic character of continuity and change in goverment-business relations could be advanced.

The Emergence of Mass-Production Unionism

DAVID BRODY

AT THE coming of the New Deal, American organized labor was an arrested movement. Membership was slightly under three million in 1933. The unionized portion of the non-agricultural labor force—one-tenth—remained unchanged after thirty years. It was not only a matter of numbers. Labor strength was limited to the needle trades, public utilities (excluding communications), coal-mining, building construction, and the railroads. A vacuum existed in manufacturing, above all, in the mass-production sector. Organized labor had not breached the industries characterized by the giant firm; by multiplant operation for a national market; by an advanced technology involving mechanization and division of labor; and by a work force composed primarily of unskilled and semi-skilled men. The mass-production core—iron and steel, non-ferrous metals, rubber, electrical products, chemicals and petroleum, and food-processing—seemed impervious to trade unionism.

The great breakthrough occurred after 1935. A decade later, most of the mass-production industries had experienced thorough unionization. The consequences were, of course, profound. It was, as Walter Galenson said, "a fundamental, almost revolutionary change in the power relationships of American society." [1] The accomplishment had its origin in the 1930's. But the favoring climate of that decade failed to carry the new unionism to its conclusion. Ultimately, permanent success came from the very events that ended the Great Depression and the New Deal.

The unionization of the mass-production industries still requires explanation; that is the purpose of this preliminary essay.[2]

The achievement began within the changing labor movement. The central fact, obviously, was the creation of the Congress of Industrial Organizations (initially, the Committee for Industrial Organization) as the unionizing agency for the basic industries. Several related questions claim our attention here. What was the necessity that split organized labor? What did the CIO bring to bear that had been lacking in the American Federation of Labor approach to the unionizing of mass production? And, finally, was the union effort decisive in accounting for the organization of the mass-production sector?

The irreconcilable issue seemingly was a matter of structure: industrial versus craft unionism. Industrial organization—the inclusion of all workers in an industry within one union—was a choice closed to the AF of L for several reasons. Foremost was the numerical dominance of the craft unionists: since theirs were the interests to be injured, industrial-union resolutions had never mustered a majority

1. Walter Galenson, *The CIO Challenge to the AFL* (Cambridge, 1960), p. xvii, and for growth of union membership, pp. 583–93.

2. Important recent research based on new sources has added much information on this subject. The documentation will reveal my debts. But no satisfying analysis has emerged from this scholarship. It was this conclusion which led to the undertaking of the present essay.

in AF of L conventions. The Federation was also in a constitutional bind. Jurisdiction was exclusive: only one union
could hold rights to a given category of workers. And it
was absolute: a union did not have to organize its jurisdiction in order to maintain its right. The craft unions
had a kind of property interest within the basic industries.
Beyond that was the immovable fact of trade autonomy;
the locus of power rested with the national unions. The
AF of L was a voluntary institution, William Green observed, and therefore had "no power to compel any union
or person to do anything." [3] Even the passage of an
industrial-union resolution, Philip Taft has pointed out,
"would not have forced any craft union to surrender its
jurisdiction, nor compelled unions to amalgamate with
each other." [4] There was, finally, the subtle role of *macht-
politik* within the labor movement. Themselves lacking
power, Federation officers respected it in other hands. The
power realities ordinarily favored the craft interests, and
so, therefore, did the inclination of the AF of L leadership. (William Green, agreeing as he did with the view-
point of the Lewis group, surely displayed that practical
quality when the chips came down in 1935 and after.)

These considerations remained binding during the historic debate over structure that took place in the mid-1930's.
At the AF of L convention of 1934 in San Francisco the
issue was joined over the question of chartering national
unions in the automobile, cement, aluminum, and other un-
specified mass-production fields. Industrial-union sentiment,
stimulated by recent events, forced the convention to recognize that "a new condition exists requiring organization
upon a different basis to be most effective." But the conven-

3. James O. Morris, *Conflict within the AFL: A Study of Craft
Versus Industrial Unionism, 1901–1938* (Ithaca, N. Y., 1958), p. 8.
4. Philip Taft, *The A.F. of L. in the Time of Gompers* (New York,
1957), p. 200.

tion also wanted to "fully protect the jurisdictional rights of all trade unions organized upon craft lines. . . ." [5] This second statement carried more weight. The Executive Council, to which the actual choice was left, excluded tool-, die-, and machine-making workers and parts plants from the jurisdiction of the new United Automobile Workers and maintenance and machine-installing men from the United Rubber Workers. The fateful Atlantic City convention of 1935 ratified the decision against industrial unionism.

It was a choice that John L. Lewis and his supporters could not accept. They insisted, as Charles Howard of the Typographical Union said, that "in the great mass-production industries industrial organization is the only solution." The aftermath of the 1935 convention was independent action that turned rapidly into dual unionism.

It has been hard to hold the momentous events of 1934-35 in perspective. The debate then was couched in the terminology of industrial unionism, and the outcome was the creation of a group of strong industrial unions. So it seemed to follow that the conflict over structure was the key to the formation of the CIO. That conclusion misplaces the emphasis.

The AF of L did not lack an alternative arrangement. No less than his critics, Samuel Gompers had seen the inappropriateness of the original craft structure for emerging American industrialism. Over the years, there had developed a response to mass production. Gompers had early accepted the need "to organize our fellow workers in unskilled labor."

> With the invention of new machines and the application of new forces, the division and subdivision of labor, many workers who had been employed at skilled trades find themselves with their

5. AF of L, *Proceedings* (1934), pp. 586–7.

occupations gone. . . . Thus we see the artisan of yesterday the
unskilled laborer of today.

The essential device was the federal labor union. Gathered
first into these mixed local bodies, the unorganized would be
drawn off by occupation into the appropriate national unions
or into local trade unions affiliated, as were the federal
unions, directly with the AF of L. The federal labor unions,
said Gompers, were "the recruiting ground for the trade
union movement." [6]

Besides organizing non-craft workers, the Federation
tried to alter the existing structure to make room for them.
Charters were granted to national unions covering the
unskilled and semi-skilled within single industries; for
instance, the Hod Carriers in construction and the Tin Plate
Workers in tin plate manufacture. But Gompers' preference
was for the less skilled to find a place within the "primary
unions," that is, national unions covering the occupations
specific to an industry.[7] To that end, the AF of L urged
unions to amalgamate or to accept broader jurisdictions.
The optimum result was a national union covering all occupations specific to an industry, irrespective of the skills
involved, plus common labor. Such residual jurisdictions in
fact were operative at some time in practically every mass-
production industry before the 1930's. The craft unions
were not victimized thereby. Defining its position in the
Scranton Declaration of 1901, the AF of L adhered as
closely to the "fundamental principle" of craft organization
"as the recent great changes in methods of production and

6. *Ibid.* (1897), pp. 6, 15.

7. For lack of an apt term in the literature, I have coined the
phrase "primary union" to describe organizations with residual
jurisdiction in mass-production fields. It should be noted that the
local unions of these nationals tended to be organized around trades
or departments rather than plants, as would be the case with industrial unions.

employment make possible." [8] Primary jurisdictions would not normally encompass such inter-industry occupations as teamsters, carpenters, machinists, and similar trades.

Co-ordination, finally, was encouraged. The primary and craft unions had to act together in the basic industries. As early as the Scranton Declaration, the suggestion had been made of "closely allying the sub-divided crafts" through "the organization of district and national trade councils. . . ." Much of the subsequent co-operation, particularly in joint organizing drives, was on an informal and sporadic basis. During and after World War I, national unions in meat-packing joined together only when faced with the need for common decisions. In steel, on the other hand, twenty-four national unions acted in 1918-20 through the permanent National Committee for Organizing Iron and Steel Workers. At the district level, local unions had formal bodies in the Schenectady plant of General Electric for over a decade after 1911, in meat-packing centers from 1901 to 1904 and again in Chicago from 1917 to 1920, and in steel during the union upsurge of the war period. The departments of the AF of L also promoted joint union activity. The Metal Trades Department chartered local councils and mounted co-operative organizing drives, for instance, in the automobile industry in 1914 and 1927. Inadequate though most of these ventures were, they did not show that organizational unity was unattainable under the primary-craft structural arrangement for the mass-production fields.

The AF of L was adhering to this established plan in 1935. Its advocates insisted that the formula was workable.

8. AF of L, *Proceedings* (1901), p. 240. AF of L organizing assistance, for instance, required prior agreement, as the Butcher Workmen were informed in 1915, "that when the employees of the meat trust are organized, [they] shall be assigned to their respective organizations" (AF of L Executive Council Minutes, February 21–26, 1916, p. 5).

The separation of craft workers would not, after all, be numerically important in mass production. The rubber industry was a case in point. Its labor force, according to a breakdown in the census of 1930, was composed of the following:

    559 carpenters
    395 compositors, linotypers, and typesetters
    915 electricians
 1,206 mechanics
 1,148 stationary engineers
    482 millwrights
 4,665 machinists
    805 plumbers
    300 toolmakers
 1,267 truck drivers
    456 painters and glaziers
80,835 operatives
29,123 laborers[9]

Jurisdiction over the last two categories would give a rubber workers' union nearly 90 per cent of the labor force in the industry. William Hutcheson of the Carpenters could not see why organization would be impeded by separating "a comparatively small number as compared to the total number employed in the rubber industry." And coordination could surely be made to work. John Frey was convinced that "joint negotiations and joint agreement reached through the [Metal Trades] Department forms the most effective answer to . . . the so-called industrial form of trade union organization . . . enabling an employer to negotiate but one agreement which will cover all his em-

9. Harold S. Roberts, *The Rubber Workers: Labor Organization and Collective Bargaining in the Rubber Industry* (New York, 1944), p. 98.

ployees. . . ."[10]   In September, 1934, this policy had been adopted for the metal and building trades. Both AF of L departments entered negotiations on this basis with the Anaconda Copper Company.

If not the optimum solution, the AF of L alternative nevertheless seemed adequate and reasonable. The primary-craft formula could not be ruled out as unworkable on the basis of past experience. While deprecated by Lewis adherents, it could not by itself drive the breach in the labor movement.

Nor, for that matter, could the appeal of industrial unionism. "Much has been said about principles in the war between the C.I.O. and the A.F. of L.," commented the informed labor consultant Chester M. Wright in 1939. "As I see it, the whole dispute is one involving tactics and practices. I fail to find any principles involved at any point." [11] Earlier, industrial unionism had involved fundamental differences. Its advocates had been mainly Socialists and others seeking to make the labor movement a vehicle for political action and/or basic social change. That was not the case in the 1930's. Industrial unionism then was directed only at the mass-production industries, not, as in the amalgamation movement of the early 1920's, at the entire economy. The ideological groundwork was mostly gone. John L. Lewis himself had opposed the amalgamationists of the postwar period. His emergence as industrial-union leader in the early New Deal period presumed that the debate over structure did not reflect basic differences about the role of the trade-union movement.

The antagonists were not doctrinaire even on the narrow structural issue. Bitter opponents of Lewis as they were, the Carpenters, Machinists, and Electrical Workers were

10. Philip Taft, *The A.F. of L. from the Death of Gompers to the Merger* (New York, 1959), pp. 86, 91.

11. Chester M. Wright, *Here Comes Labor* (New York, 1939), p. 47.

themselves asserting industrial jurisdiction over limited areas between 1934 and 1936.[12] For his part, Lewis was not rigid on industrial unionism. When the AF of L Executive Council was considering in February, 1935, what craft groups to exclude from an auto workers' union, Lewis pleaded that the "cavilling be deferred until in the light of what accomplishment is made in the objective we can take up the question of dividing the members, that contention over the fruits of victory be deferred until we have some of the fruits in our possession." While he retained hope in the AF of L, Lewis did not commit himself to industrial unionism.[13]

It was not in itself of importance. Lewis was a pragmatist in the dominant tradition of American trade unionism. Labor leaders responded, as William Green said, to "the fact, not a theory but a situation actually existing. . . ."[14] The formation of the CIO was a drastic measure which, from Lewis' standpoint, had to yield a commensurate return. The structural reform of industrial unionism was not such a return. Nor, in fact, was it absolutely precluded from the pragmatic labor movement. Industrial unions could find a place—as did the United Mine Workers of America itself—within the AF of L. The Butcher Workmen had put the fact neatly back in 1922 when the issue over requesting industrial jurisdiction in meat-packing arose. It would be better, the convention decided, first to unionize the industry "and then by reason of the strength that would accompany such an organization, take and retain control over all men of whatever craft

12. Morris, *Conflict Within the AFL*, p. 177; Robert A. Christie, *Empire in Wood: A History of the Carpenters' Union* (Ithaca, N.Y., 1956), chap. ix; Mark Perlman, *The Machinists: A New Study in American Trade Unionism* (Cambridge, 1961), pp. 90–91.

13. Taft, *A. F. of L. from the Death of Gompers*, pp. 105, 107; AF of L, *Proceedings* (1934), p. 588.

14. Taft, *A. F. of L. from the Death of Gompers*, p. 106.

employed in the industry." [15]   The obstacles to that first point—not the second—were the operative ones in 1935.

What excited Lewis and his adherents was a concrete objective: the organization of the mass-production industries.   That accomplished, the structural issue would resolve itself and would, in any case, not be of great moment.   "The fundamental obligation is to organize these people," Lewis insisted. The resulting problems should be considered "after we had accomplished organization and not before, after the fact of organization has been accomplished [,] not tie on reservations that will in themselves deter an effective campaign." [16]   This revealed the heart of the crisis: would the AF of L take the measures necessary for the organization of mass-production workers?

Industrial unionism fitted into this larger context. The immense influence of the idea sprang from the contemporary assessment of the psychology of industrial workers. "I know their state of mind," William Green asserted, speaking of the automobile workers. ". . . If you tell them to go here, you here and you there, you will never get anywhere. They are so closely related and inextricably interwoven they are mass minded." [17]   In her perceptive *Industrial Valley*, Ruth McKenney described the problem as she saw it in Akron rubber plants.

> . . . The machinists and the electricians kept coming to the Federal local meetings. [The AFL organizer] could never make them understand they were supposed to stay away, supposed to belong to a separate union. He could never teach them that their interests were different from the common ordinary rubberworker. Stubbornly and stupidly they clung to the Federal locals.[18]

15. Amalgamated Meat Cutters and Butcher Workmen of North America, *Proceedings* (1922), pp. 18, 35, 81–82.

16. Taft, *A. F. of L. from the Death of Gompers*, p. 107.

17. *Ibid.*; AF of L, *Proceedings* (1934), p. 592.

18. Ruth McKenney, *Industrial Valley* (New York, 1939), p. 109.

Industrial unionists had here an explanation for the failure to hold the thousands of industrial workers who had flocked into the AF of L federal unions in 1933. Sidney Hillman noted, for example, that during the NRA period over 40,000 rubber workers had been organized. Then the AF of L "started to divide those workers among the different unions claiming jurisdiction over them. As a result of that procedure, the membership of the rubber workers union fell as low as 3,000." [19]

The problem was *tactical*. Since industrial labor was "mass minded," the first stage of organization had to be on a mass basis. "Vice President Lewis said there is a psychology there among the men . . . ," read the minutes of the February, 1935, meeting of the AF of L Executive Council. "What he has in mind [is that] the time to quarrel over jurisdiction is after we organize the men rather than before." [20] William Green shared Lewis' view. The mass-production industries should be organized "as best we can, then after they are organized if the question [arises] on the jurisdiction of an international union, perhaps by education we can bring about respect among these workers of the jurisdiction of the national and international unions." [21]

That reasoning explained the hopefulness following the San Francisco convention of 1934. The objectives then enunciated seemed irreconcilable: to protect craft jurisdictions and to organize mass-production fields on "a different basis." But an apparent accommodation had emerged from the many hours of talks off the floor of the convention. The Executive Council was "directed to issue charters for

19. Mathew Josephson, *Sidney Hillman: Statesman of American Labor* (New York, 1952), p. 385.
20. AF of L Executive Council Minutes, January 29–February 14, 1935, p. 213. I have utilized the Council minutes in this account. I have, however, thought it more helpful to give references to Taft or Galenson except in instances in which selections from the minutes do not appear in those secondary sources.
21. Taft, *A. F. of L. from the Death of Gompers*, p. 91.

National or International Unions"—the instructions did not specify precise jurisdictions. Second, "for a provisional period" the chartered unions should be under AF of L direction "in order to protect and safeguard the members of such National and International Unions as are chartered. . . ." Both these points—temporary AF of L control and an undefined jurisdiction—were included in John L. Lewis' seven-point program for an automobile union which was presented to the Executive Council in February, 1935. And there was a final point:

> That all questions of overlapping jurisdiction on the automobile parts and special crafts organizations encountered in the administration policy be referred to the Executive Council for consideration at such time as the Council may elect to give these questions consideration.[22]

"This proposal is in strict conformity with the action of the A. F. of L. convention of 1934," Lewis explained, "and in proposing it I intend that if this policy does an injury to any international union that the union thus affected will have the right to take up these questions with the Executive Council of the American Federation of Labor and I assume that judgment will be rendered in conformity with . . . the record of the previous actions of the Council." [23]

Confronting the proposal, the craft leaders could not accept it. Dan Tobin of the Teamsters saw "some merit"

22. *Ibid.*, p. 105; AF of L, *Proceedings* (1935), pp. 94–96, 538. At the San Francisco convention of 1934, Lewis' explanation of the industrials union resolution was thoroughly unrevealing, no doubt for good tactical reasons. The most he would say, when pressed, was that the jurisdictional decisions rested with the Executive Council (to which he and his supporter David Dubinsky were being added). But see the speech of Mathew Woll, AF of L, *Proceedings* (1934), pp. 593–94; also, the editorial in the *American Federationist*, XLI (November, 1934), 1177.

23. AF of L Executive Council Minutes, January 29–February 14, 1935, pp. 68–69, 218–19.

in Lewis' view and was willing to permit a "dispensation for six months or so in the hope we will unscramble them later on. . . ." [24] But others, above all Wharton of the Machinists, had higher stakes in the automobile field. They were responding to the realities of the American labor movement: could they successfully exert their jurisdictional rights *after* organization had occurred on an industrial basis? In fact, they had grown critical even of the standard AF of L practice of placing skilled recruits in federal unions because these recruits then became reluctant to transfer to the appropriate craft unions.[25] William Hutcheson of the Carpenters thought the jurisdictional question "should be straightened out now to avoid trouble." [26] The Executive Council so decided: specific groups were excluded from the jurisdiction of the Auto Workers and, at the next Council meeting, of the Rubber Workers. In essence, the craft unions were refusing to gamble—at long odds—their vested rights in order to unionize mass-production workers. Tobin put the fact bluntly: "We are not going to desert the fundamental principles on which these organizations have lived and are living to help you organize men who have never been organized." [27]

The jurisdictional problem was only the most visible of the obstacles to effective action. National unions with old-line leadership had primary jurisdiction in a number of basic industries—most importantly, the Amalgamated Association of Iron, Steel and Tin Workers. The industrial bloc agreed with Green's view that "the officers of the

24. *Ibid.*, pp. 214–15.

25. See Morris, *Conflict within the AFL*, pp. 152–58; Sidney Fine, "The Origins of the United Automobile Workers, 1933–35," *Journal of Economic History*, XVIII (September, 1958), 254–55.

26. AF of L Executive Council Minutes, January 29–February 14, 1935, p. 213.

27. AF of L Executive Council Minutes, April 30–May 7, 1935, p. 124.

Amalgamated cannot organize these workers with their own resources or with the set-up as is. . . . The change has been taking place but the Amalgamated has been standing committed to its old tradition policy." Lewis urged the chartering of another national union with jurisdiction over steel. The craft unionists refused to abrogate the sacred rights of an autonomous union, as William Hutcheson said, "even if it was in bad straits." [28] They were willing to permit others to mount a steel campaign, but the bulk of the steelworkers would have to go into an organization which had amply proved its incapacity. Exclusive jurisdiction and trade autonomy seemed to be immutable principles.

Finally, the necessary resources were not being directed to the organization of the basic industries. The income of the labor movement accumulated in the national unions, not in the Federation. President Green was able to augment his organizing staff by only fifteen in the critical year 1933. The affiliated unions were unwilling either to raise the per capita going to the AF of L or to expend adequate funds directly in the organizing effort. (The response to Green's appeal in March, 1936, for funds for a steel drive totaled $8,625 from five unions.) The flabbiness of the financial support could be gauged by the later reaction to the CIO threat: AF of L organizing expenses during 1937–39 were triple those of 1933–35.[29] Nor were the unions with jurisdiction in the basic industries roused to a common effort. No joint drives were mounted in 1933–34 that would compare to those of earlier years in steel, autos, textiles, and meat-packing. The AF of L convention of 1934 instructed the Executive Council not only to charter national unions in mass-production industries but to inaugurate a union

28. Taft, *A. F. of L. from the Death of Gompers*, p. 116.
29. Morris, *Conflict within the AFL*, p. 162.

drive in steel. The Council had done nothing beyond passing a resolution by the time of the fateful convention of 1935.

At bottom, the AF of L was experiencing a crisis of will. Lewis bitterly commented in May, 1935, "that some six months have gone by since we adopted that resolution in San Francisco and there still remains the fact that there has been no administration of that policy, no execution of the promissory note that this Federation held out to the millions of workers in the mass-production industry. . . . Neither do I understand there is any immediate desire to carry out that policy. . . . " [30] The choice rested with the controlling craft unionists. And they were not really committed to organizing the mass-production workers. Dan Tobin of the Teamsters, for instance, spoke contemptuously of "the rubbish that have lately come into other organizations." A widespread feeling was, as Mathew Woll said in 1934, that the industrial workers were "perhaps unorganizable." Tobin was saying in February, 1936, that "there isn't a chance in the world at this time to organize the steelworkers." [31]

To John L. Lewis, the basic obstacle was the indifference of the craft leaders. They were the object of his plea at the 1935 convention:

> Why not make a contribution to the well-being of those who are not fortunate enough to be members of your organizations? . . . The labor movement is organized upon a principle that the strong shall help the weak. . . . Is it right, after all, that because some of us are capable of forging great and powerful organizations of

30. AF of L Executive Council Minutes, April 30–May 7, 1935, p. 115.

31. *Ibid.*, p. 174; Taft, *A. F. of L. from the Death of Gompers*, p. 118; Edward Levinson, *Labor on the March* (New York, 1938), p. 84; also, the speech of A. O. Wharton, AF of L, *Proceedings* (1935), pp. 569–72.

skilled craftsmen in this country that we should lock ourselves up in our own domain and say, "I am merely working for those who pay me"?

The AF of L had to choose between becoming "an instrumentality that will render service to all of the workers" and resting "content in that comfortable situation that has prevailed through the years. . . ." Convinced at last that the craft bloc preferred the second path, Lewis saw independent action as the only remedy to "twenty-five years of constant, unbroken failure." [32]

Mass-production unionization merged with industrial unionism only when hope was lost in the AF of L. Actually, this began to happen months before the Atlantic City convention of 1935. Lewis started to shift his ground after the defeat of his program for an auto union at the February meeting of the Executive Council. At the May meeting, he did not try to apply his compromise formula to the Rubber Workers. Rather, he wanted "the jurisdiction granted to the organization to cover all workers employed throughout the rubber industry." Nothing was said at the subsequent convention either in Lewis' arguments or in the Minority Report about the postponement of jurisdictional questions until after the achievement of mass-production organization (although there were such intimations in the speeches of Lewis' supporters Charles Howard and Sidney Hillman).[33] The full commitment to industrial unionism became evident

32. AF of L, *Proceedings* (1935), pp. 534, 536, 541.

33. *Ibid.*, pp. 526, 746; AF of L Executive Council Minutes, April 13–May 7, 1935, pp. 113–16. At the May meeting of the Council a resolution was offered to postpone the jurisdictional decision on the Rubber Workers until after they had formed an international and drawn up a constitution with a proposed jurisdiction. This compromise came not from Lewis but, significantly, from AF of L Secretary Morison, probably with Green's backing. The craft majority refused this alternative, as well as Lewis' offer to exclude "those engaged in new construction work." (*Ibid.*, pp. 135–39.)

in Lewis' offer of $500,000 toward an AF of L steel-organizing fund on February 22, 1936. One condition was that "all steel workers organized will be granted the *permanent* right to remain united in one international union." [34]

Having opted for independent action, Lewis had every reason to espouse industrial unionism: it was a desirable structural reform; it would draw in unions such as the Oil Workers and the Mine, Mill and Smelter Workers that were having jurisdictional troubles within the AF of L;[35] and, above all, it would serve as a rallying cry in the union rivalry and in the organizing field. But industrial unionism remained a subordinate consideration. When the occasion demanded, it was sacrificed to the necessities of the organizing task and to the inevitable ambitions for the CIO as an institution.[36] Nor did industrial unionism fulfill the expectations of earlier advocates. No real transformation was worked in the objectives of the labor movement. Differing in some ways, the rival federations were, as Chester Wright insisted, "brothers under the skin," and the passage of twenty years was time enough to permit them to join in a merger.

The CIO had been created with the fixed purpose of organizing the mass-production industries. Liberated from past practice and vested interest, the effort could be made with optimum effectiveness. Starting fresh, the CIO thoroughly exploited its opportunity.

34. Galenson, *CIO Challenge to AFL*, p. 79 (my italics).

35. See, for example, Vernon H. Jensen, *Nonferrous Metals Industry Unionism, 1932–1954: A Story of Leadership Controversy* (Ithaca, N.Y., 1954), chap. iii; Lowell E. Gallaway, "The Origin and Early Years of the Federation of Flat Glass Workers of America," *Labor History*, II (Winter, 1962), 100–102.

36. In some instances, for example, CIO unions attempted to keep groups out of bargaining units if a close election was forthcoming or in order to avoid trouble with the strategic Teamsters. (11 NLRB 950 [1939], 14 NLRB 287 [1939], 16 NLRB 334 [1939], 21 NLRB 1189 [1940].)

The previous restrictions were immediately thrown off. The separation of skilled men no longer, of course, constituted an impediment to organization. Funds in massive amounts were now injected in some areas. The Steel Workers Organizing Committee received in six years $1,619,613 from outside sources, as well as the services of many organizers who remained on the payrolls of other unions.[37] In part, the money came as direct contributions from affluent CIO affiliates. The Mine Workers and the Clothing Workers, frankly anxious for the organization of industries related to them, directed most of their assistance to steel and textiles, respectively. The rest of the CIO income came from a high per capita tax of five cents a month. Proportionately, the investment far surpassed what had been possible within the AF of L (although, it should be noted, the latter in response was doing likewise). Finally, the CIO was able to build the new industrial unions, particularly those which first took the form of organizing committees, free from the restricting hand of the past. There were instances, notably in steel and textiles, where AF of L unions with old-line leaders came over to the CIO, but they were held to subordinate roles. Able officials were recruited from men rising from the ranks or, as in the case of steel, from experienced unionists elsewhere in the CIO.

The job of organizing was meanwhile changing radically. First, mass-production workers were bursting with militancy. The upsurge of NRA-inspired unionism, for instance, was very largely spontaneous. At the time, it seemed to William Green "a sight that even old, tried veterans of our movement never saw before." Another official believed it would surpass in "numbers, intensity, and duration" the union experience of World War I.[38] Even before the CIO, popular militancy was expressing itself in internal resist-

37. Galenson, *CIO Challenge to AFL*, p. 110.
38. Morris, *Conflict within AFL*, p. 147.

ance to AF of L policies and/or in independent unionism, and in rank-and-file strikes such as that at the Toledo Chevrolet plant in April, 1935.[39] The second change followed from the Wagner Act. For the first time, workmen had the legal right to express through majority rule their desires on the question of union representation. On the counts of both rank-and-file sentiment and federal law, success came to depend on the union appeal, hitherto of secondary importance, to the workingmen. To this requirement, the CIO responded brilliantly.

The ingredients of success were unremitting effort and a mastery of the techniques suited to the special conditions of the mass-production industries. A pool of effective organizers for this work could be drawn from CIO affiliates, above all, the Mine Workers; from left-wing groups; and from militants within the industrial ranks. In addition to using the standard methods, CIO organizers emphasized rank-and-file participation. These were the instructions to a group of adherents in Fort Worth on how to organize their Armour plant:

> It takes Organizers inside the plant to Organize the plant.
>
> The Committee that organized the Oklahoma City plant was a voluntary committee established inside the plant.
>
> You cannot wait for the National Organizer to do all the work. . . . You people here can have a Union, but you will have to work to build it.

Typically, an intricate network of unpaid posts was established in CIO plants, so that "more men are given responsibility, and our organization becomes more powerful and

39. On the experience in automobiles, see Fine, "Origins of the United Automobile Workers," *passim*, and Sidney Fine, "The Toledo Chevrolet Strike of 1935," *Ohio Historical Quarterly*, LXVII (1958), 326–56.

more closely knit." The aim was to avoid "bureaucratic" rule by putting the leadership, as one organizer said, not in a few hands, but in "the whole body, in one, acting as one." [40]

Another significant CIO tactic arose out of sensitivity to the deep-seated resentments of the workers. At the plant level, grievances characteristically received aggressive support. When the men saw "how the CIO was fighting to protect workers' rights . . . ," a Packinghouse Workers' official explained, they flocked into the organization. Direct action was another expression of CIO militancy. Sudden strikes and slowdowns, although often against official policy, were frequently encouraged by local officers. For, as one functionary observed of the stoppages at the Armour Chicago plant, they "demonstrated to all, union members and non-union members, that the CIO had plenty of stuff on the ball and that there was no such thing as waiting for something to happen." [41]

The effectiveness of the CIO had another dimension. The basic industries had drawn the newcomers and underprivileged of American society. Eastern Europeans and then, when the flow of immigrants was stopped by World War I, migrants from the South filled the bottom ranks of mass-production labor. The colored workers had unquestionably been among the chief obstacles to earlier union efforts. William Z. Foster, who had taken a leading part in the AF of L drives of World War I, admitted that "we could not win their support. It could not be done. They were constitutionally opposed to unions, and all our forces could

40. Joint Executive Board Minutes, Oklahoma City and Ft. Worth Locals, Packinghouse Workers Organizing Committee, August 9, 1942; District 2 Conference Minutes, PWOC, January 14, 1940, Files of United Packinghouse Workers of America; *People's Press*, July 23, 1938.

41. Arthur Kampfert, "History of Unionism in Meat Packing," MSS in UPWA Files; *CIO News. Packinghouse Edition*, November 5, 1938, p. 8.

not break down that opposition." [42] The problem was of diminishing magnitude in the 1930's. Negro workers, mostly new arrivals from the South fifteen years before, had gone through a lengthy adjustment. In addition, racial tensions had largely abated. There would be no counterpart to the Chicago race riot of 1919 which had disrupted the union drive in the stockyards. Yet the Negro workers still required special treatment.

Here again the CIO capitalized fully on the opportunity. It became an aggressive defender of Negro rights. After a foothold had been gained in the Armour Chicago plant, for example, one of the first union victories was to end the company practice of "tagging" the time cards of colored employees: "the Stars will no longer offend the Negro workers of Armour & Co." The initial informal agreement at the Swift plant included a company pledge to hire Negroes in proportion to their numbers in the Chicago population.[43] The AF of L could not match these zealous efforts. From the start, Gompers had insisted on the necessity of organizing the colored workers, not out of concern for "social or even any other kind of equality," but to insure that they would not "frustrate our every effort for economic, social and political improvement." [44] This view prevailed, before as well as during the New Deal, wherever the membership of Negroes was essential to the success of a union. But many craft affiliates could afford to exclude or segregate such workers, and the Federation reluctantly accepted what it could not prevent. Besides being tainted by discrimination, the AF of L failed to crusade even where it favored racial equality. Doing so, the CIO swept the Negroes in mass

42. Chicago Commission on Race Relations, *The Negro in Chicago* (Chicago, 1922), p. 429.

43. *CIO News. Packinghouse Edition*, January 2, 1939, p. 2; Kampfert, "History of Unionism in Meat Packing."

44. Gerald N. Grob, "Organized Labor and the Negro Worker, 1865–1900," *Labor History*, I (Spring, 1961), 168.

production into its ranks. The same sensitivity to non-economic factors marked the CIO approach to immigrant and female labor and to the fostering of public support through political work and such communal activities as the "back of the yards" movement in the Chicago packing-house district.

The labor movement thus generated an effective response in the basic industries. A further question remains: Was this the decisive change? It does not seem so. More than the incapacity of organized labor had prevented earlier success. Had everything else remained constant, the CIO effort alone would not have resulted in permanent unionization of the mass-production sector—nor, for that matter, would it even have been attempted.

The sense of urgency was significant. At his last AF of L convention, John L. Lewis told Powers Hapgood that a union drive in the basic industries in the past "would have been suicide for organized labor and would have resulted in complete failure. But now, the time is ripe; and now the time to do those things is here. Let us do them."[45] The American system of industrial relations was being profoundly shaken during the mid-1930's. "Conditions as they exist now," Charles Howard told the Atlantic City convention, "make it more necessary, in my opinion, for effective organization activity than at any time during the life of the American Federation of Labor." [46]

In retrospect, employer resistance looms largest in accounting for the long years of union failure in mass production. The sources of that hostility need not be explored here. Suffice it to say that American industrialists found compelling reasons and, more important, adequate means for resisting labor organization. Lewis noted the "great

45. Hapgood quoting Lewis in Saul Alinsky, *John L. Lewis: An Unauthorized Biography* (New York, 1949), p. 80.
46. *Ibid.*, p. 70; AF of L, *Proceedings* (1935), p. 525.

concentration of opposition to the extension and logical expansion of the trade union movement."

> Great combinations of capital have assembled great industrial plants, and they are strong across the borders of our several states from the north to the south and from the west in such a manner that they have assembled to themselves tremendous power and influence. . . .

"There is no corporation in America more powerful than these corporations—General Motors and Ford," William Green said respectfully. "Everybody knows their financial strength. . . . It is a fact we have always recognized." [47] No real possibility of countering the resources and advantages available to industry had earlier existed; the power balance had been overwhelmingly against labor.

In the 1930's, a new legal framework for industrial relations emerged. In the past, the right to organize had fallen outside the law; unionization, like collective bargaining, had been a private affair. Within normal legal limits, employers had freely fought the organization of their employees. Now that liberty was being withdrawn. World War I had first raised the point. The National War Labor Board had protected workers from discrimination for joining unions and thus contributed substantially to the temporary union expansion of the war period. The lesson was inescapable. Unionization in the mass-production industries depended on public protection of the right to organize. The drift of opinion in this direction was discernible in the Railway Labor Act of 1926 and the Norris-LaGuardia Act of 1932. But the real opportunity came with the advent of the New Deal. Then key union spokesmen, notably Green and Lewis, pressed for the insertion of the famous section 7a in

47. AF of L, *Proceedings* (1935), p. 535; AF of L Executive Council Minutes, January 29–February 14, 1935, p. 64, also, for example, p. 213.

the National Industrial Recovery Act. After an exhilarating start, section 7a foundered; loopholes developed and enforcement broke down long before the invalidation of the NRA. But the intent of section 7a was clear, and it soon received effective implementation.

"If the Wagner bill is enacted," John L. Lewis told the AF of L Executive Council in May, 1935, "there is going to be increasing organization. . . ."[48] The measure, enacted on July 5, 1935, heavily influenced Lewis' decision to take the initiative that led to the CIO. For the Wagner Act did adequately protect the right to organize through a National Labor Relations Board clothed with powers of investigation and enforcement. Employer opposition was at long last neutralized.

The Act made it an unfair labor practice for an employer "to interfere with, restrain, or coerce employees in the exercise" of "the right of self-organization." This protection unquestionably freed workers from fear of employer discrimination. Stipulation cases required the posting of such notices as the following at a Sioux City plant:

> The Cudahy Packing Company wants it definitely understood that . . . no one will be discharged, demoted, transferred, put on less desirable jobs, or laid off because he joins Local No. 70 or any other labor organization. . . . If the company, its officers, or supervisors have in the past made any statements or taken any action to indicate that its employees were not free to join Local No. 70 or any other labor organization, these statements are now repudiated.[49]

Even more persuasive was the reinstatement with back pay of men discharged for union activities. The United Auto Workers' cause at Ford was immensely bolstered in

48. Taft, *A. F. of L. from the Death of Gompers*, pp. 89-90.
49. 31 NLRB 967–68 (1941).

1941 by the rehiring of twenty-two discharged men as the result of an NLRB decision which the company had fought up to the Supreme Court. By June 30, 1941, nearly twenty-four thousand charges of unfair labor practices—the majority involving discrimination—had been lodged with the NLRB.[50] More important in the long run, vigorous enforcement encouraged obedience of the law among employers. Assured of their safety, workers flocked into the unions.

The law also resolved the knotty problems of determining union representation. During the NRA period, company unions had been widely utilized to combat the efforts of outside organizations. The Wagner Act now prohibited employers from dominating or supporting a labor union. Legal counsel at first held that "inside" unions could be made to conform with the law by changing their structure, that is, by eliminating management participation from the joint representation plans. The NLRB, however, required the complete absence of company interference or assistance. Few company unions could meet this high standard, and large numbers were disestablished by NLRB order or by stipulation. In meat-packing, for instance, the Big Four companies had to withdraw recognition from over fifteen company unions. Only in the case of some Swift plants did such bodies prevail over outside unions in representation elections and become legal bargaining agents.[51] Besides eliminating employer-dominated unions, the law put the selection of bargaining representatives on the basis of majority rule. By mid-1941, the NLRB had held nearly six thousand elections and cross-checks involving nearly two million workers. Given a free choice, they overwhelmingly preferred a union to no union (the latter choice resulting in

50. Harry A. Millis and Emily Clark Brown, *From the Wagner Act to Taft-Hartley* (Chicago, 1950), p. 77.

51. James R. Holcomb, "Union Policies of Meat Packers, 1929–1943" (Master's thesis, University of Illinois, 1957), pp. 101–2, 124, 139, 161–62.

only 6 per cent of elections in 1937 and, on the average, in less than 20 per cent up to the passage of the Taft-Hartley Act). Having proved its majority in an "appropriate" unit, a union became the certified bargaining agent for all employees in the unit.

An unexpected dividend for union organization flowed from the Wagner Act. In the past, the crisis of mass-production unions had occurred in their first stage. Rank-and-file pressure normally built up for quick action. Union leaders faced the choice of bowing to this sentiment and leading their organizations into suicidal strikes—as happened on the railroads in 1894, in the stockyards in 1904, and in steel in 1919—or of resisting the pressure and seeing the membership melt away or break up in factional conflict —as occurred in meat-packing after World War I. The Wagner Act, while it did not eliminate rank-and-file pressures, eased the problem. A union received NLRB certification on proving its majority in a plant. Certification gave it legal status and rights which could be withdrawn only by formal evidence that it lacked majority support. Defeat in a strike did not in any way affect the status of a bargaining agent. Restraint, on the other hand, became a feasible policy. The CIO unions as a whole were remarkably successful in resisting workers' demands for national strikes in the early years, although not in preventing local trouble. The resulting dissidence could be absorbed. The Packinghouse Workers Organizing Committee, for instance, was in continual turmoil from 1939 to 1941 because of the conservative course of Chairman Van A. Bittner; but internal strife did not lead to organizational collapse there or elsewhere. NLRB certification permitted labor leaders to steer between the twin dangers—external and internal—that earlier had smashed vigorous mass-production unionism.

Years later, the efficacy of the Wagner Act was acknowledged by an officer of the most hostile of the major packing firms: ". . . The unions would not have organized Wilson [and Company] if it had not been for the Act." [52] That judgment was certainly general in open-shop circles.

Yet the Wagner Act was not the whole story. For nearly two years while its constitutionality was uncertain, the law was virtually ignored by antiunion employers. And after the Jones and Laughlin decision in April, 1937, the effect was part of a larger favoring situation. John L. Lewis was not reacting to a single piece of legislation. He saw developing in the mid-1930's a general shift toward unionization.

The change was partly in the workers themselves. Their accommodation to the industrial system had broken down under the long stretch of depression. The resulting resentment was evident in the sitdown strikes of 1936-37, which involved almost half a million men. These acts were generally not a calculated tactic of the union leadership; in fact, President Sherman Dalrymple of the Rubber Workers at first opposed the sitdowns. Spontaneous sitdowns within the plants accounted for the initial victories in auto and rubber.[53] Much of Lewis' sense of urgency in 1935 sprang from his awareness of the pressure mounting in the industrial ranks. A local auto-union leader told Lewis in May, 1935, of talk about craft unions' taking skilled men from the federal unions. "We say like h—— they will and if it is ever ordered and enforced there will be one more independent union." [54] Threats of this kind, Lewis knew, would surely become actions under existing AF of L policy,

52. James D. Cooney, in Holcomb, "Union Policies of Meat Packers," p. 173.

53. Galenson, *CIO Challenge to AFL*, pp. 135 ff., 269 ff.; Roberts, *Rubber Workers*, pp. 144 ff.; McKenney, *Industrial Valley*, Part III. On the spontaneous character of the decisive shutdown of the Ford River Rouge complex, see Irving Howe and B. J. Widick, *The UAW and Walter Reuther* (New York, 1949), pp. 100–101.

54. Fine, "Origins of the United Automobile Workers," p. 280.

and, as he warned the Executive Council, then "we are facing the merging of these independent unions in some form of national organization." [55] That prophecy, Lewis was determined, should come to pass under his control. The CIO succeeded in large measure because it became the vehicle for channeling the militancy released by the Great Depression.

The second factor that favored union organization was the impact of the depression on the major employers. They had operated on a policy of welfare capitalism: company paternalism and industrial-relations methods were expected to render employees impervious to the blandishments of trade unionism.[56] The depression forced the abandonment of much of this expense and, beyond that, destroyed the workers' faith in the company's omnipotence on which their loyalty rested. Among themselves, as an official of Swift and Company said, industrialists had to admit that grounds existed for "the instances of open dissatisfaction which we see about us, and perhaps with us. . . ." [57]

The depression also tended to undermine the will to fight unionization. Anti-union measures were costly, the La Follette investigation revealed. The resulting labor troubles, in addition, cut deeply into income. The Little Steel companies, Republic in particular, operated significantly less profitably in 1937 than did competitors who were free of strikes. Economic considerations seemed most compelling, not when business was bad, but when it was getting better. Employers then became very reluctant to jeopardize the anticipated return of profitable operations. This apparently influenced the unexpected decision of U. S. Steel to

55. Taft, *A. F. of L. from the Death of Gompers*, pp. 89–90. See also, for example, Howard's speech, AF of L, *Proceedings* (1935), p. 525.

56. See, for example, Irving Bernstein, *The Lean Years: A History of the American Worker, 1920–1933* (Boston, 1960), chap. iii.

57. F. I. Badgeley, *National Provisioner*, October 28, 1933, pp. 82–84.

recognize the Steel Workers Organizing Committee. In 1937 the Steel Corporation was earning substantial profits for the first time during the depression; net income before taxes that year ultimately ran to 130 million dollars. And the first British purchases for defense were just then in the offing. During the upswing, moreover, the competitive factor assumed increasing importance. Union firms had the advantage of avoiding the disruptions incident to conflict over unionization. Certainly a decline of 15 per cent in its share of the automobile market from 1939 to 1940 contributed to the Ford Company's retreat of the following year.[58]

Finally, the political situation—the Wagner Act aside— was heavily weighted on the side of labor. Management could no longer assume governmental neutrality or, under stress, assistance in the labor arena. The benefits accruing to organized labor took a variety of forms. The Norris-LaGuardia Act limited the use of injunctions that had in the past hindered union tactics. A federal law prohibited the transportation of strikebreakers across state lines. The *Thornhill* decision (1940) declared that antipicketing laws curbed the constitutional right of free speech. Detrimental governmental action, standard in earlier times of labor trouble, was largely precluded now by the emergence of sympathetic officeholders on all levels, from the municipal to the national. Indeed, the inclination was in the opposite direction. The response to the sitdown strike illustrated the change. "Well, it is illegal," Roosevelt commented. "But shooting it out and killing a lot of people because they have violated the law of trespass . . . [is not] the answer. . . . There must be another way. Why can't those fellows in General Motors meet with the committee of workers?"[59]

58. Galenson, *CIO Challenge to AFL*, pp. 93–94, 108–9, 182.
59. Frances Perkins, *The Roosevelt I Knew* (New York, 1946), p. 322.

This tolerance of unlawful labor acts, as sitdowns were generally acknowledged to be, could not have happened at any earlier period of American history. These were negative means of forwarding the labor cause.

But political power was also applied in positive ways. The La Follette investigation undermined antiunion tactics by exposure and, among other ways, by feeding information on spies to the unions.[60] At critical junctures, there was intercession by public officials ranging from President Roosevelt and Labor Secretary Perkins down to Mayor Kelly of Chicago. Governor Frank Murphy's role in the General Motors controversy is only the best known of a number of such mediating contributions to the union cause.[61] At the start of the CIO steel drive Pennsylvania's Lieutenant-Governor Thomas Kennedy, a Mine Workers' officer, announced that organizers were free to move into steel towns and that state relief funds would be available in the event of a steel strike. The re-election of Roosevelt in 1936 no doubt cast out lingering hopes; many employers bowed to the inevitable after F.D.R.'s smashing victory with labor support.

These broader circumstances—rank-and-file enthusiasm, economic pressures on management, and the political condition—substantially augmented the specific benefits flowing from the Wagner Act. In fact, the great breakthroughs at U. S. Steel and General Motors in early 1937 did not result from the law. The question of constitutionality was resolved only some weeks later. And the agreements them-

60. Robert R. R. Brooks, *When Labor Organizes* (New Haven, 1937), p. 72.

61. J. Woodford Howard, "Frank Murphy and the Sit-Down Strikes of 1937," *Labor History*, I (Spring, 1960), 103–40; Barbara W. Newell, *Chicago and the Labor Movement: Metropolitan Unionism in the 1930's* (Urbana, Ill., 1961), pp. 178–79; George Mayer, *Floyd B. Olson* (Minneapolis, 1951), pp. 159-60. For a summary of New Deal "sensitivity" to labor, see Milton Derber and Edwin Young (eds.), *Labor and the New Deal* (Madison, Wis., 1957), chap. v.

selves did not accord with the provisions of the Wagner Act. The unions dared not utilize procedures for achieving certification as bargaining agents in the auto and steel plants. Lee Pressman, counsel for the SWOC, later admitted that recognition could not then have been won "without Lewis' brilliant move" in his secret talks with U. S. Steel's Myron C. Taylor.

> There is no question that [the SWOC] could not have filed a petition through the National Labor Relations Board . . . for an election. We could not have won an election for collective bargaining on the basis of our own membership or the results of the organizing campaign to date. This certainly applied not only to Little Steel but also to Big Steel.[62]

Similarly, the *New York Times* reported on April 4, 1937: "Since the General Motors settlement, the union has been spreading its organization rapidly in General Motors plants, which were weakly organized at the time of the strike." The NLRB could not require either U. S. Steel or General Motors to make agreements with unions under those circumstances. Nor did the companies grant the form of recognition contemplated in the Wagner Act, that is, as *exclusive* bargaining agents. (This would have been illegal under the circumstances.) Only employees who were union members were covered by the two agreements. These initial CIO victories, opening the path as they did for the general advance of mass-production unionism, stemmed primarily from the wider pressures favorable to organized labor.

The Wagner Act proved indecisive for one whole stage of unionization. More than the enrollment of workers and the attainment of certification as bargaining agent was needed in unionization. The process was completed only

62. Alinsky, *Lewis*, p. 149.

when employers and unions entered bona fide collective bargaining. But this could not be enforced by law. Meaningful collective bargaining was achievable ultimately only through the interplay of non-legislative forces.

The tactics of major employers had shifted significantly by the 1920's. Their open-shop doctrine had as its declared purpose the protection of workingmen's liberties. "We do not believe it to be the wish of the people of this country," a U. S. Steel official had said, "that a man's right to work shall be made dependent upon his membership in any organization." [63]   Since the closed shop was assumed to follow inevitably from collective bargaining, the refusal to recognize unions was the fixed corollary of the open shop. The argument, of course, cut both ways. Open-shop employers insisted that their employees were free to join unions (whether or not this was so). The important fact, however, was that the resistance to unionism was drawn tight at the line of recognition and collective bargaining. That position had frustrated the attempt of the President's Industrial Conference of October, 1919, to formulate principles for "genuine and lasting cooperation between capital and labor." The union spokesmen had withdrawn in protest against the insistence of the employer group that the obligation to engage in collective bargaining referred only to shop committees, not to trade unions.[64]   In effect, the strategy was to fight organized labor by withholding its primary function.

Federal regulation of labor relations gradually came to grips with the question of recognition and collective bargaining. During World War I, the NWLB only required employers to deal with shop committees. Going further, the NRA granted employees the right to "bargain collectively

63. David Brody, *Steelworkers in America: The Non-Union Era* (Cambridge, 1960), p. 176.

64. Lewis L. Lorwin and Arthur Wubnig, *Labor Relations Boards: The Regulation of Collective Bargaining under the National Industrial Recovery Act* (Washington, D.C., 1935), pp. 13–18.

through representatives of their own choosing. . . ." This was interpreted to imply an obligation of employers to deal with such representatives. The major failing of section 7a was that the NRA did not implement the interpretation. In practice, determined employers were able, as earlier, to escape meaningful negotiation with trade unions.[65] It seems significant that the permanent union gains of the NRA period came in those areas—the coal and garment industries—where collective bargaining did not constitute a line of employer resistance. Profiting by the NRA experience, the Wagner Act established the procedure for determining bargaining agents and the policy of exclusive representation and, by the device of certification, withdrew recognition from the option of an employer.

But recognition did not mean collective bargaining. Section 8 (5) did require employers to bargain with unions chosen in accordance with the law. Compliance, however, was another matter. In the first years, hostile employers attempted to withhold the normal attributes of collective bargaining. When a strike ended at the Goodyear Akron plant in November, 1937, for example, the company insisted that the agreement take the form of a "memorandum" signed by the mediating NLRB regional director, not by company and union, and added that "in no event could the company predict or discuss the situation beyond the first of the year." [66] (Although the Rubber Workers' local had already received certification, it would not secure a contract for another four years.) Westinghouse took the position that collective bargaining "was simply an opportunity for representatives of the employees to bring up and discuss problems affecting the working force, with the final decision

65. On the difficulties over this question in the automobile industry, see Irving Fine, "Proportional Representation of Workers in the Automobile Industry," *Industrial and Labor Relations Review*, XIII (January 1959), 182–205.

66. Roberts, *Rubber Workers*, p. 223.

reserved to the company. It rejected the notion of a signed agreement because business conditions were too uncertain. . . ."[67] Some companies—for instance, Armour in April, 1941—unilaterally raised wages while in union negotiations. The contractual forms were resisted: agreements had to be verbal, or take the form of a "statement of policy," or, if in contractual terms, certainly with no signatures. These blatant evasions of the intent of section 8 (5) were gradually eliminated: a series of NLRB and court rulings prohibited the refusal to negotiate or make counteroffers, the unilateral alteration of the terms of employment, and opposition to incorporating agreements into written and signed contracts.

The substance proved more elusive than the externals of collective bargaining. "We have no trouble negotiating with Goodyear," a local union president observed, "but we can never bargain. The company stands firmly against anything which does not give them the absolute final decision on any question."[68] The law, as it was interpreted, required employers to bargain "in good faith." How was lack of good faith to be proved? The NLRB tried to consider the specific circumstances and acts, rather than the words, of the employer in each case. That cumbersome procedure was almost useless from the union standpoint. Delay was easy during the case, and further evasion possible afterward. Barring contempt proceedings after a final court order, moreover, the employer suffered no penalties for his obstruction; there was no counterpart here for the back-pay provisions in dismissal cases. The union weakness was illustrated at Wilson & Co. The Cedar Rapids packing plant had been well organized since the NRA period, but

67. Twentieth Century Fund, *How Collective Bargaining Works: A Survey of Experience in Leading American Industries* (New York, 1945), pp. 763–64.
68. Roberts, *Rubber Workers*, p. 247.

no agreement was forthcoming from the hostile management. In 1938 the union filed charges with the NLRB. Its decision came in January, 1940, and another year was consumed by the company's unsuccessful appeal to the Circuit Court. The negotiations that followed (interrupted by a strike which the union lost) led nowhere because, a union official reported, Wilson "as always . . . tried to force the Union to accept the Company's agreement or none at all." [69] The contract which was finally consummated in 1943 resulted neither from an NLRB ruling nor from the free collective bargaining that was the aim of the Wagner Act. Clearly, "good faith" was not to be extracted from recalcitrant employers by government fiat.

The collective-bargaining problem had a deeper dimension. The bitter-enders themselves constituted a minority group in American industry. For every Westinghouse, Goodyear, Ford, and Republic Steel there were several major competitors prepared to abide by the intent of the law and enter "sincere negotiations with the representatives of employees." But, from the union standpoint, collective bargaining was important for the results it could yield. Here the Wagner Act stopped. As the Supreme Court noted in the Sands case, "from the duty of the employer to bargain collectively . . . there does not flow any duty . . . to accede to the demands of the employees." [70] No legal force sustained the objectives of unions either in improving wages, hours, and conditions or in strengthening their position through the union shop, master contracts, and arbitration of grievances.

The small utility of the law in collective bargaining was quickly perceived by labor leaders. The CIO packing-house

69. National Wilson Conference Minutes, PWOC, February 14, 1942, UPWA Files. See also, 19 NLRB 990 (1940).

70. Quoted in Joseph Rosenfarb, *The National Labor Policy and How It Works* (New York, 1940), p. 197.

union, for instance, did not invoke the Wagner Act at all in its three-year struggle with Armour. The company, in fact, objected to the intercession of Secretary of Labor Perkins in 1939 on the ground that the union had not exhausted, or even utilized, the remedies available through the NLRB.[71] The dispute actually did involve issues which fell within the scope of the Wagner Act. But the union clearly was seeking more effective ways—federal pressure in this case—of countering Armour's reluctance to negotiate and sign contracts. For the prime union objective was a master contract covering all the plants of the company organized by the union, a concession which could only be granted voluntarily by the company. Collective bargaining, both the process itself and the fruits, depended on the working of the other advantages open to the unions in the New Deal era.

Where negotiation was undertaken in "good faith," there were modest initial gains. The year 1937, marking the general beginning of collective bargaining in mass production, saw substantial wage increases as the result of negotiations and/or union pressure. In steel, the advances of November, 1936, and March, 1937, moved the unskilled hourly rate from 47 cents to 62½ cents. In rubber, average hourly earnings rose from 69.8 cents to 76.8 cents; in automobiles, from 80 to 93 cents. Other gains tended to be slender. The U. S. Steel agreement, for instance, provided the two major benefits of time-and-a-half after eight hours and a grievance procedure with arbitration. The vacation provision, on the other hand, merely continued an existing arrangement, and silence prevailed on many other questions. The contracts were, in contrast to later ones, very thin documents.[72] Still, the first fruits of collective bargaining were encouraging to labor.

71. *New York Times*, September 12, 1939.

72. For an analysis of the U. S. Steel agreement, see Robert R. R. Brooks, *As Steel Goes . . .: Unionism in a Basic Industry* (New Haven, 1940), chap. viii.

Then the economy faltered again. In 1938 industrial unions had to fight to stave off wage cuts. They succeeded in most, but not all, cases. Rates were reduced 15 per cent at Philco after a four months' strike. Less visible concessions had to be granted in some cases. For example, the SWOC and UAW accepted changes which weakened the grievance procedure at U. S. Steel and General Motors.[73] The mass-production unions were, in addition, hard hit by the recession. Employment fell sharply. The UAW estimated that at the end of January, 1938, 320,000 auto production workers were totally unemployed and most of the remainder of the normal complement of 517,000 were on short time. The union's membership was soon down to 90,000. It was the same story elsewhere. In the Chicago district of the SWOC, dues payments fell by two-thirds in the twelve months after July, 1937 (that is, after absorbing the setback in Little Steel).[74] Declining membership and, in some cases, internal dissension rendered uncertain the organizational viability of the industrial unions. And their weakness in turn further undermined their effectiveness in collective bargaining. They faced a fearful choice. If they became quiescent, they would sacrifice the support of the membership. If they pressed for further concessions, they would unavoidably become involved in strikes. By so doing, they would expose their weakened ranks in the one area in which labor legislation permitted the full expression of employer hostility—and in this period few even of the law-abiding employers were fully reconciled to trade unionism.

Collective bargaining was proving a severe obstacle to the new mass-production unions. The Wagner Act had little value here; and the other favoring circumstances had declining effectiveness after mid-1937. Hostile employers were

73. *Ibid.*, p. 211; Galenson, *CIO Challenge to AFL*, p. 158.
74. Galenson, *CIO Challenge to AFL*, p. 157; Newell, *Chicago and the Labor Movement*, p. 144.

evading the requirement of negotiating in good faith. For the larger part, the industrial unions achieved the first approximation of collective bargaining. But from 1937 to 1940 very little more was forthcoming. The vital function of collective bargaining seemed stalled. The situation was, in sum, still precarious five years after the formation of the CIO.

John L. Lewis had made something of a miscalculation. The promise of the New Deal era left mass-production unionism short of permanent success. Ultimately, two fortuitous circumstances rescued the industrial unions.

The outbreak of World War II finally ended the American depression. By 1941, the economy was becoming fully engaged in defense production. Corporate profits before taxes leaped from 6½ billion dollars in 1939 to 17 billion in 1941. The number of unemployed fell from 8½ million in June, 1940, to under 4 million in December, 1941. It was this eighteen-month period that marked the turning point for the CIO. Industry's desire to capitalize on a business upswing, noted earlier, was particularly acute now; and rising job opportunities and prices created a new militancy in the laboring ranks. The open-shop strongholds began to crumble. Organization came to the four Little Steel companies, to Ford, and to their lesser counterparts. The resistance to collective bargaining, where it had been the line of conflict, was also breaking down. First contracts were finally being signed by such companies as Goodyear, Armour, Cudahy, Westinghouse, Union Switch and Signal. Above all, collective bargaining after a three-year gap began to produce positive results. On April 14, 1941, U. S. Steel set the pattern for its industry with an increase of ten cents an hour. For manufacturing generally, average hourly earnings from 1940 to 1941 increased over 10 per cent and weekly earnings 17 per cent; living costs rose only 5 per cent. More than wages was involved. Generally, initial contracts were thoroughly renegotiated for the first time, and this produced a wide range of improvements in vacation, holiday, and seniority provisions and in grievance procedure. Mass-production workers could now see the tangible benefits flowing from their union membership. These results of the defense prosperity were reflected in union growth: CIO membership jumped from 1,350,000 in 1940 to 2,850,000 in 1941.[75]

The industrial unions were arriving at a solid basis. That achievement was insured by the second fortuitous change. American entry in the war necessitated a major expansion of the federal role in labor-management relations. To prevent strikes and inflation, the federal government had to enter the hitherto private sphere of collective bargaining. The National War Labor Board largely determined the wartime terms of employment in American industry. This emergency circumstance, temporary although it was, had permanent consequences for mass-production unionism. The wartime experience disposed of the last barriers to viable collective bargaining.

For one thing, the remaining vestiges of anti-unionism were largely eliminated. The hard core of resistance could now be handled summarily. In meat-packing, for instance, Wilson & Co. had not followed Armour, Swift, and Cudahy in accepting collective bargaining. In 1942 the NWLB ordered the recalcitrant firm to negotiate a master contract (Wilson was holding to the earlier Big Four resistance to company-wide bargaining). Years later in 1955, a company official was still insisting that Wilson would not have accepted "a master agreement if it had not been for the war.

75. Joel Seidman, *American Labor from Defense to Reconversion* (Chicago, 1953), pp. 27, 31, 32; Galenson, *CIO Challenge to AFL,* p. 587; on contract terms, Twentieth Century Fund, *How Collective Bargaining Works, passim.*

Such an agreement is an unsatisfactory arrangement; today or yesterday." [76] Subsequent negotiations having yielded no results, a Board panel itself actually wrote the first Wilson contract.[77]

Beyond such flagrant cases, the NWLB set to rest an issue deeply troubling to the labor-management relationship in mass production. With few exceptions, the open shop remained dogma even after the acceptance of unionism. "John, it's just as wrong to make a man join a union," Benjamin Fairless of U. S. Steel insisted to Lewis, ". . . as it is to dictate what church he should belong to." [78] The union shop had been granted in auto by Ford only; in rubber, by the employers of a tenth of the men under contract;[79] in steel, by none of the major producers (although they had succumbed under pressure in the "captive mines"). The issue was profoundly important to the new unions. The union shop meant membership stability and, equally significant, the full acceptance of trade unionism by employers. The NWLB compromised the charged issue on the basis of a precedent set by the prewar National Defense Mediation Board. Maintenance-of-membership prevented members from withdrawing from a union during the life of a contract. Adding an escape period and often the dues checkoff, the NWLB had granted this form of union security in 271 of 291 cases by February, 1944. The CIO regarded maintenance-of-membership as a substantial triumph. And, conversely, some employers took the measure, as Bethlehem and Republic Steel asserted, to be a "camouflaged closed shop." Among the expressions of resentment was the indication in contracts, following the example of Montgomery

76. Holcomb, "Union Policies of Meat Packers," p. 172.

77. 6 War Labor Reports 436–41 (1943).

78. Benjamin F. Fairless, *It Could Only Happen in the United States* (New York, 1957), p. 38.

79. Roberts, *Rubber Workers*, p. 310.

Ward, that maintenance-of-membership was being granted "over protest." [80] This resistance, however, was losing its force by the end of the war. The union shop then generally grew from maintenance-of-membership.

The war experience also served a vital educational function. A measure of collective bargaining remained under wartime government regulation. Both before and after submission of cases to the NWLB, the parties involved were obliged to negotiate, and their representatives had to participate in the lengthy hearings. From this limited kind of confrontation, there grew the consensus and experience essential to the labor-management relationship. Wartime education had another aspect. The wage-stabilization policy, implemented through the Little Steel formula by the NWLB, tended to extend the issues open to negotiation. Abnormal restraint on wages convinced labor, as one CIO man said, that "full advantage must be taken of what leeway is afforded" to achieve "the greatest possible gains. . . ." [81] As a result the unions began to include in their demands a variety of new kinds of issues (some merely disguised wage increases) such as premium pay, geographical differentials, wage-rate inequalities, piece-rate computation, and a host of "fringe" payments. Thus were guidelines as to what was negotiable fixed for use after the war and a precedent set that would help further to expand the scope of collective bargaining. The collapse of economic stabilization then also would encourage the successive wage increases of the postwar rounds of negotiation. However illusory these gains were in terms of real income, they endowed the industrial unions with a reputation for effectiveness.

80. Seidman, *American Labor from Defense to Reconversion,* chap. vi.

81. Officers' Report, 2nd Wage and Policy Conference, July 8–10, 1943, PWOC, UPWA Files.

Finally, the wartime restrictions permitted the groping advance toward stable relations to take place in safety. The danger of strikes that might have pushed the parties back to an earlier stage of hostilities was eliminated. Strikes there were in abundance in the postwar period, but these could then be held to the objective of the terms of employment, not the issue of unionism itself. Nothing revealed more of the new state of affairs than the first major defeat of an industrial union. The packing-house strike of 1948 was a thorough union disaster in an industry traditionally opposed to trade unionism. Yet the United Packinghouse Workers of America recovered and prospered. As one of its officials noted with relief, it was the first time in the history of the industry that a " 'lost' strike did not mean a lost union." [82]

Unionization thus ran its full course in mass production. The way had been opened by the New Deal and the Great Depression. The legal right to organize was granted, and its utilization was favored by contemporary circumstances. John L. Lewis seized the unequalled opportunity. Breaking from the bounds of the labor establishment, he created in the CIO an optimum instrument for organizing the mass-production workers. These developments did not carry unionization to completion. There was, in particular, a failure in collective bargaining. In the end, the vital progress here sprang fortuitously from the defense prosperity and then the wartime impact on labor relations. From the half-decade of war, the industrial unions advanced to their central place in the American economy.

82. *Packinghouse Worker*, August 20, 1948, p. 7.

Poverty in Perspective

ROBERT H. BREMNER

IN THE MIDDLE of the nineteenth century an English visitor reported that the most obvious feature of American life was "the nearly entire absence, certainly of the appearance, and in a great degree of the reality, of poverty." "It is the blessed privilege of the United States," said Lord Carlisle, "that they have not, as a class, any poor among them." Gushing abundance struck him as the characteristic of the land, general ease and comfort the condition of the great bulk of the people. Yet Englishmen, he thought, looked healthier, stouter, rosier, and jollier than Americans. The United States, he concluded, quoting an American informant, was "probably the country in which there was less misery and less happiness than in any other of the world." [1]

Since Carlisle's day, and no doubt before, a host of observers, imported and domestic, have cited material abundance and emotional starvation as the twin phenomena

---

1. "Lord Carlisle's Lecture at Leeds," *Littell's Living Age*, XXVIII (1851), 197, 203. George William Frederick Howard, Seventh Earl of Carlisle (1802–1864), visited the United States and Canada in 1841–42. He wrote the preface for the English edition of *Uncle Tom's Cabin* (London, 1853).

of American culture. To say that riches cannot buy happiness is trite, but creative writers, journalists, philosophers, and social scientists say it every day, sometimes with such conviction, eloquence, or erudition that they earn reputations for profundity. Multimillionaires like Andrew Carnegie used to contrast the tribulations of the rich with the advantages of the poor; retired army officers still denounce the yearning for individual and social—but not national—security; and everybody laughs or shudders at the American appetite for the light taste, chewing-enjoyment, and the soft crust. Nobody, however, has as yet succeeded in convincing the American people that poverty buys happiness. The common attitude still seems to be that if we are going to be unhappy we might as well take advantage of such comforts as credit cards and trading stamps procure. "I've been rich and I've been poor," said a popular singer, "and believe me, rich is better."

The extent of poverty in the United States has always been a disputed subject. By comparison with the misery in which so large a portion of the world's population lives and dies, America has no poverty. But obviously part of the American people are poor, and some portion of them are miserably poor, when compared with the rest of their countrymen. The poverty they suffer imposes handicaps on them and their children and casts a shadow on the happiness of the nation.

The American poor are periodically rediscovered, each time with a sense of shock. Their plight is usually presented as a novel problem—and perhaps it is, for each generation views poverty from a changed perspective and sees it in a new light. It may be useful, therefore, to summarize the voluminous literature on the subject produced during the past six decades and review what leading authorities have had to say about the extent, meaning, causes, and consequences of poverty in modern America.

For more than sixty years after 1900 serious and informed students have asserted there was no justification for the survival of poverty in a country as rich, free, progressive, and productive as the United States. Paradoxically, those who were most firmly convinced that poverty was unnecessary generally arrived at high estimates of its extent, while those who assumed the laws of God, nature, or human nature decreed a certain amount of economic hardship usually denied poverty was a serious problem in the United States. But the study of poverty abounds in paradox. For example, nearly anything said of wealth might also be said of poverty. Like wealth, poverty is a condition some people inherit and others acquire; it can be deserved or undeserved, a blessing or an affliction; and it is hard to define: X is poor in comparison to Y and rich in comparison to Z. Paradox aside, something can be said of poverty that cannot be said of wealth: poverty means want, wealth means surplus.

The particular want of the American poor was money. From the turn of the century to the 1960's expert witnesses agreed that insufficient income was the crux of the poverty problem. Obvious and inescapable as the conclusion seemed, its acceptance represented a departure from the nineteenth-century tendency to emphasize moral factors and dependency as the central issues in poverty. Over the years, in governmental and academic parlance, "low-income status" all but supplanted "poverty." As a practical matter, since the lower depths of degradation were easy to recognize, only the upper limits of low income had to be defined. Beginning at the bottom of the social scale poverty extended upward to whatever level of income the observer deemed appropriate.

After 1900 investigators drew the poverty line at annual earnings ranging from $460 at the start of the century, to $2,000 around 1929, and $4,000 in the late 1950's and early

1960's.[2] The progressive elevation of the line reflected the
rising cost of living as well as higher standards of need
and want. As definitions broadened and the general population increased, estimates of the number of people in poverty also mounted. In 1904 Robert Hunter declared that no
less than 10 million and perhaps as many as 15 to 20 million
Americans lived in poverty; a generation later in 1933, I.
M. Rubinow estimated that the number was 25 million;
and in 1963 Dwight Macdonald set the figure at 42.5
million.[3] Needless to say other students arrived at other
estimates. There was general agreement, however, that in
relation to total population the poor declined from at least
one-third of all the people in the country in the mid-1930's
to about one-fifth in 1960.[4]

The qualitative standards twentieth-century students
used to define and describe poverty were perhaps even more
significant than the quantitative. In *Poverty* (1904), Robert Hunter described the poor as people whose earnings
were insufficient to provide the food, clothing, and shelter
needed to maintain physical efficiency.[5] Hunter took this
definition from two English students, Alfred Marshall and

2. Robert Hunter, *Poverty* (New York, 1904), p. 52; Maurice
Leven, Harold G. Moulton, and Clark Warburton, *America's Capacity
to Consume* (Washington, D.C., 1934), pp. 55–56; Conference on Economic Progress, *Poverty and Deprivation in the U.S.: The Plight of
Two-Fifths of a Nation* (Washington, D.C., 1962), p. 2.

3. Hunter, *Poverty*, pp. v–vi, 12–13, 25; I. M. Rubinow, "Poverty,"
Encyclopaedia of the Social Sciences, XI (New York, 1937), 285–87;
Dwight Macdonald, "Our Invisible Poor," *New Yorker*, January 19,
1963, p. 94.

4. Robert J. Lampman, *The Low Income Population and Economic
Growth* (Washington, D.C., 1959), pp. 4–5; Michael Harrington, *The
Other America: Poverty in the United States* (New York, 1962),
p. 182; Herman P. Miller, "Is the Income Gap Closed? 'No'." *New
York Times Magazine*, November 11, 1962, p. 50 and "New Definitions
of Our 'Poor'," *New York Times Magazine*, April 21, 1963, p. 11;
Conference on Economic Progress, *Poverty and Deprivation in the
U.S.*, pp. 2, 20–22.

5. Hunter, *Poverty*, pp. 5–9.

B. Seebohm Rowntree. Both Marshall and Rowntree distinguished between the income necessary for merely sustaining life and the larger amount required to keep human beings in efficient working order, but they differed on the content of the efficiency standard. Marshall stressed the items which should be included among the "necessaries," Rowntree noted the many "desirables" (such as postage, newspapers, entertainment, travel, and education) which had to be excluded. At best (and it was better than mere subsistence) the physical-efficiency standard provided for human needs on about the same level as those of reasonably well-tended steam engines.[6]

Rigorous as the physical-efficiency standard was it brought a substantial number of independent but poorly paid workers within the definition of poverty. No doubt that this is why Hunter, a social worker and settlement resident, adopted it. He rejected the notion, common among late nineteenth-century reformers, that poverty became a social problem only when the poor applied for relief or charity. He devoted a sizable portion of his book to the problems of pauperism, but he was not really interested in paupers and he did not find their lot a challenging subject of research. "Paupers," he said, "are not, as a rule, unhappy. They are not ashamed; they are not keen to become independent; they are not bitter or discontented." Vastly more important and much more distressing, in Hunter's opinion, was the condition of self-supporting toilers in factories, mines, and sweatshops who, in spite of their best efforts, received "too little of the common necessities to keep themselves at their best, physically." Too often confused either with the willfully idle, or with moderately well-paid artisans, these toilers comprised an almost forgotten class.

6. Alfred Marshall, *Principles of Economics* (London, 1890), pp. 120–21; B. Seebohm Rowntree, *Poverty: A Study of Town Life* (London, 1901), pp. 86–87, 132.

They worked hard but lived miserably, always on the verge of want and constantly exposed to accident, sickness, unemployment, and other hardships which might cost them their independence—that is, make them seek assistance. "The decision to apply for public aid," said Hunter, "is perhaps the greatest crisis in the life of the poor." Once driven or enticed into pauperism, the poor were irreclaimable.[7]

In the thirty years after 1904, Hunter's successors lifted the poverty line well above the minimum necessary for maintaining physical efficiency. Even before American entry into World War I, students defined poverty to include persons whose incomes were inadequate to support "a normal standard of living," "decent and wholesome life," and "a fair amount of comfort and . . . a certain degree of mental in addition to physical efficiency."[8] At the start of the 1920's John Gillin brought the idea of "social efficiency" into the definition. People were poor, Gillin write in *Poverty and Dependency* (1921), if either because of inadequate earnings or because of unwise expenditures they were unable to "function usefully" according to the prevailing standards of society.[9] The most striking advance in the poverty line, however, came during the Great Depression. I. M. Rubinow, in *The Quest for Security* (1934), identified the poor as the millions of wage-workers and salaried employees whose earnings fell below "the level of the true American standard of life." To Rubinow the "true American standard" provided for comfort, recreation, education, and participation

7. Hunter, *Poverty*, pp. 3, 5–6, 71.

8. Owen R. Lovejoy, "Report of the Committee on Standards of Living and Labor," *Proceedings* of the National Conference of Charities and Correction, 1912, p. 388; Jacob Hollander, *The Abolition of Poverty* (Boston and New York, 1914), p. 2; Maurice F. Parmelee, *Poverty and Social Progress* (New York, 1916), p. 91.

9. John Lewis Gillin, *Poverty and Dependency. Their Relief and Prevention* (New York, 1921), p. 23. See also Robert W. Kelso, *Poverty* (New York, 1929), p. 3.

in group activities. "In short," Rubinow declared, "it means opportunity to *enjoy life*." [10]

At the start of the twentieth century William Dean Howells commented that poverty was not the lack of things but the fear and dread of want. With rising standards and expectations of living, insecurity—once the prerogative of the upper and middle classes—spread through nearly all levels of society. Reformers had long contrasted the anxiety of struggling white-and-blue-collar workers with the indifference of ne'er-do-wells who had given up the struggle for independence. In the presidential campaign of 1928, Herbert Hoover called fear of poverty, old age, and unemployment "the greatest calamities of human kind." [11] It was not until the 1930's, however, when millions of Americans lived in actual want, that insecurity—the fear and dread of want—became a crucial social issue. "Although we have suffered neither revolution, famine nor war, and our country is surfeited with food and goods," wrote Abraham Epstein in 1933, "insecurity stalks the land and misery prevails to a degree we never before experienced." [12]

No one enumerated the various conditions of American poverty as succinctly or as movingly as Franklin Roosevelt did in his Second Inaugural Address. His dramatic phrase, "one-third of a nation ill-housed, ill-clad, ill-nourished," climaxed a series of short paragraphs in which he cited insufficiency, insecurity, indecent living conditions, inequality, and—characteristically—low-purchasing power as chal-

10. I. M. Rubinow, *The Quest for Security* (New York, 1934), pp. 8, 16.

11. "The Worst of Being Poor" [William Dean Howells], *Harper's Weekly*, XLVI (1902), 261. Hoover is quoted in the *New York Times*, October 23, 1928.

12. Abraham Epstein, *Insecurity: A Challenge to America* (New York, 1933), p. 657.

lenges to democracy.[13] Yet even while listing the nation's economic ills, President Roosevelt affirmed faith in the possibility of translating national wealth into "a spreading volume of human comforts hitherto unknown" and of raising the lowest standard of living "far above the level of mere subsistence." [14]

In 1944, when war prosperity had vastly altered the national economic and social picture, Roosevelt called on the Congress and people of the United States to begin laying plans for "the establishment of an American standard of living higher than ever before known." No matter how high the general level of prosperity, he said, we cannot be content if some fraction of the population—whether one-third, one-fifth, or one-tenth—"is ill-fed, ill-clothed, ill-housed and insecure." [15] Roosevelt's message on an Economic Bill of Rights (January 11, 1944) outlined the essentials of a security standard: a useful and remunerative job; earnings sufficient to provide food, clothing, and recreation; a decent home; adequate medical care; protection against the economic hazards of old age, sickness, accident, and unemployment; and a good education. These rights, in the President's words, constituted "a new basis of security and prosperity." [16]

In the two decades after 1944 the majority of the American people moved in the direction Roosevelt pointed, toward "new goals of human happiness and well-being." The

13. Samuel I. Rosenman (comp.), *The Public Papers and Addresses of Franklin D. Roosevelt*, VI (New York, 1941), pp. 4–5. Roosevelt's estimate of one-third of the nation in poverty was conservative. According to a report issued by The National Resources Committee, *Consumer Incomes in the United States: Their Distribution in 1935–36* (Washington, D.C., 1938), two-thirds of the twenty-nine million families studied had yearly incomes under $1500.

14. Rosenman (comp.), *Public Papers and Addresses of Franklin D. Roosevelt*, VI, 4.

15. *Ibid.*, XIII (New York, 1950), 40–41.

16. *Ibid.*, p. 41.

essentials of security, although not secured for all, were accepted—as Roosevelt had said—"so to speak," as rights. In the 1960's, students defined poverty much as they had in earlier years: economic inability to maintain minimum standards of health, housing, food, clothing, and education.[17] But the minimum standards were higher because the normal standard, enjoyed and expected by the bulk of the population, provided comforts and conveniences no previous generation had known. Hence, as numerous troubled observers noted, the psychological hardships of poverty, the consciousness of inequality and feeling of inferiority, were as burdensome and possibly more galling than ever.[18] Measured by objective physical standards the condition of the American poor was deplorable. It became even sorrier when—as was increasingly the custom—wants and needs were measured by cultural standards. Poverty, an economist wrote in 1958, "is the sense of deprivation stemming from inability to possess or consume what others have." [19] Five years later a *New Yorker* correspondent, in a widely-praised article, summed up the case: "Not to be able to afford a movie or a glass of beer is a kind of starvation—if everybody else can." [20]

During the twentieth century the elaborate charts of the causes of poverty and dependency which late nineteenth-

17. Gabriel Kolko, *Wealth and Power in America* (New York, 1962), p. 70; Harrington, *The Other America*, p. 179.

18. Harrington, *The Other America*, p. 179; Max Lerner, *America as a Civilization: Life and Thought in the United States* (New York, 1957), p. 337; John Kenneth Galbraith, *The Affluent Society* (Boston, 1958), pp. 323–24; Miller, "Is the Income Gap Closed? 'No'," p. 50, and "New Definitions of Our 'Poor'," p. 11. Cf. Walter E. Weyl, *The New Democracy* (New York, 1912), p. 221, n. 1.

19. Moses Abramovitch, "Economic Goals and Social Welfare in the Next Generation," in Committee for Economic Development, *Problems of United States Economic Development*, I (New York, 1958), p. 196.

20. Macdonald, "Our Invisible Poor," p. 132.

century reformers drew went out of fashion. Their place was taken by equally elaborate but matter-of-factly-worded catalogues of the "characteristics" of the low-income population. The characteristics most often cited at mid-century were old age, youth, broken families (especially those headed by women), physical handicap or infirmity, low educational attainment, non-white status, non-employed status, residence in depressed rural areas and decaying industrial communities, and low-paid, unskilled employment in industry, retail stores, service trades, and agriculture.[21] Low wages and income loss stemming from unemployment, sickness, accident, old age, and death or desertion of breadwinner had been recognized as causes of want for many years. Rural distress came to the fore in the 1930's; the poverty of depressed areas and racial minorities received more attention after World War II than in earlier years. On the other hand, after about 1930, immigration and "hereditary degeneracy" ceased to be regarded, as they had been in the first two decades of the century, as important factors in poverty.[22] Personality defects, such as laziness and immorality, although still cited as characteristics of the poor, were increasingly thought to be as much results as causes of poverty.[23]

21. U. S. Congress Joint Committee on the Economic Report, *Characteristics of the Low-Income Population and Related Federal Programs* (Washington, D.C., 1955); Lampman, *Low Income Population and Economic Growth*, pp. 4–12.

22. Robert Hunter, Maurice Parmelee, John L. Gillin, and Thomas Nixon Carver all expressed concern about immigration and favored restriction. See, for example, Hunter, *Poverty*, pp. 261–317. Later writers, however, including Dwight Macdonald and Michael Harrington, have praised the energy of the immigrants of 1890–1910 and have lamented the seeming lack of aspiration of the internal migrants (Negroes, Puerto Ricans, and "poor whites") of the 1950's. For changing attitudes on "hereditary degeneracy" see James L. and Katherine M. Ford, *The Abolition of Poverty* (New York, 1937), pp. 49–66.

23. W. D. P. Bliss (ed.), *The Encyclopedia of Social Reform* (New York and London, 1898), pp. 1072–75; Thomas Sewall Adams and

Until the 1920's the study of poverty was nearly always associated with social reform. The fundamental causes of poverty, as reformers then saw them, were social, the remedies political: tenement-house legislation, abolition of child labor, maximum-hour and minimum-wage laws, assured compensation for industrial accidents, social insurance, stricter regulation or prohibition of liquor sales, and immigration restriction. The poor could not protect themselves against "dying wages," "famine for work," and the hazards of employment in "wildcat industries," but society could if it would. Hence it was "social recklessness" that reformers deplored, the heavy costs of inaction and neglect that alarmed them. Poverty was not only unnecessary but unjust. It was caused by society's failure to protect the weak against exploitation by the strong and from destruction by the impersonal forces of modern economic life.[24]

Opinion on the cause and cure of poverty took a new turn in the early 1920's following publication by the National Bureau of Economic Research of an authoritative study of the amount and distribution of the national income. Wesley C. Mitchell, the guiding spirit of the Bureau, had a scholar's distaste for "the savage dependence on catastrophes for progress," and he deemed reform by agitation or class struggle "a jerky way of moving forward, uncomfortable, and wasteful of energy."[25] The method Mitchell proposed was quantitative analysis of social processes, with constant

Helen L. Sumner, *Labor Problems* (New York, 1905), pp. 151–53; Charles Horton Cooley, *Social Organization: A Study of the Larger Mind* (New York, 1909), p. 292.

24. Hunter, *Poverty*, p. 98; Edward T. Devine, "The Dominant Note of the Modern Philanthropy," *Proceedings* of the National Conferences of Charities and Correction, 1906, pp. 4–5; Walter Rauschenbusch, *Christianity and the Social Crisis* (New York, 1907), p. 217; Lovejoy, "Report of the Committee on Standards of Living and Labor," p. 381; Weyl, *The New Democracy*, p. 321.

25. Mitchell is quoted in Arthur F. Burns, *The Frontiers of Economic Knowledge* (Princeton, N.J., 1954), p. 63,

improvement and conscious application of analysis to matters affecting social welfare. The Bureau's study was prompted in part by Mitchell's and his associates' desire to learn whether the national income was adequate to provide a decent living for all Americans. The findings were not reassuring. National and per capita income had increased in the decade after 1909 and both were greater in the United States than in other countries. Otherwise neither the size nor the distribution of income offered grounds for complacency. The estimated national income in 1918—$61 billion—was so distributed that almost half of the total went to the fortunate fifth of the population whose incomes were in excess of $1,700 a year. Even if national income had been more equitably distributed, $61 billion was not large enough to provide bountifully for a population in excess of one hundred million.[26]

The lesson economists drew from these findings was the need for boosting national income by expanding production. If we seek to abolish inequalities, and thereby curtail production, wrote Henry R. Seager, a long-time advocate of social insurance, "instead of making the poor richer we may merely cause us all to grow poorer together." [27] In *The Tragedy of Waste* (1925), Stuart Chase, no apologist for inequality, said his book was based on the assumption not enough goods and services were normally produced to keep the majority of American families above the poverty line. "A subsistence level standard for the whole population is billions of dollars—and millions of tons of physical goods— short of being won." [28] Even as Chase wrote, however, a

26. National Bureau of Economic Research, Inc., *Income in the United States: Its Amount and Distribution, 1909–1919* (2 vols.; New York, 1921–22) I, pp. ix, 146–47.

27. Henry R. Seager, "Income in the United States," *Survey,* XLVII (1921), p. 270.

28. Stuart Chase, *The Tragedy of Waste* (New York, 1925), pp. 265, 268.

new industrial revolution, promising and bringing new quantities of both necessities and luxuries, was under way. In 1929, while admitting "recent developments may appear less satisfactory in retrospect than they appear at present," Wesley Mitchell cited advances in per capita income as evidence that since 1921 Americans had found ways of producing more physical goods per hour of labor than ever before.[29]

Not poverty but prosperity was the preoccupation of the 1920's—and perhaps of all decades. Certainly the recovery of prosperity was the goal of government and people in the 1930's. In both the 1920's and 1930's the state of the national economy was a more challenging issue than the condition of the poor, and in each the elimination of poverty was presented as a matter of economic necessity quite as much as of social justice. In the years between the wars, the trouble with the poor was simply that they were too numerous; their chief fault was that they did not buy enough. Expansion of purchasing power was as essential to the national welfare in the ten years after 1929 as increased productivity had seemed in the preceding decade. The extravagance of the rich does not hurt the poor, Stuart Chase commented after five years of depression, but the rich suffer when the poor are hard up—because "the spending power of the masses, even more than their earning power," keeps the economic system going. Gilbert Seldes made the same point. Poverty will not be abandoned for moral reasons, he wrote in 1936. "It will be abandoned because poverty is the great enemy of the large-scale productive system or because the victims of poverty will organize themselves to destroy the system entirely."[30]

29. President's Conference on Unemployment, Committee on Recent Economic Changes, *Recent Economic Changes in the United States* (2 vols.; New York, 1929), II, pp. 862, 909.

30. Stuart Chase, *The Economy of Abundance* (New York, 1934), pp. 293–94; Gilbert Seldes, *Mainland* (New York, 1936), p. 307.

During the Depression the insecurity of the average man and woman loomed as a more pressing problem than the special needs of the poor. Through various stratagems the New Deal attempted to solve the nation's economic woes by bringing purchasing power and production into a working relationship. President Roosevelt, always concerned with recovery, consistently sought a business-like justification even for humanitarian reforms. He was interested in the poor not only for their own sake, but because their poverty, expressed in inability to buy the products of farm and factory, denied work and productiveness, strength and security, to the rest of the nation. The sympathetic but unsentimental attitude of the New Deal era to poverty was well expressed in the *Final Report* of the Temporary National Economic Committee, published in 1941:

> . . . Many of our more serious problems of economic imbalance are due to the sad plight of more than a third of our people whose meager incomes, unstable employment, unhealthful living conditions, and limited cultural opportunities constitute a substantial drag on the economy's forward march toward recovery and expansion.[31]

For a dozen years after 1941 the economy went forward, fast and far, despite the drag of a substantial amount of poverty. High employment, rapid economic growth, and the stabilizers built into the economy during the New Deal reduced but did not eliminate poverty. In the decade following 1953, a period marred by recessions, increasing unemployment, and a slowing-down of the rate of economic growth, the drag of poverty once again became noticeable. The aged, migrants, sharecroppers, persons of low skill and little education, newcomers to great cities, and victims of

31. United States Temporary National Economic Committee, *Final Report and Recommendations* (Washington, D.C., 1941), p. 21.

technological progress or of racial prejudice either did not participate in or fell behind in the general advance. Oddly but characteristically these groups were called "the new poor." As in the past one school of thought maintained the proper way to correct economic distress was "by raising the productivity of those at the bottom of the income scale rather than by transferring income from the rich to the poor." Another school, increasingly vocal after the mid-fifties, called for a more direct attack on inequality through governmental action to increase purchasing power, raise living standards, strengthen social security, and improve public services.[32]

"Modern democrats recognize that the abolition of poverty is the most immediate question before the world today," wrote Walter Lippman in 1914.[33] Fifty years later the Cold War, the population explosion in already hungry continents, and the emergence of proud new poverty-stricken nations made the question even more urgent. As the world moved further into the second half of the twentieth century, the great powers competed not only in missiles and moon-shots but in the well-being of their people, and sought friends on the basis of their efficiency in meeting human needs. Meanwhile advances in the social sciences gave the study of poverty new dimensions. Instead of being regarded solely as a physical or economic condition, poverty came to be viewed as an emotional, cultural, intellectual, and political problem of grave importance in both developed and undeveloped areas of the earth.

32. Harrington, *The Other America*, p. 10. The quotation about raising the productivity of those at the bottom of the income scale is from Burns, *Frontiers of Economic Knowledge*, p. 137; the other school is best represented by Galbraith, *The Affluent Society*, pp. 328–31; Max Lerner, *America as a Civilization*, pp. 337–39; Conference on Economic Progress, *Poverty and Deprivation in the U.S.*, p. 1.

33. Walter Lippmann, *Drift and Mastery* (New York, 1914), p. 258.

In these circumstances the truism that poverty is itself the most general and abiding cause of poverty took on fresh meaning. In the United States a host of issues directed popular and scholarly attention to the obstinate, weed-like character of poverty. The challenge and frustrations of foreign economic assistance, the efforts of individuals and organizations to help the people of poor countries break the vicious circle of poverty, and—at home—clamor over the "welfare mess" and investigations of "hard core" relief families, perplexing problems of urban renewal and area redevelopment, the fight for racial equality, and widely publicized surveys of social status and mobility—all contributed, in various ways, to awareness of poverty's tendency to perpetuate itself. Along with this awareness, and partly inspired by it, came a revival of interest in a long-neglected class, the very poor in the lowest layer of society.

In 1904 Robert Hunter called poverty a "culture bed for criminals, paupers, vagrants, and for such diseases as inebrity, insanity, and imbecility." In the 1960's anthropologists, and those influenced by their work, were content to call poverty a culture. Oscar Lewis, in *The Children of Sanchez* (1961), described the culture of the very poor as "a way of life, remarkably stable and persistent, passed down from generation to generation along family lines." Michael Harrington, applying the culture concept to the American poor, asserted in *The Other America* (1962): "Poverty in the United States is a culture, an institution, a way of life." [34] Lewis, like Hunter before him, believed that wherever the miserably poor happened to live, whether in Mexico City or Harlem, Glasgow or Paris, their way of life was strikingly similar, and vastly different from the

34. Hunter, *Poverty*, pp. 64–65; Oscar Lewis, *The Children of Sanchez* (New York, 1961), p. xxiv; Harrington, *The Other America*, p. 16.

behavior expected or demanded as normal by the dominant culture.[35]

The economic attributes of the culture of poverty, as Lewis and Harrington reported them in the 1960's—unemployment, underemployment, low wages, unskilled employment, child labor, no savings, buying in small quantities, borrowing from loan sharks, and use of secondhand furniture and clothing—had a familiar ring. Hunter, Jacob Riis, and Charles Loring Brace had found similar conditions among the very poor slum dwellers of their day. The same was true of bad housing, sickness, and high death rates in the culture of poverty. Earlier students had customarily used words like shiftlessness, improvidence, drunkenness, immorality, irresponsibility, brutality, and lawlessness when writing of "paupers" or "the dangerous classes." Lewis and Harrington avoided the judgmental language of their predecessors but recorded similar characteristics: lack of aspiration, present-time orientation, alcoholism, early initiation into sex, consensual marriage, desertion of mothers and children, violence in settling disputes, hostility to outsiders, mistrust of government, and hatred of the police.[36]

The difference between the new and older observers of the culture of poverty lay not in findings but in interpretation and attitude. Earlier students had seen poverty negatively, as deprivation of such necessities as work, privacy, decency, health, and self-respect. The new writers presented poverty positively, as a style of life adopted to meet the problems of a particular environment and to make existence in that environment bearable. Robert Hunter, as noted above, hated the conditions which drove the poor into

35. Lewis, *Children of Sanchez*, pp. xxv-xxvii, and *Five Families: Mexican Case Studies in the Culture of Poverty* (New York, 1959), p. 2; Hunter, *Poverty*, pp. 3-4.

36. Lewis, *Children of Sanchez*, pp. xxvi-xxvii; Harrington, *The Other America*, pp. 16-17.

pauperism, but he could not summon up much sympathy for paupers. "There is no mental agony here," he wrote, "they do not work sore; there is no dread; they live miserably but they do not care." Michael Harrington, dealing with the same kind of people, was convinced that they did care and that they experienced "mental suffering" of a kind unknown among the more fortunate classes.[37] Lewis and Harrington had as much sympathy for the miserables, and as much tolerance for their failings, as Hunter and his generation had for the struggling toilers.

The favorable response of critics and readers to Lewis's and Harrington's books suggested fairly widespread concern, or at least curiosity, about the lives of desperately poor people. Accounts of low life have often found a market among middle-class readers. But considered in connection with other trends the new interest in an old problem could be interpreted as the opening of another chapter in the study of poverty. By the latter half of the twentieth century the United States had at last reached a stage of economic and social development which permitted its people to turn their thoughts and apply their skills to the treatment of the oldest, saddest, and stubbornest forms of want. Hopefully, it could be anticipated that in the years ahead these kinds of want would be studied as respectfully, and the sufferers' needs met at least as effectively, as earlier generations had examined and provided for other conditions of poverty.

37. Hunter, *Poverty*, p. 4; Harrington, *The Other America*, p. 2.

NOTES ON THE CONTRIBUTORS

JOHN BRAEMAN, Assistant Professor of History at Brooklyn College, is author of *The Road to Independence* and is completing a biography of Albert J. Beveridge.

ROBERT H. BREMNER, Professor of History at Ohio State University, is author of *From the Depths, the Discovery of Poverty in the United States*.

DAVID BRODY is Assistant Professor of History at Columbia University and author of *Steelworkers in America: The Nonunion Era*.

RICHARD S. KIRKENDALL, Associate Professor of History at the University of Missouri, has written widely on the New Deal and is now preparing a biography of Harry S. Truman.

ARTHUR M. JOHNSON is Associate Professor of Business History at Harvard University, editor of the *Business History Review*, and author of *The Development of American Petroleum Pipelines*.

WILLIAM E. LEUCHTENBURG, Professor of History at Columbia University, is the author of *Franklin D. Roosevelt and the New Deal, 1932–40* and *The Perils of Prosperity, 1914–1932*.

RICHARD W. LEOPOLD is William Smith Mason Professor of American History at Northwestern University and author of *Growth of American Foreign Policy: A History,* and *Elihu Root and the Conservative Tradition*.

EVERETT WALTERS is Vice-President for Academic Affairs, Boston University. His publications include *Joseph Benson Foraker: An Uncompromising Republican*.

INDEX